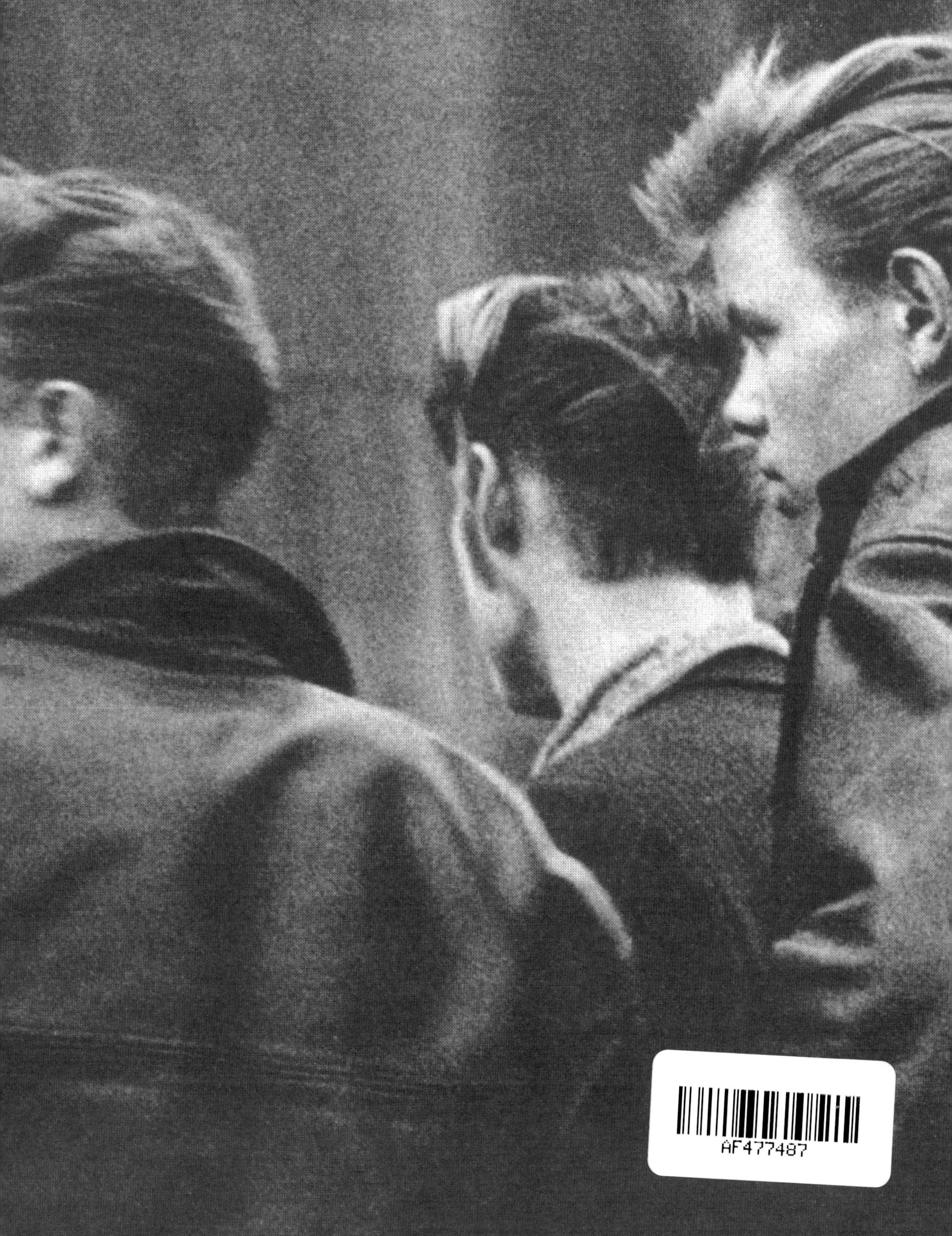
AF477487

Steven · Morrissey
384 · Kings Rd
STRETFORD
Manchester - M32 8GW
✝

Dear Person,
So nice to know there's another
soul out there, even if it _is_
Glasgow.
Does being Scottish bother
you? Manchester is a lovely
little place, if you happen to
be a bedridden deafmute.
I'm unhappy, hope you're
unhappy too.
    In poverty,
        Steven

Camera Report
The Smiths Karaoke
Saturday, 17th March 2007 (Jakarta)

#	No	Name	Song	Take	Timecode in	Timecode out	Notes
#1	1.	Arian	"Panic"	(T1)	01:00:10:01	01:02:49:19	
	2.			(T2)	01:02:49:19	01:05:24:19	
	1.	Arian	"The Boy..."	(T1)	01:05:24:19	01:07:34:20	→NG
	2.			(T2)	01:07:34:20	01:11:14:15	
	1	NZL	"Golden Lights"	(T6)	01:11:14:15	01:11:45:15	→NG
	2.	(Re-take)		(T7)	01:11:45:15	01:12:51:19	→NG
	3.			(T8)	01:12:51:19	01:15:50:24	
	4.			(T9)	01:15:50:24	01:18:51:03	
	5.			(T10)	01:18:51:03	01:21:51:04	→No sound record.
	6.			(T11)	01:21:51:04	01:24:54:24	
	7.			(T12)	01:24:54:24	01:25:09:15	→NG
	8.			(T13)	01:25:09:15	01:28:13:14	
	9.			(T14)	01:28:13:14	01:29:00:11	→NG
	10.			(T15)	01:29:00:11	01:32:03:12	→OK *
	11.			(T16)	01:32:03:12	01:35:09:22	
	1.	Chucky	"Half a Person"	(T5)	01:35:09:22	01:35:49:23	→NG
	2.	(Re-take)		(T6)	01:35:49:23	01:39:38:00	
#2	3.			(T7)	02:00:09:01	02:04:04:04	
	4.			(T8)	02:04:04:04	02:07:54:02	
	5.			(T9)	02:07:54:02	02:11:40:06	
	6.			(T10)	02:11:40:06	02:15:30:20	
	7.			(T11)	02:15:30:20	02:15:52:04	→NG
	8.			(T12)	02:15:52:04	02:19:41:13	→OK *
	1.	Renya & Reza	"There's a Light"	(T1)	02:19:41:13	02:23:44:10	
	2.	Renya	"Panic"	(T1)	02:23:44:10	02:26:17:17	
	3			(T2)	02:26:17:17	02:28:53:23	
	4.			(T3)	02:28:53:23	02:31:30:02	
	5.			(T4)	02:31:30:02	02:32:33:22	
	6.			(T5)	02:32:33:22	02:35:21:19	
	7			(T6)	02:35:21:19	02:39:04:17	
#3	8.			(T7)	03:00:10:03	02:02:52:23	
	1.	Kenya	"Asleep"	(T1)	08:02:52:23	03:07:29:16	
	1.		"Panic"	(T8)	03:07:29:16	03:10:05:12	
	1.	Adit	"London"	(T1)	03:10:05:12	03:12:32:22	
	1.	Adam Fauzan	"Ask"	(T1)	03:12:32:22	03:14:36:09	
	2.			(T2)	03:14:36:09	03:18:15:01	
	~~1.~~	~~Hedar~~	~~"Panic"~~	~~(T1)~~	~~03:18:15:01~~		
	1.	Chucky	"Half a Person"	(T13)	03:18:15:01	03:22:02:15	
	1.	Hedar	"Panic"	(T1)	03:22:02:15	03:22:34:20	→NG
	2.			(T2)	03:22:34:20	03:23:29:14	
	3.			(T3)	03:23:29:14	03:26:00:09	
	1.	Wilman	"There's a Light"	(T1)	03:26:00:09	03:30:04:05	
	1.	Suseng	"Half a Person"	(T1)	03:30:04:05	03:30:58:02	→NG
	2			(T2)	03:30:58:02	03:30:31:04	→NG
	3			(T3)	03:30:31:04	03:35:22:10	
	1.	Taufan, Pbanta, Arif	"Big Mouth"	(T1)	03:35:22:10	03:38:52:16	
#4	1.	Taufan = friends	"Panic"	(T1)	04:00:10:02	04:02:50:20	
	1	Taufan = friend	"There's a Light"	(T1)	04:02:50:20	04:06:58:02	
	1.	Insan	"There's a Light"	(T1)	04:06:58:02	04:10:59:09	
	1.	Suseng	"That Jolie..."	(T1)	04:10:59:09	04:14:59:04	
	1.	Gery	"There's a Light"	(T1)	04:14:59:04	04:19:03:01	
	1	Lupo	"The Boy..."	(T1)	04:19:03:01	04:20:12:01	
	2.	Adam		(T2)	04:20:12:01	04:23:47:02	
	1.	Adam	"Half a Person"	(T5)	04:23:47:02	04:27:33:11	

Note : T : Take 1, 2, 3 ... etc.
       NG : No Good.

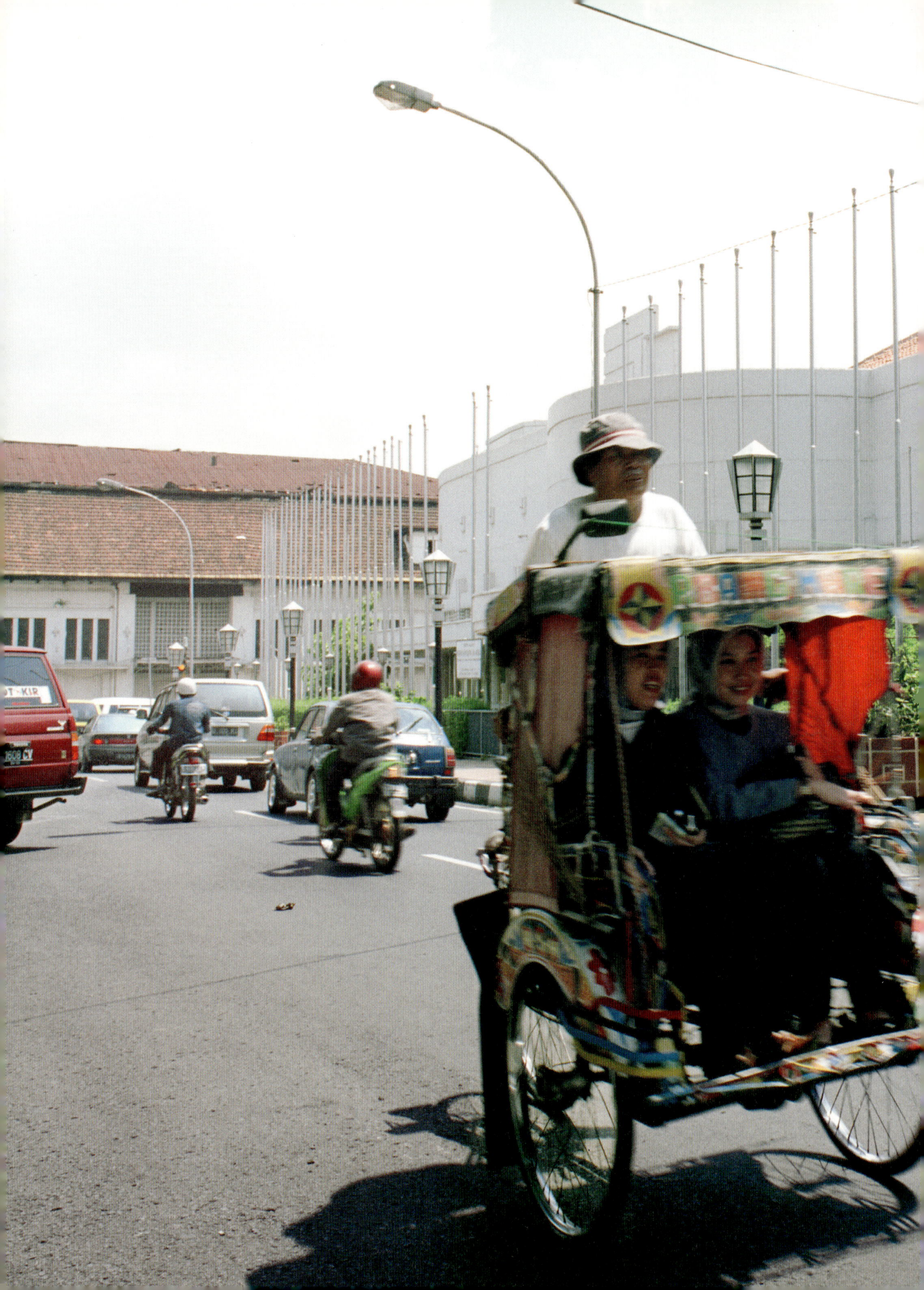

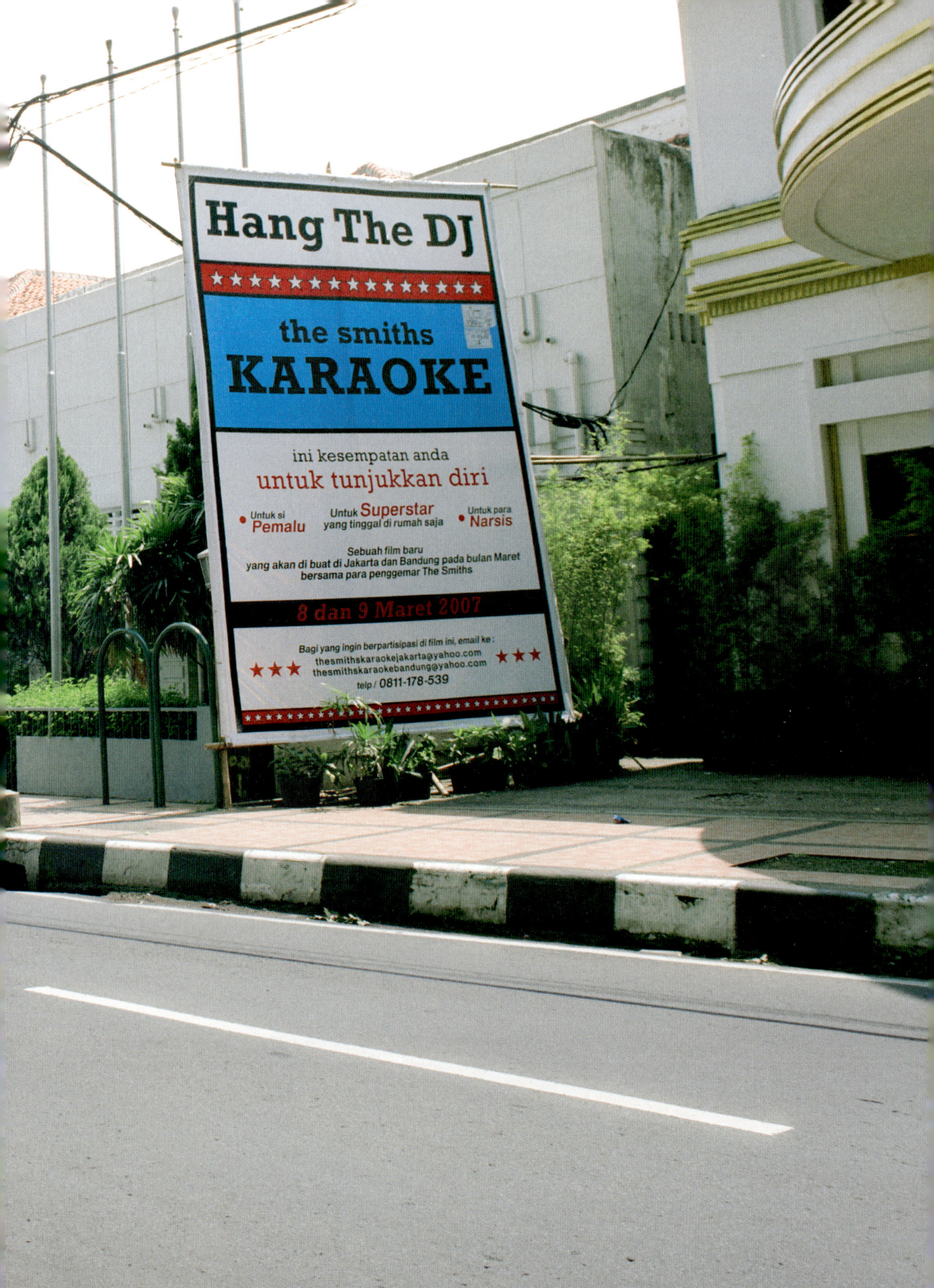

Hang The DJ
the smiths
KARAOKE
ini kesempatan anda
untuk tunjukkan diri
Untuk si Pemalu
Untuk Superstar yang tinggal di rumah saja
Untuk para Narsis
Sebuah film baru
yang akan di buat di Jakarta dan Bandung pada bulan Maret
bersama para penggemar The Smiths
8 dan 9 Maret 2007
Bagi yang ingin berpartisipasi di film ini, email ke :
thesmithskaraokejakarta@yahoo.com
thesmithskaraokebandung@yahoo.com
telp / 0811-178-539

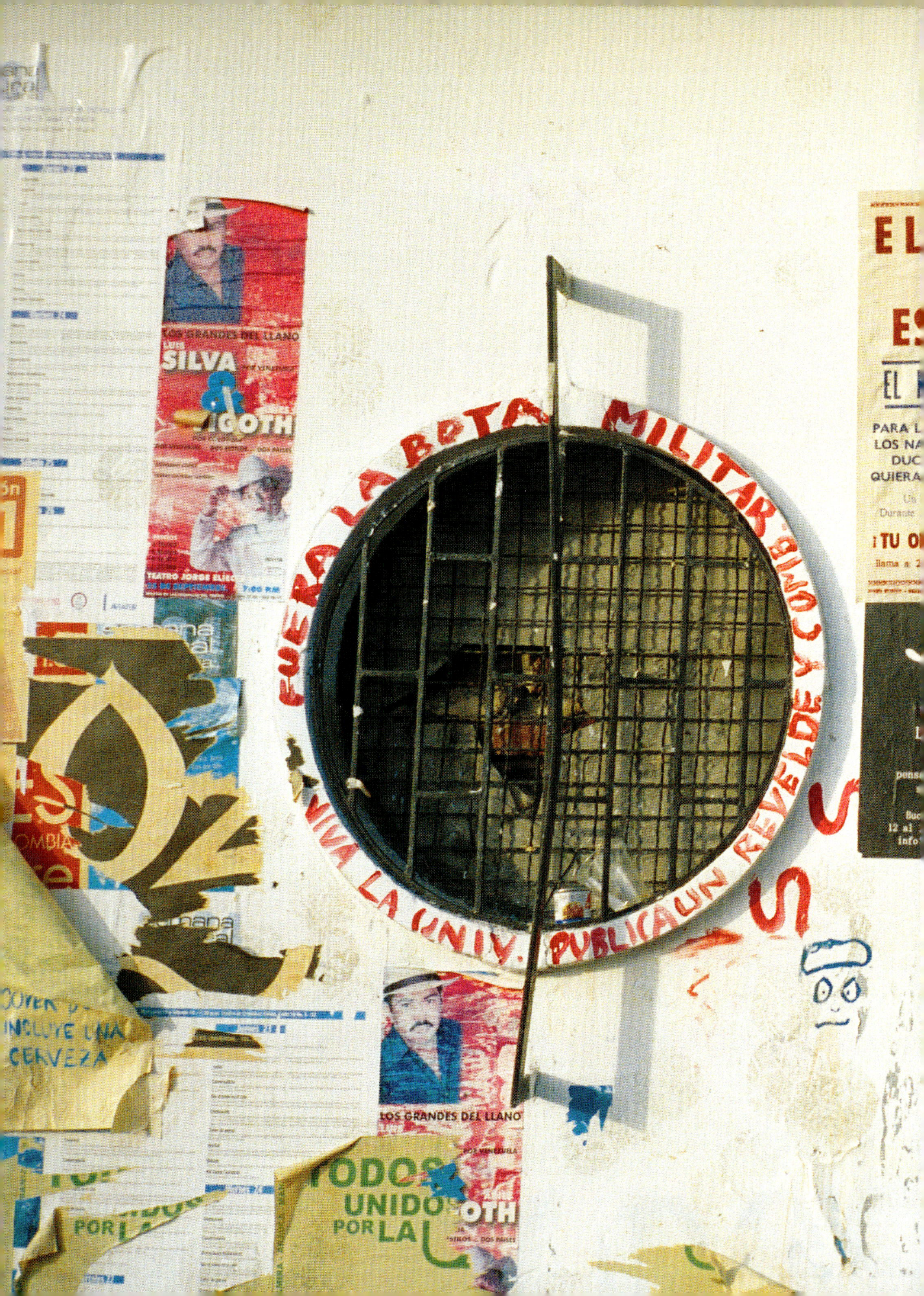
FUERA LA BOTA MILITAR
VIVA LA UNIV. PUBLICA UN REVELDE Y CUMB
LOS GRANDES DEL LLANO
LUIS SILVA
IGOTH
TEATRO JORGE ELIÉC
7:00 P.M.
COVER
INCLUYE UNA
CERVEZA
LOS GRANDES DEL LLANO
TODOS
UNIDOS
POR LA
EL
ES
EL
PARA L
LOS NA
DUC
QUIERA
¡TU O

PARO
CIONAL
Contra ... los impuestos
...nsiones
UNDO
O
HARÁ
DE LOS SMITHS
LOS INSATISFECHOS,
S ESTRELLAS DE LA
A) POR UNA NOCHE
AD DE BRILLAR!
ilovethesmiths@michica.org
Hang The DJ
Hang The DJ
Hang The DJ
EL KARAOKE DE LOS SMITHS
PARA LOS TIMIDOS, LOS INSATISFECHOS,
LOS NARCISOS, LAS ESTRELLAS DE LA
DUCHA Y TODOS AQUELLOS QUE
QUIERAN SER OTRO(A) POR UNA NOCHE
Un Nuevo Karaoke Video que se Grabará
Durante Noviembre con Fans de los Smiths en Bogotá
¡TU OPORTUNIDAD DE BRILLAR!
llama a: 2451040   email: ilovethesmiths@michica.org
PRESENTA EL CICLO:
LUGAR:
HORA:
PELICULA: Taller
FECHA: Nov 1/2004
SALUD Y ANARQUIA PARA TOD@S

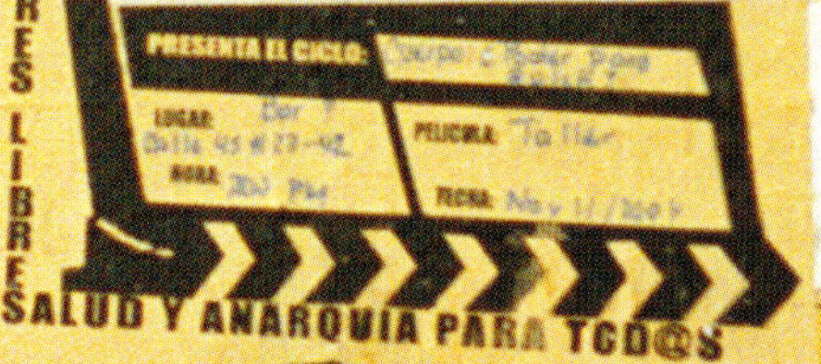
Daniel Hendler   Adriana Aizenberg   Jorge D'Elía
EL
ABRAZO
PARTIDO
a film by Daniel Burman

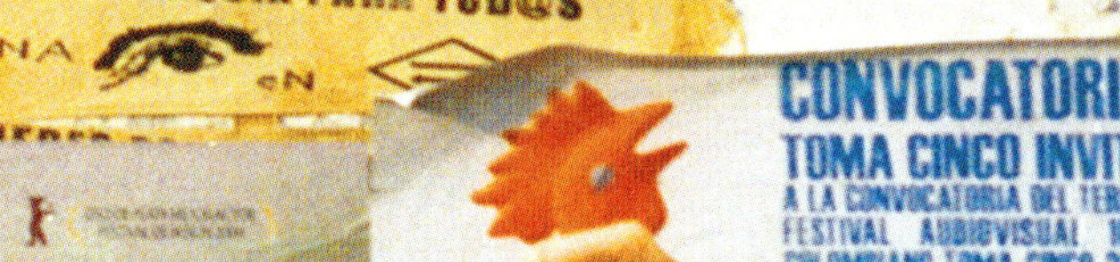

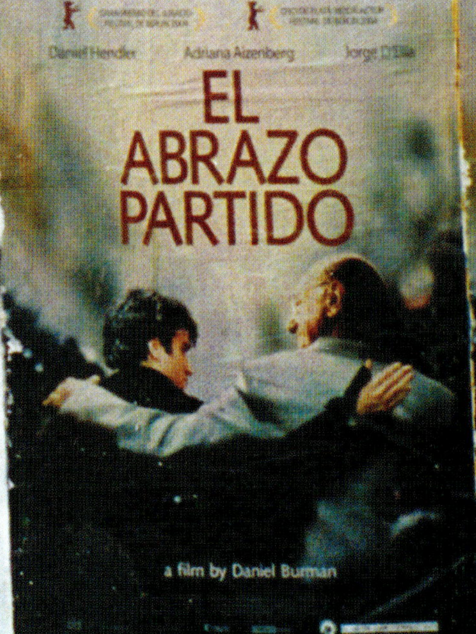
Daniel Hendler   Adriana Aizenberg   Jorge D'Elía
EL
ABRAZO
PARTIDO
a film by Daniel Burman

CONVOCATORIA
TOMA CINCO INVITA
A LA CONVOCATORIA DEL TERCER
FESTIVAL AUDIOVISUAL 100%
COLOMBIANO TOMA CINCO 2005
CONVOCATORIA A
PREMIOS
INSCRIPCIÓN B
MAYOR INFORMACIÓN
TOMA CINCO

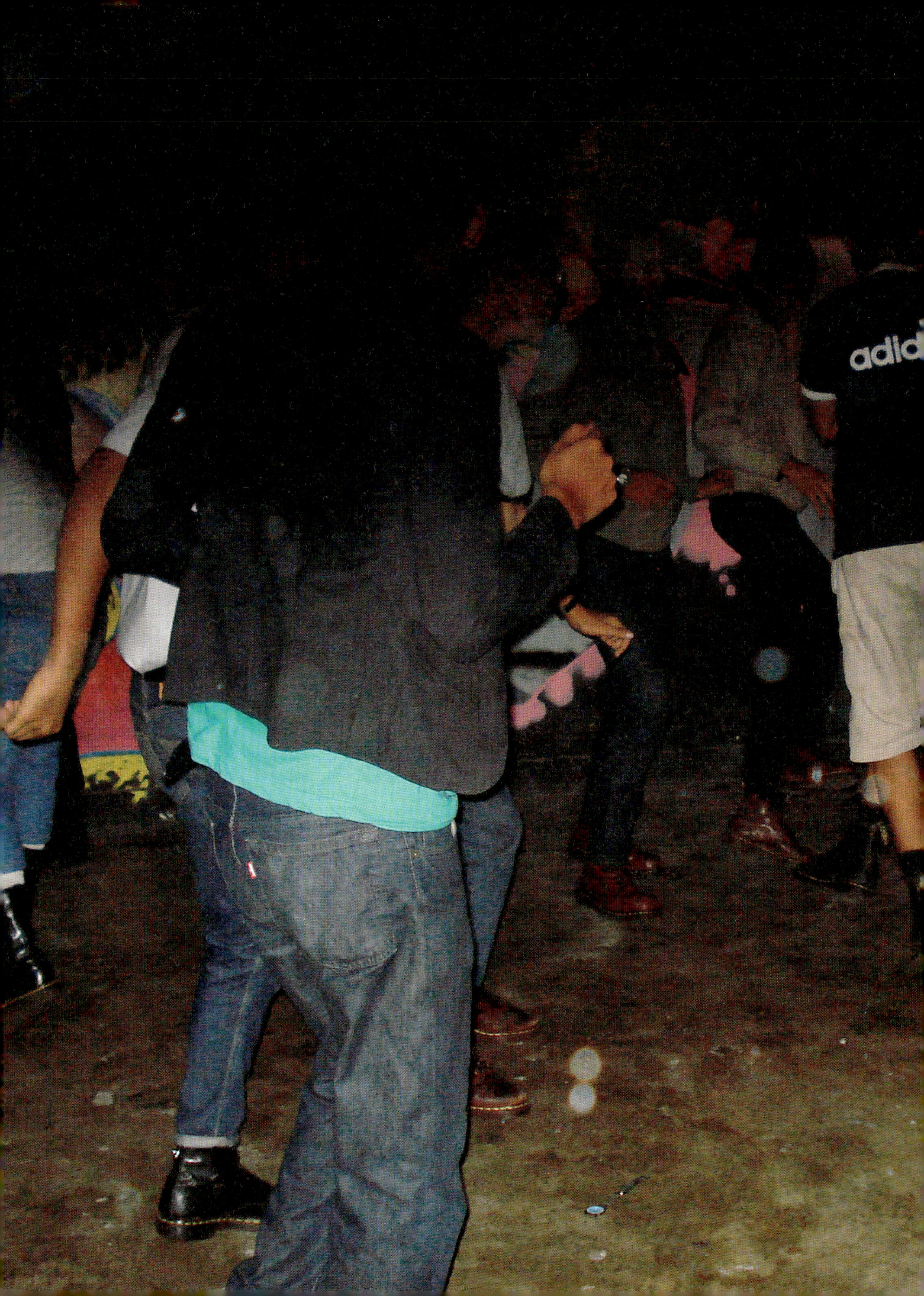

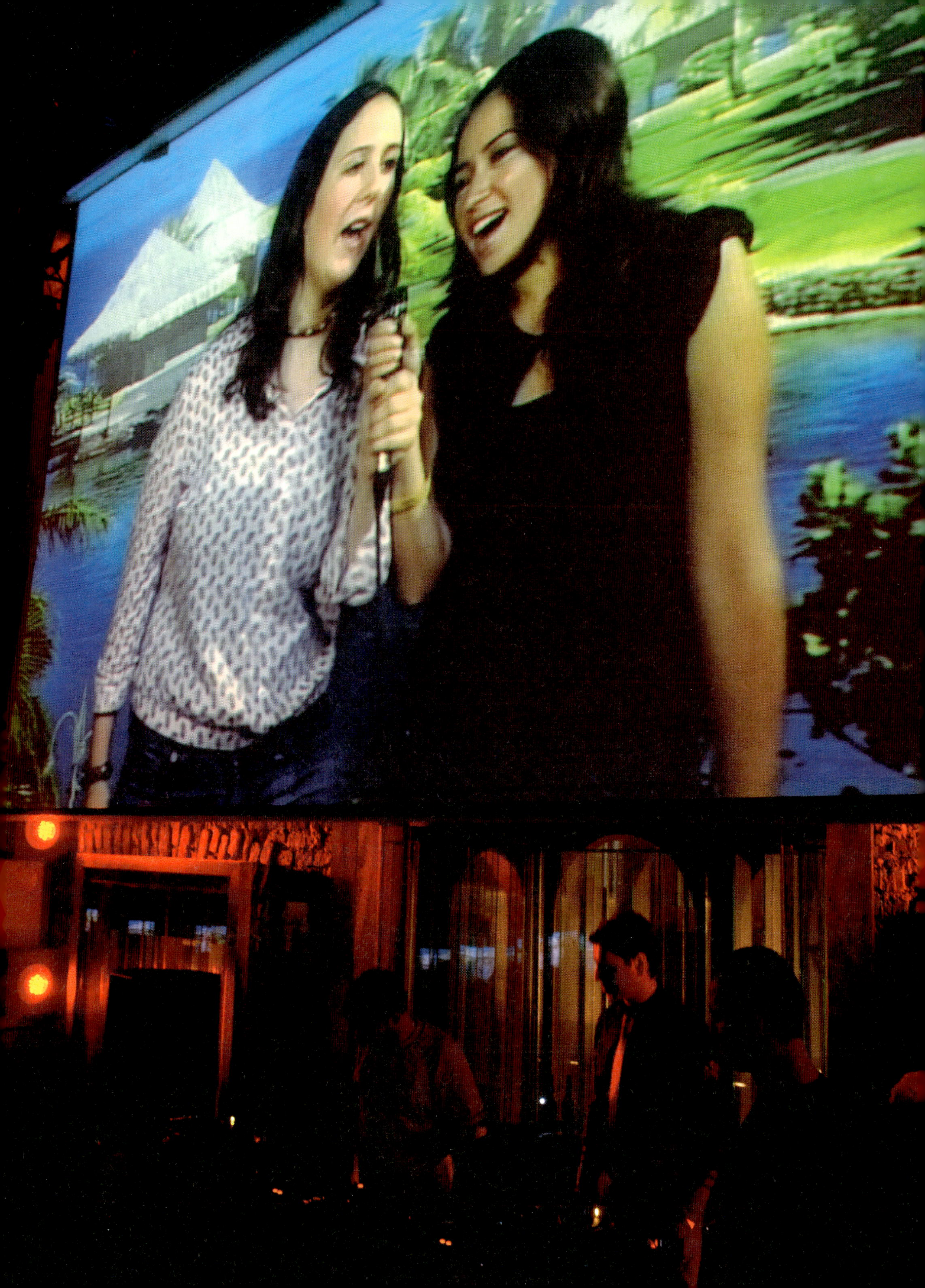

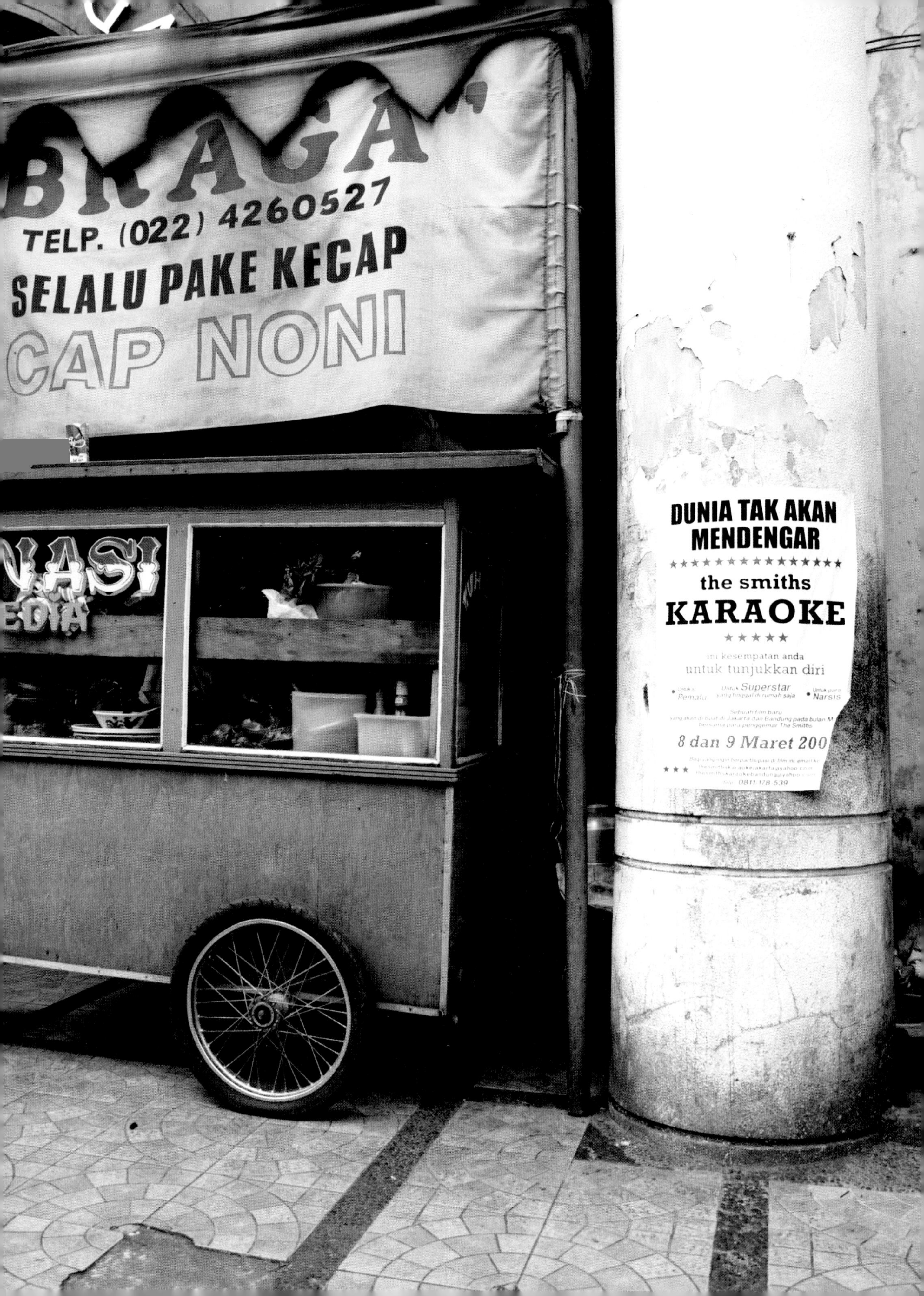

BRAGA'
TELP. (022) 4260527
SELALU PAKE KECAP
CAP NONI
NASI
EDIA
DUNIA TAK AKAN
MENDENGAR
the smiths
KARAOKE
ini kesempatan anda
untuk tunjukkan diri
Untuk Superstar Untuk para
Pemalu yang tinggal di rumah saja Narsis
Sebuah film baru
yang akan di buat di Jakarta dan Bandung pada bulan M
bersama para penggemar The Smiths
8 dan 9 Maret 200
thesmithskaraokejakarta@yahoo.com
thesmithskaraokebandung@yahoo.com
0811-178-539

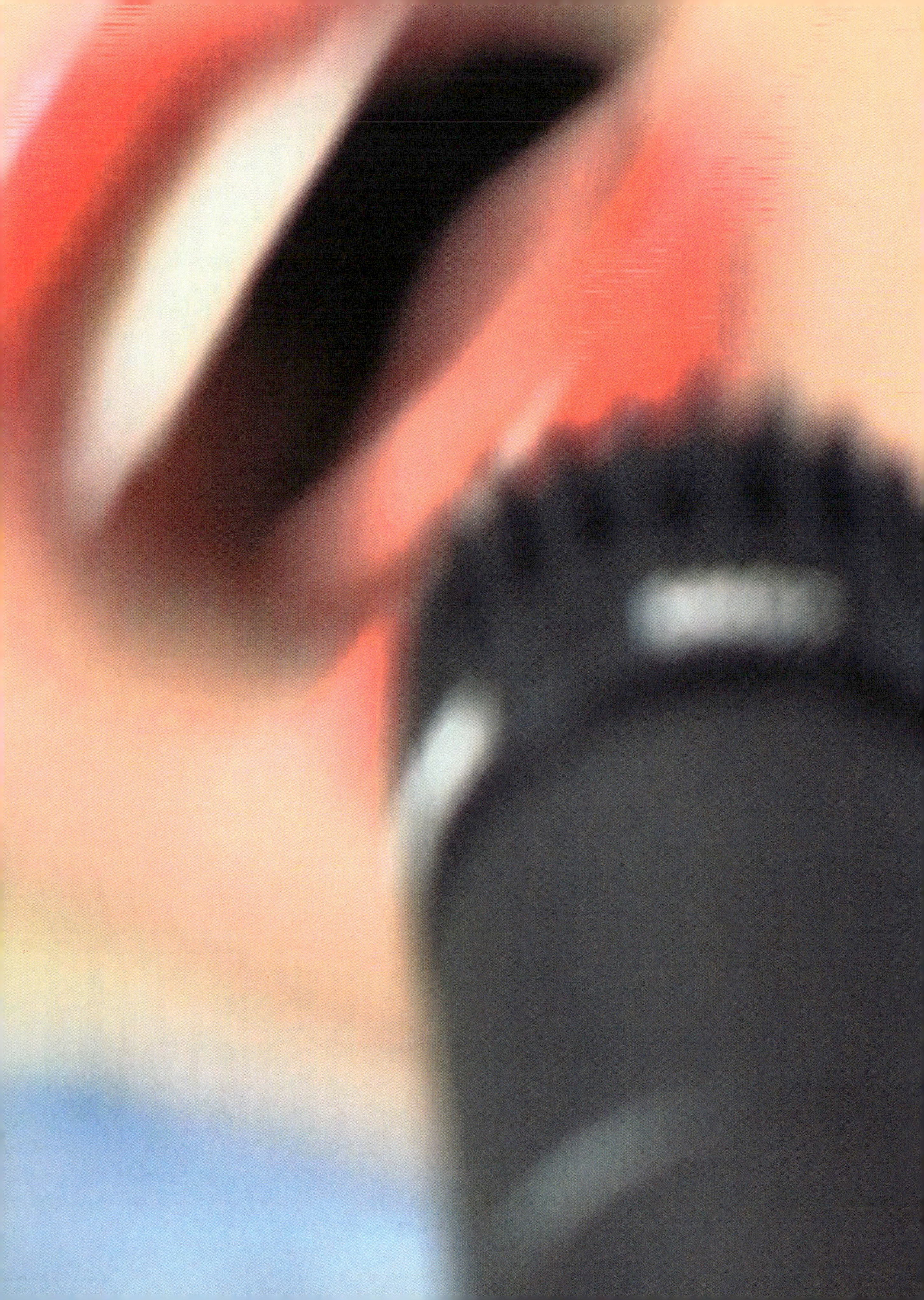

Phil Collins
the world won't listen

Suzanne Weaver

With contributions by
Bruce Hainley
Liz Kotz
Simon Reynolds

Dallas Museum of Art
Yale University Press, New Haven and London

This catalogue has been published in conjunction with
the exhibition *Phil Collins: the world won't listen*,
organized by the Dallas Museum of Art, November 9, 2007 — March 23, 2008.

Edited by Suzanne Weaver and Siniša Mitrović

Exhibition support is provided by the Contemporary Art Fund through
the gifts of an anonymous donor, Arlene and John Dayton, Laura and Walter Elcock,
Amy and Vernon Faulconer, Kenny Goss and George Michael, Nancy and Tim Hanley,
Marguerite Hoffman, Suzanne and Patrick McGee, Allen and Kelli Questrom,
Cindy and Howard Rachofsky, Deedie and Rusty Rose, Gayle and Paul Stoffel,
and Sharon and Michael Young.

This exhibition is number 52 in the *Concentrations* series, annual support
provided by the Donor Circle Membership Program through leadership gifts
of Gail and Dan Cook, Claire Dewar, Nancy and Tim Hanley, Caren Prothro,
and Cindy and Howard Rachofsky. Air transportation provided by American Airlines.

Publication of the exhibition catalogue was underwritten in part
by Shady Lane Productions and by Gayle and Paul Stoffel.

Contents

Director's Foreword

John R. Lane
The Eugene McDermott Director

Phil Collins, who was shortlisted for Tate Britain's prestigious Turner Prize in 2006,
has made a notable impact on the international contemporary art scene in a short span
of time. While still in graduate school at the University of Ulster, Belfast, in the late
1990s, he began an extraordinary journey, which continues today, creating videos and
photographs of people in places marked by political, social, and cultural turmoil and
change, such as Belgrade, San Sebastián, Baghdad, and Ramallah. With rigor, insight,
and sensitivity, Collins uniquely combines art, music, and popular culture to create
compelling real situations, from a two-day dance marathon to a press conference in
which people are afforded an opportunity to present a story that differs from what is
portrayed in commercial or official media.

As part of and in an expansion of the Dallas Museum of Art's ongoing program
Concentrations, a series of project-based exhibitions featuring the work of leading
younger international and American artists, Collins's three-part video installation
the world won't listen will be shown for the first time. Beginning in 2004, this video
trilogy has been a monumental undertaking for the artist, who spent extended periods
of time in each of three culturally different countries, researching, lecturing, building
sets, and filming, with the filming followed by an intensive and extensive editing period.
In each city, Collins went on radio and television, visited dance clubs, and posted flyers
to invite participants to come and perform karaoke versions of tracks from the 1987
album *The World Won't Listen* by the highly influential British indie band The Smiths.
The first chapter was filmed in Bogotá, Colombia, where Collins worked with local
musicians to produce a fully functioning karaoke machine; the second was filmed in
Istanbul, Turkey, and was included in the Ninth International Istanbul Biennial; and
the third was filmed in Jakarta and Bandung, Indonesia. Many Smiths fans, an almost
cultlike worldwide phenomenon, showed up and, with courage and heart, performed
their favorite lyrics by the band's iconic lead singer Morrissey. Engaging on several levels,
the world won't listen is a sympathetic, occasionally heartbreaking, and, at times, funny
portrait of humanity. It offers a poignant look at one's desire and struggle for expression
or, as the artist has said, at "the sweet agony of self-fulfillment and self-limitation."

Many people have contributed to the success of Collins's first presentation of
the completed work as a synchronized three-channel installation, the way in which the
artist envisioned it at the outset. We thank Suzanne Weaver, the Nancy and Tim Hanley
Associate Curator of Contemporary Art, for inviting the artist to present his work at the
Dallas Museum of Art and, in close collaboration with him, planning and realizing this
exhibition and publication. Her thoughtful conversation with Collins, which is included
in the catalogue, enriches our understanding of the artist's background, ideas, and process.

We acknowledge with sincere appreciation Siniša Mitrović for his insightful and crucial guidance and assistance at every stage of the project. We thank Sue MacDiarmid for her expert coordination of the audiovisual installation and exhibition design of the Dallas presentation. We are grateful to the catalogue essayists, who have helped to create a valuable contribution to the study of contemporary art and culture: Simon Reynolds, for his analysis of the seductive power of The Smiths and Morrissey; Bruce Hainley, for his illumination of the political implications of *the world won't listen*; and Liz Kotz, for her assessment of the aesthetics and art historical context of Collins's work.

For their commitment to and support of this project, our thanks go to Tanya Bonakdar Gallery, New York, Victoria Miro Gallery, London, and Kerlin Gallery, Dublin. For their contribution to the making of this publication, we extend our appreciation to the designers Scott Williams and Henrik Kubel of A2/SW/HK; to the copyeditor Frances Bowles; and to Patricia Fidler and Carmel Lyons, representatives of Yale University Press. The exhibition and publication were produced through the efforts of Dallas Museum of Art staff members Jill Bernstein, Jennifer Bueter, Vince Jones, Lance Lander, Michael Mazurek, Holly Morgan, Debra Phares, Bonnie Pitman, Elayne Rush, Kevin Todora, Tamara Wootton-Bonner, Eric Zeidler, and Jeff Zilm, each of whom played an important, much appreciated role.

We offer our gratitude to the contributors to the Contemporary Art Fund, Arlene and John Dayton, Laura and Walter Elcock, Amy and Vernon Faulconer, Kenny Goss and George Michael, Nancy and Tim Hanley, Marguerite Hoffman, Suzanne and Patrick McGee, Allen and Kelli Questrom, Cindy and Howard Rachofsky, Deedie and Rusty Rose, Gayle and Paul Stoffel, Sharon and Michael Young, and an anonymous donor, for their support of the exhibition and accompanying catalogue; to Gail and Dan Cook, Claire Dewar, Nancy and Tim Hanley, Caren Prothro, and Cindy and Howard Rachofsky for their support of the *Concentrations* series through their generous leadership gifts, a part of their Donor Circle membership; and to Gayle and Paul Stoffel for special additional support for the catalogue.

Our greatest thanks are due to Phil Collins for his inspiring imagination and generous spirit. His remarkable video work *the world won't listen* expands the possibilities of art and its ability to foster a deeper comprehension of the world and ourselves.

Artist's Acknowledgments

Suzanne Weaver and everyone at the Dallas Museum of Art, Bruce Hainley, Liz Kotz, Simon Reynolds, Scott Williams and Henrik Kubel at A2/SW/HK

Tanya Bonakdar, James Lavender, Erin Manns, Rachel Helfand, Anna Mustonen, Kathy Stephenson, Darragh Hogan, Brid McCarthy, and everyone at Tanya Bonakdar Gallery, New York, Victoria Miro Gallery, London, and Kerlin Gallery, Dublin

the production crews in all three countries

Julián Garcia, Salvador Gomezcaceres, Adelaida Herrera, Humberto Junca, Alejandro Mancera, Rosaura Pérez, Ligia Rodríguez, María Isabel Rueda, Francisco Toquica, Catalina Torres, María Antonia Vélez Serna, Charlie's Bar, Bogotá, Espacio la Rebeca, Bogotá, and Gabinete, Bogotá

Mete Avunduk, Metin Belgin, Murat Beşer, Ayşe Bulutgil, Serhat Ersöz, Charles Esche, Çiler Geçici, Hatice Güleryüz, Jülide Gürbuz, Idil Kartal, Vasıf Kortun, Hakan Liç, Filiz Örgen, November Paynter, Yeşim Tabak, Necati Tüfenk, Balans Music Hall, Istanbul, and Peyote Bar, Istanbul

Reza "Asung" Afisina, Pipin Aldiana, Dade Black, Ade Darmawan, Felix Dass, Rio Farabi, Saleh bin Husein, Jimi Multhazam, Satria Nurbambang, Karlina Octaviany, Oomleo, Ryan Pelor, Wendi Putranto, Grace Samboh, Yoko Sari, Hanin Sidhartawas, Karina Sugardha, Lenah Susiantu, Nasta Sutardjo, David Tarigan, Keke Tumbuan, Aksara Records, Jakarta, Bintang 41 Studio, Bandung, The Brandals, Déjà Vu, Jakarta, Gedung Merdeka, Bandung, Goodnight Electric, Polypony, everyone at Ruangrupa, Trax FM, The Upstairs, West Pacific, Jakarta, White Shoes & Couples Company, and Mentos

Jim Lambie, Kenny MacLeod, Daniel Mora, Chris Nelms, Danny Saunders, Maps and Official Publications Unit, Glasgow University Library, Glasgow, and Metro Imaging Ltd., London

Siniša & Ringo

and a very special thank you to the brave ones

This book is dedicated to Gugi Ljubonović.

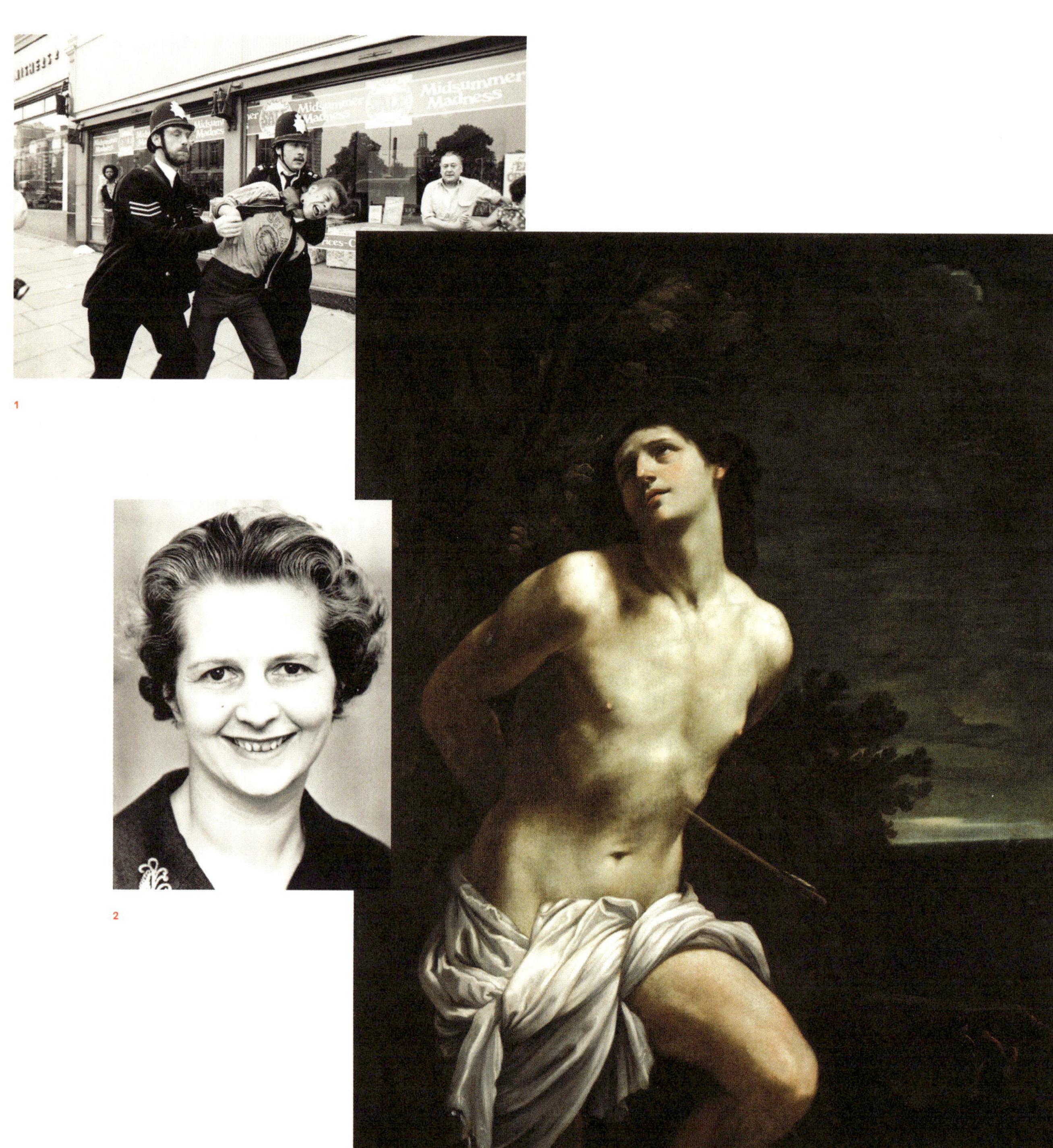

1

2

3

Simon Reynolds

It is now a critical commonplace to describe The Smiths as "the most important British band since The Beatles." The pairing makes sense on several levels. Both groups are famous for introducing Englishness into rock, yet their creative cores — the songwriting partnerships of Lennon/McCartney and Morrissey/Marr — were actually of Irish descent. Both bands came from northern industrial cities — Liverpool and Manchester — famous for a native cocky swagger typically accompanied by a sarky contempt for southern England, seen as effete and bourgeois. There's a sonic similarity between the groups: if The Smiths never sounded exactly Beatlesy, they definitely harked back to the sixties, to the guitar jangle of The Byrds (the American Beatles) and the focused aesthetic of the two-and-a-half-minute single. The Smiths were fixated on the sixties-redolent idea of the Hit Single as public event and accordingly released a large number of singles that weren't on their albums, just as The Beatles and other 1960s bands did — a compulsion that went against the grain of eighties record business practices, when singles figured merely as loss-leading promotional tools for selling albums, the industry's prime source of profit.

The Beatles/Smiths link is less about similarities and parallels, though, or even about an equivalence in terms of the quality of their respective bodies of work, than about the keen and widely felt sense that The Smiths somehow caught the zeitgeist of their decade as The Beatles did with theirs. Curiously, though, The Smiths achieved this by rejecting everything that defined eighties pop: synthesizers and drum machines, white R&B mannerisms and funk-derived dance rhythms, videos (which they refused, at first, to make, albeit soon capitulating). In a larger sense, the band's image, lyrics, and values represented a sort of protest vote against Thatcher-Reagan and the popular culture that came with the conservative backlash. Opposing the garish glitz of the early eighties New Romantic movement (Culture Club, Duran Duran, et al.), The Smiths espoused ordinariness — from their mundane name to their dressed-down look of denim and rockabilly quiffs to the gritty imagery of the songs. Yet in their own black-and-white-cinema and intensely literate way, they were glamorous, and singer/lyricist Morrissey was massively influenced by glam rock: New York Dolls, Bowie, Sparks, T.Rex. Compared with the pseudo-decadent Euro-chic of the New Romantics, The Smiths offered a true romanticism, mired in grim and grimy reality (lovers kiss under iron bridges, end up with "sore lips") yet reaching out for transcendence. This was music for depressive dreamers, people for whom the shortfall between dreams and the all-enveloping drabness was the source of endless pangs.

If you were one of these Smiths fans, you knew they were THE band of their era, "the only band that matters" (as CBS had once hyped The Clash in America). But this was a minority view. Records by Simple Minds, U2, Dire Straits, George Michael — to name only their British contemporaries — vastly outsold The Smiths' releases. If, in the group's homeland, Smiths fans were the party of permanent opposition, elsewhere in the world, to be a Smiths fan meant belonging to a delusional sect. This is where The Smiths-as-Beatles analogy falls apart. Compared with the Fab Four's global impact and (almost) unbroken chain of number-one singles, The Smiths were a largely British phenomenon and even there their singles tended to land in the charts somewhere between number thirty and the edge of the Top Ten. They wouldn't linger long either, in some cases dropping off the charts after three or four weeks — a sign that only the diehardcore were buying (typically rushing out to get the single the week it was released). Smiths singles often went down the chart immediately after the band had appeared on Britain's weekly *Top of the Pops* show, a reversal of what usually happened following exposure to ten million viewers. The fey flamboyance of Morrissey's dancing seemed to be especially aggravating to the general public. Way more people abhorred The Smiths than adored them.

—

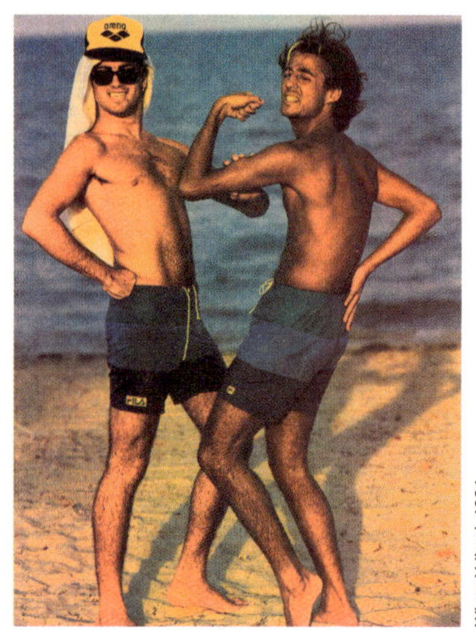

Wham! Miami, 1984

Nineteen eighty-three, the year that The Smiths started to get attention, was the peak of the New Pop moment in British music. New Pop referred to a strategy of "entryism" adopted by postpunk musicians, which involved embracing a more glossily commercial sound while abandoning the independent label sector in favor of major companies, in order to achieve the broadest mainstream impact. The Smiths went the opposite direction, signing to the country's leading indie label, Rough Trade (once ultrahip but by this point deemed dowdy, worthy, ineffectual — just like the Labour Party). Morrissey and his bandmates had easily as much burning ambition and starlust as New Pop groups like Scritti Politti (who defected from Rough Trade to Virgin). Quixotically, The Smiths aimed for the pop firmament via a label that, try as it might, consistently lacked the distribution and promotional power to propel its acts into the stratosphere. It was almost as though The Smiths were unconsciously setting themselves up for perpetual frustration, engineering their own exile — which is not such a fanciful thought when you consider how much Morrissey reveled in martyrdom.

In February 1987, almost four years into their time with Rough Trade, The Smiths released a compilation album, a mixed bag of singles and B-sides from 1985 and 1986, a period during which they struggled desperately to break into the Top Ten. Its title, *The World Won't Listen*, speaks to the band's sense of thwarted destiny. One inclusion was a scrapped single intended for January 1987 release, "You Just Haven't Earned It Yet, Baby." Although the song is a sarcastic anthem of disaffection for Smiths fans (the "it" is the endlessly receding possibility of love and happiness), the title actually comes from a remark uttered by Rough Trade boss Geoff Travis, increasingly exasperated by Morrissey's kvetching about the label's failure to make The Smiths into superstars. Despite the considerable amount of ego-affirming fan worship and critical adulation the band had received, Morrissey remained bitterly disappointed. Perhaps Travis grasped

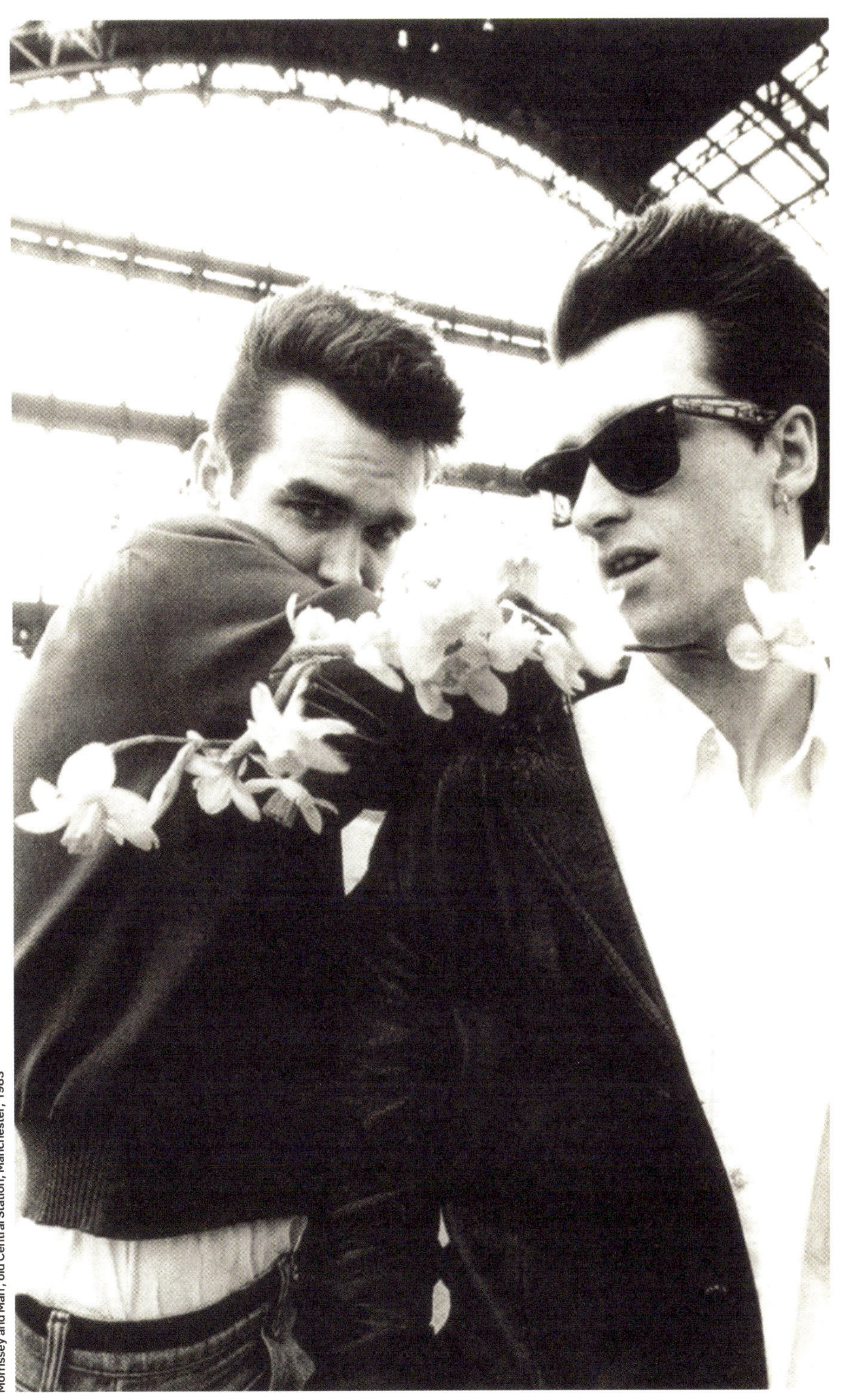

Morrissey and Marr, old Central Station, Manchester, 1983

1

John Pilger, *Heroes*
(London: Jonathan Cape, 1986).

that he always would be. Being unrequited, an outcast, was integral to Morrissey's mindset, his worldview. The smarting sense of injustice and neglect from his youth as a weirdo-nobody had simply been transposed to the larger arena of pop music. The unearned "it" stood for some impossibly total state of prestige and recognition destined to stay out of reach.

The following month, March 1987, The Smiths released another compilation, the title, *Louder Than Bombs*, apparently expressing frustrated megalomania. Put together by their American label Sire as a primer for new fans, this was a U.S.-only anthology (although inevitably legions of British devotees bought it as an import). The phrase "louder than bombs" sometimes gets sourced in Alan Sillitoe's novel *The Loneliness of the Long-Distance Runner* (made into one of the black-and-white British "kitchen sink" realist films of the 1960s that Morrissey adored), and it has been attributed to a Vietnamese man, quoted in John Pilger's book *Heroes*, who recalls children and old folks singing as they cowered from American bombardments: "singing is louder than bombs."[1] But most likely the phrase comes from "louder than bombs or screams or the inside ticking of remorse, . . ." a line in one of Morrissey's favorite books, *By Grand Central Station I Sat Down and Wept* by Elizabeth Smart, a novel he pillaged extensively for other Smiths songs. This torrid testament of (almost completely) unrequited love is a big clue to Morrissey's psychology and aesthetic. Unrequited and, better still, unrequited-able love is a Morrissey song staple because longing — yearning across an unbridgeable gulf — is an end in itself.

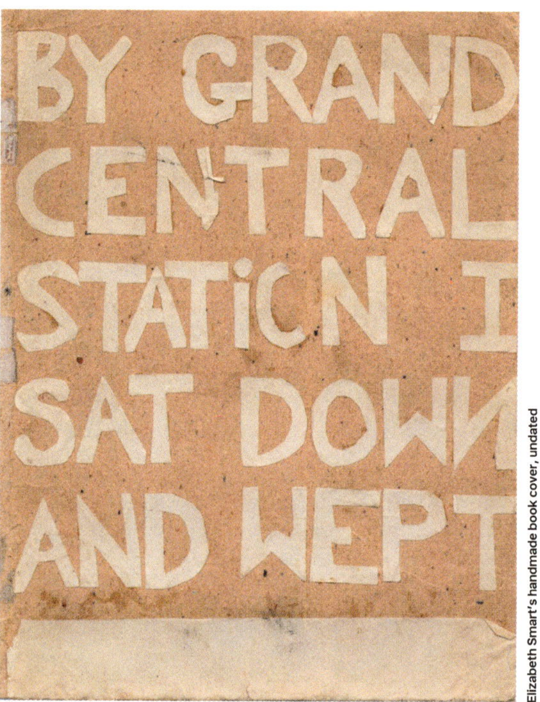

Elizabeth Smart's handmade book cover, undated

2

Morrissey, interview by Paul Morley, *Blitz* magazine (London), April 1988.

3

B-side to the twelve-inch version of "This Charming Man," 1983. The song is said to be inspired by Morrissey's close companion Linder (Linda Sterling) of the Manchester postpunk experimental pop band Ludus.

4

Morrissey, interview by Morley.

Part of what made Morrissey a dissident in the eighties — the pop decade of Madonna, Prince, George "I Want Your Sex" Michael — was his avowed celibacy, probably the single most perplexing and preposterous thing for the antifans. While many assumed it was a pose or just a cloak for closeted homosexuality, there remains the possibility that Morrissey really did believe in abstinence. Partly because the reality of consummation could never live up to his romantic ideals; partly because celibacy engenders a sort of perpetual polymorphous buzz of pent-up libido, as enjoyed by the mystic monks of the Middle Ages. Morrissey once declared, "all those thing like love, sex, sharing a life with somebody, are actually quite vague. Being only with yourself can be much more intense."[2] This is not the same as solipsism, because for Morrissey, the Other remains crucial, as the instigator of desire. But for this yearning to become suspended necessitates wanting the one you can't have (like Elizabeth Smart and her married lover), which in Morrissey's case could mean a heterosexual man or equally involve an intense but noncarnal admiration for a woman (as in the awesome and awestruck "Wonderful Woman," an early Smiths B-side pivoting around the chorus "what to be done with her?" — a line that can be read in a couple of ways).[3] Morrissey's bizarre and unprecedented (in pop) insistence on both his omnisexuality and his celibacy sealed a sort of pact with his fans. It guaranteed that he would stay as unloved and unlovable as they believed they were and would always be. But it also ensured that he would remain utterly out of reach (because even if, by fan cunning and strategy, you could get close to Morrissey . . . well . . .). It's the ultimate tease.

The agony of the unrequited is that they've got so much love and nobody to give it to. Morrissey proposes that intransitive state of anguished ardor as an ideal for living. The starkest articulation of this stance came long after The Smiths broke up, in his 1994 song "I Am Hated for Loving." With his sonorous croon gliding through a near-ambient haze of golden guitar-chimes, whispery backing vocals, and his own multitracked moans and murmurs, Morrissey seems to be wrapping himself *in himself*, weaving a womb-world of serenely regal narcissism: "I still don't belong / To anyone — *I am mine*." The title "I Am Hated For Loving," repeated throughout the song and also twisted to "I am haunted for wanting," is intriguing. The proximity of "hate" and "love" recalls Paul Weller's lyric for The Jam's "Start," in which the boy in the song makes a brief and affirming connection with another idealistic youth who, like him, "loves with a passion called hate."

That line captures the polarized black/white vision of adolescence, where the world is divided into holy and corrupt. And it fits Morrissey and his fans like a glove. As much as the fans identify with the singer's eternally unreciprocated amorousness, Morrissey is also loved for hating. The singer claimed that he always knew from the response at their early gigs that The Smiths would be big: "It was more than I expected. There were lots and lots of people ready to identify with what I was feeling. Hatred! Hating everything but not being offensively hateful. It was like hate from quite gentle people."[4] He titled his 1988 solo debut *Viva Hate* and in an interview at the time declared that he was disappointed in pop because of a dearth of negativism and "serious

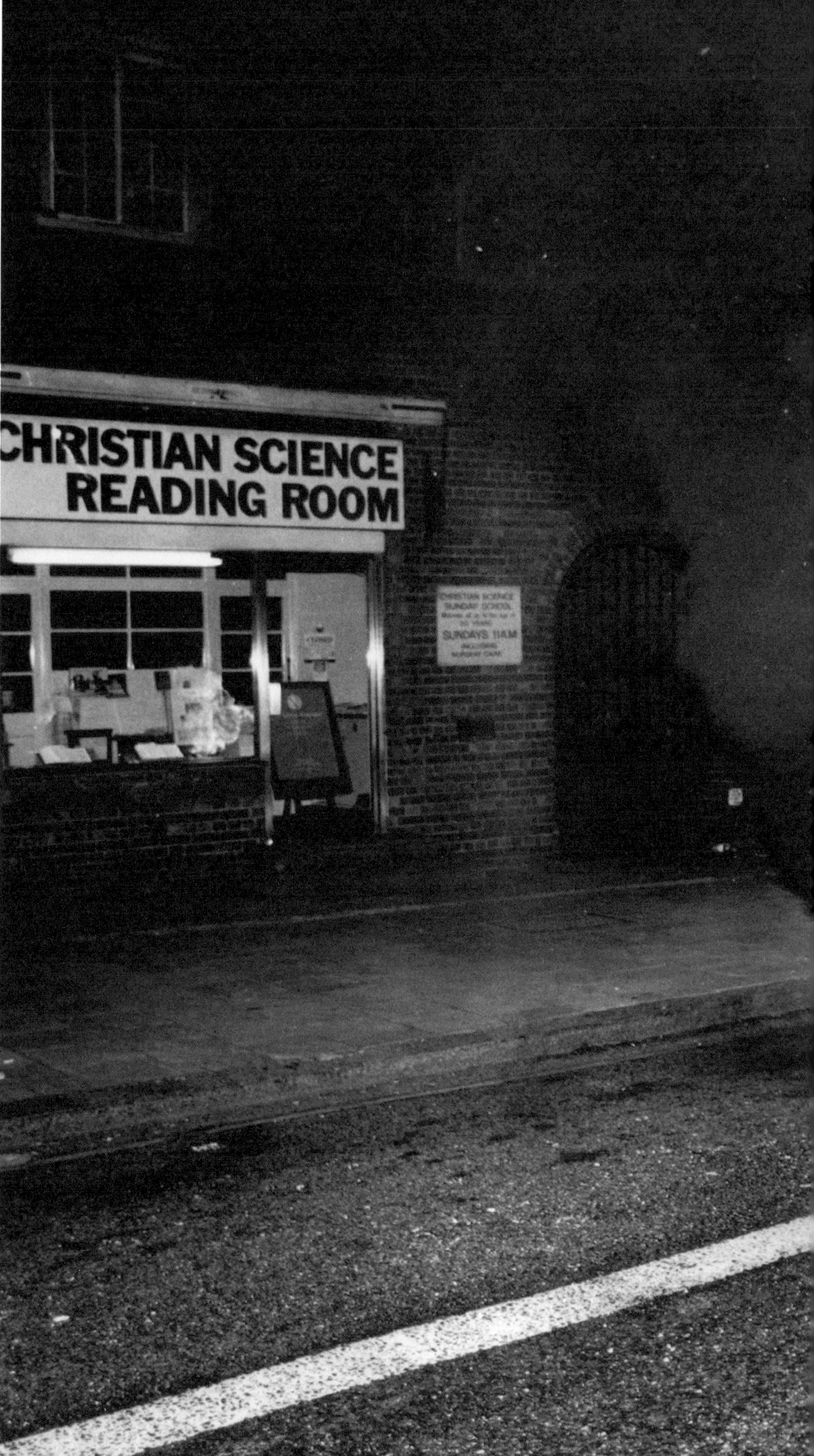

Car blazes during Brixton riots, London, 1984

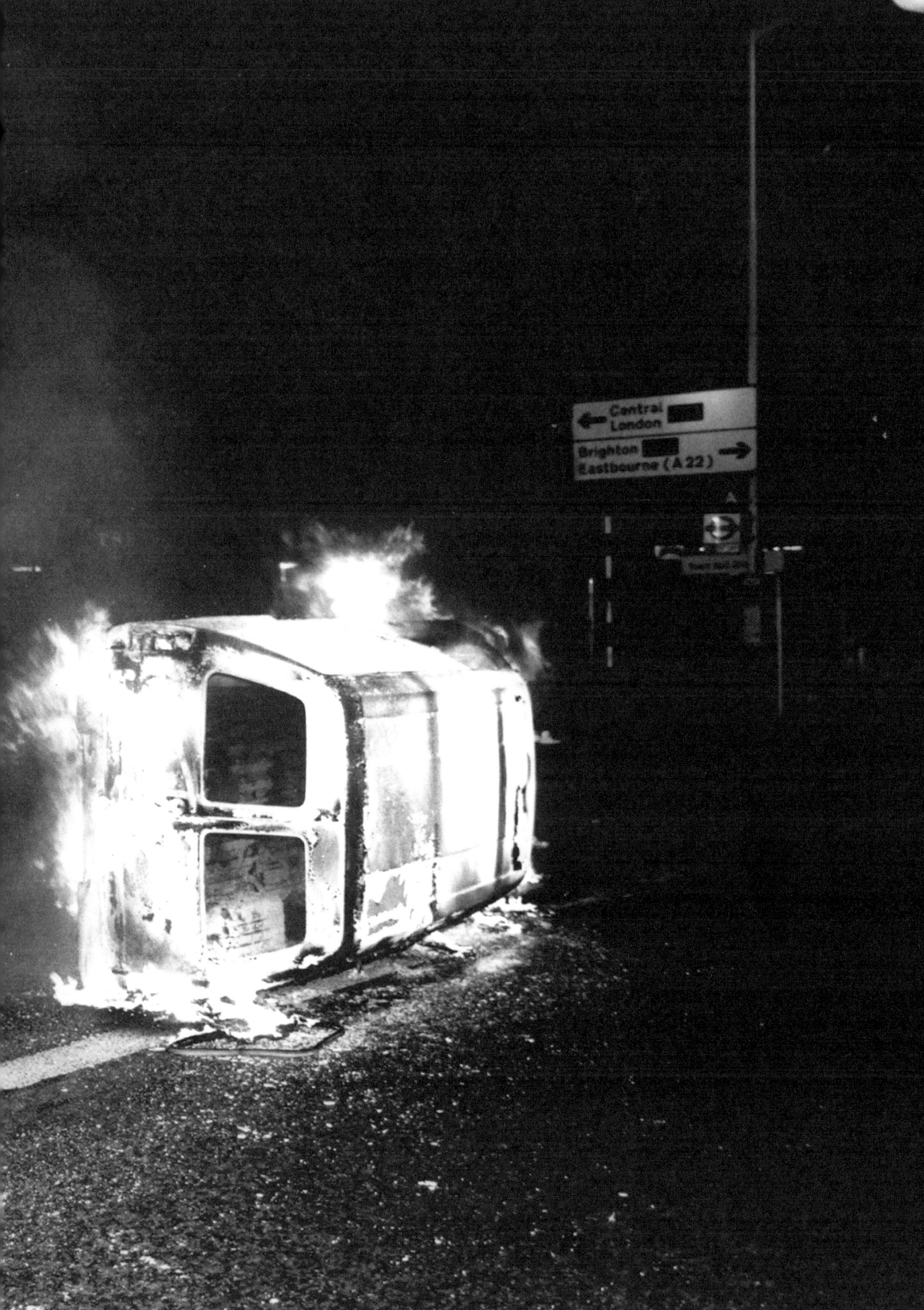

Central London
Brighton
Eastbourne (A 22)

5

Morrissey, interview by Simon Reynolds, *Melody Maker* magazine (London), March 12 and March 19, 1988; reprinted in Simon Reynolds, *Bring the Noise: 20 Years of Writing About Hip Rock and Hip Hop* (London: Faber and Faber, 2007), 75.

6

In a British TV interview around the time of the song's release, Morrissey explained that "the thorn's the music industry and all these people who just would never believe anything I said. Tried to get rid of me. Wouldn't play the records. So I think we've reached a stage where we feel if they don't believe me now, will they ever believe me? . . . What more can a poor boy do?" (Morrissey, interview with Margi Clarke, Glasgow Barrowlands, September 25, 1985; broadcast on Channel 4 television station, October 25, 1985).

7

Mark Simpson, *Saint Morrissey: A Portrait of This Charming Man by an Alarming Fan* (New York: Touchstone, 2003), chapter 3.

statements. . . . I feel I should look about and see streams of groups being angry and hateful."[5] Pop fandom, for Morrissey, has always been inseparable from disgust and dismay about all the other crap cluttering up the charts, hence his virulent dismissals of hip-hop ("a stench"), reggae ("vile") and techno-rave (mechanistic, inhuman), along with a more general contempt for the vast bulk of pop and rock on account of the wit-less vapidity of the lyrics.

Morrissey regards himself as a thorn in pop's side, a perpetual reminder of its underachievement and shoddiness. Yet in one of the singles corralled on *The World Won't Listen*, it's Morrissey who's "The Boy With The Thorn In His Side."[6] The language seems simple enough on the surface — "The boy with the thorn in his side / Behind the hatred there lies / A murderous desire for love" —but it contains peculiar depths. The title is generally taken as an allusion to Saint Sebastian, the early Christian martyr depicted in paintings as a half-naked youth tied to a post by the Romans and pierced with arrows (as a result becoming an image of eroticized suffering and a gay icon). "The hatred" could be the shower of insult and injury that batters Morrissey, but it makes more sense as a reference to his own hatred for the world, which is really a "murderous" (later "plundering") longing for love. On its first pass, the verse has Morrissey, in the first-person singular, wondering how people can look in his eyes and not apprehend the truth of his misery; coming around for a second time, it's pluralized to "we."

> *How can they see the Love in our eyes*
> *And still they don't believe us?*
> *And after all this time*
> *They don't want to believe us*
> *And if they don't believe us now*
> *Will they ever believe us?*

The capitalization of *Love* in the lyric sheet is intriguing. Is this the love that dare not speak its name? Or something unspeakable and mystical, a love that bypasses all plausible partners, and flesh and blood itself? A kind of desire within desire(s), an ardor for the Absolute that can be fulfilled only in dreams or in death? One of the most penetrating and provocative books on the singer, *Saint Morrissey* by Mark Simpson, harps on his Catholic background.[7] Another single on *The World Won't Listen* is "Big Mouth Strikes Again," in which Morrissey makes a jokey but not entirely unserious comparison between himself and Joan of Arc.

The notion of sacrificing yourself on behalf of a principle, risking life or limb for the sake of words, has intense romantic allure to Morrissey. Sometimes the "truth" in question is a (forbidden or denigrated) love: "I'll fight to the last breath" ("Hand In Glove"), "I'd jump in front of a flying bullet for you" ("What Difference Does It Make?"), "to die by your side / well the pleasure, the privilege is mine" ("There Is A Light That

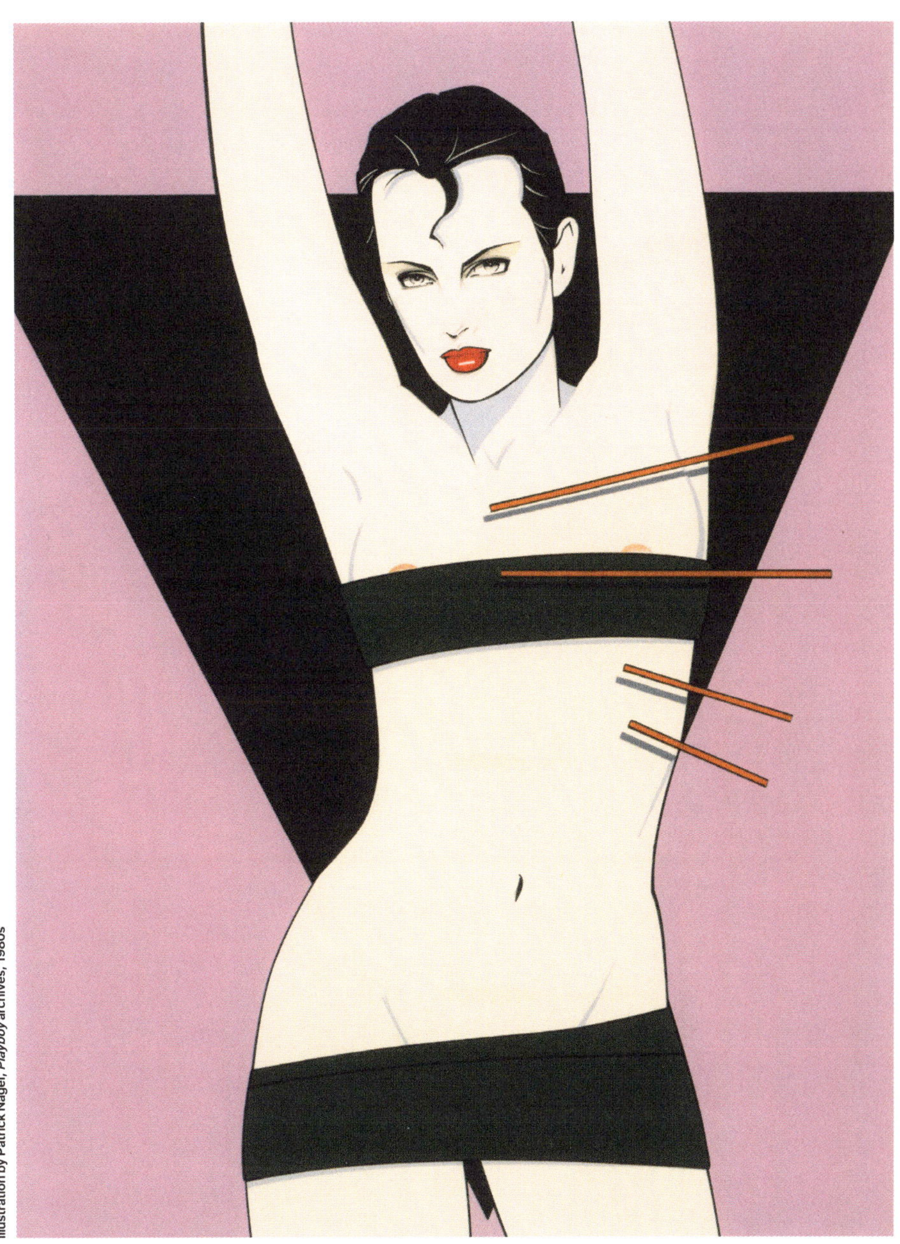

Never Goes Out"). Another form of self-martyrdom in the name of Truth is suicide, sung about with tender empathy in *The World Won't Listen*'s "Asleep" and "That Joke Isn't Funny Anymore." The heretical truth here is the suicide's defiant disbelief in the commonsensical faith in life as a good never to be relinquished, a gift horse whose teeth should remain unexamined. Suicide is the ultimate passive-aggressive act. Marianne Faithfull, whose "Come And Stay With Me" was the first pop single bought by the child

8

Quoted in Antti Nylén, "Me and Morrissey:
Notes on the Essence and Effects of
a Voice," *Eurozine*, August 23, 2004. http://
www.eurozine.com/articles/2004-08-24
-nylen-en.html.

9

Morrissey, interview by Reynolds; reprinted
in Reynolds, *Bring the Noise*, 78.

10

Morrissey, interview by Paul du Noyer,
Frontline magazine, 1985; http://
www.geocities.com/SoHo/Square/9076/
smiths/articles/goon.html.

11

Morrissey, interview, *New Musical Express*
(London), 1991; quoted in Nylén, "Me and
Morrissey."

Morrissey, once said that if she hadn't been a heroin addict — essentially a form of slow suicide, a controlled death-in-life, the sustained suppression of one's vital(ity) signs — she would have been a terrorist. Her utopian rage had to either implode or explode.

Morrissey has frequently expressed admiration for active-aggressive expressions of utopian impatience. In one 1987 interview he called for "Direct Action" as "the only thing that can save the world" (but with typical and wonderful lack of proportion equated the trifling teenpop irritant Tiffany with nuclear waste as problems that require "a few bricks . . . to be thrown").[8] The scenario of popular justice revenging itself on the tyrannical crops up in the form of not one but two songs involving execution: one concerns the so-called trivial domain of pop, the other the far more urgent realm of politics. In 1986's "Panic," Morrissey beseeches "hang the deejay" (the crime: playing music that "says nothing to me about my life"). *Viva Hate*'s "Margaret On The Guillotine" imagines the beheading of Prime Minister Thatcher. In interviews, Morrissey insisted the song was neither a joke nor a silly fantasy:

> "You'd like to see her dead?"
> "Instantly."
> "In a cruel, bloody sort of way?"
> "Yes."
> "Would you carry out the execution?"
> "I have got the uniform, ready."[9]

In an earlier interview, he expressed disappointment that the IRA bombing of the Brighton hotel in which members of the British government were staying during the Conservative Party conference of 1984 had failed to kill Thatcher. And on The Smiths' last album *Strangeways, Here We Come*, the song "A Rush And A Push And The Land Is Ours" took its title from a call for armed resistance made by the Irish nationalist poet Speranza. This was the pseudonym of Jane Francesca Agnes, a.k.a. Lady Wilde — the mother of Oscar Wilde, Morrissey's hero and supreme role model.

This entwining of anticolonial revolution and dandy defiance in the figures of Wilde mother and son almost too perfectly sources Morrissey's revolt against reality. His art — which includes the songs, but also the record covers with their rich iconography of Morrissey's pantheon of pop culture heroes, and the singer's entire persona as expressed through countless interviews — constitutes a form of subaltern retaliation, a reprisal against everyone who ever slighted or disregarded him, tried to hold him back or down. In 1985 Morrissey talked of success as "absolutely and entirely a form of revenge" and one that tasted "remarkably sweet. I like the taste, yes. More please!"[10] In 1991 Morrissey informed the *New Musical Express*, "No matter what people say, I've won. In a strange sense, the battle is over. It was over when *Viva Hate* went in at Number One."[11]

—

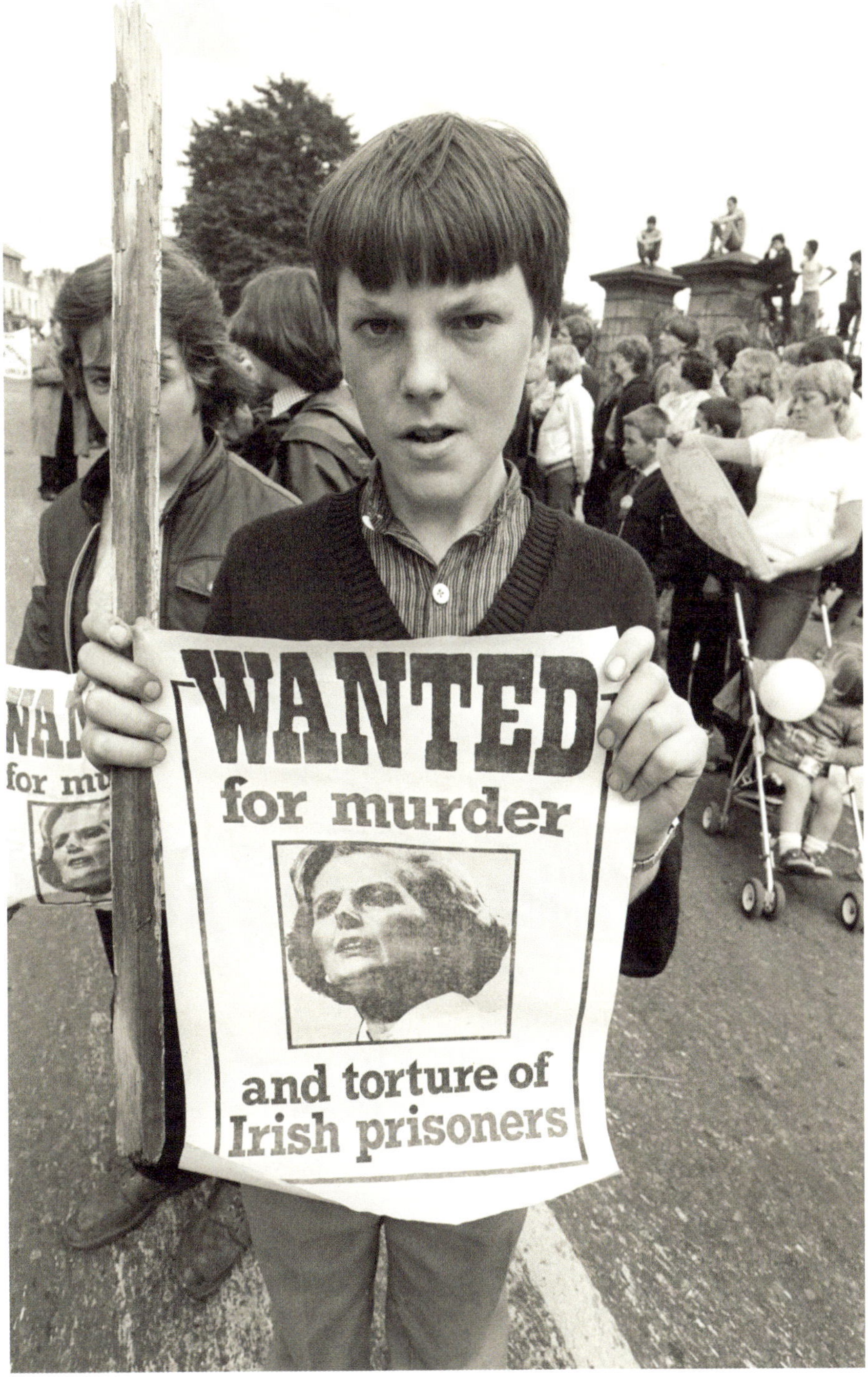

Demonstration in Belfast on tenth anniversary of internment, August 10, 1981

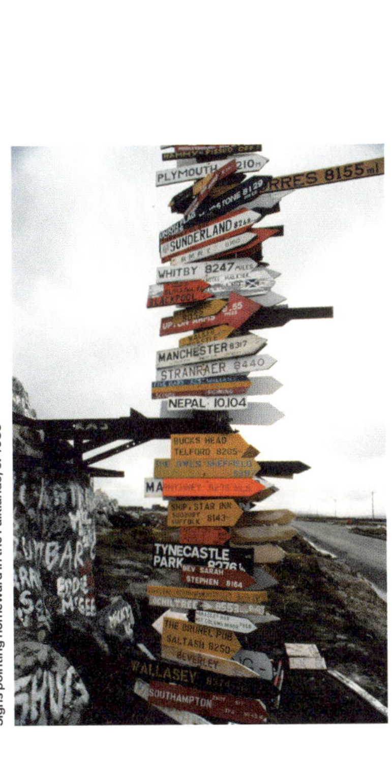

Signs pointing homeward in the Falklands, c. 1985

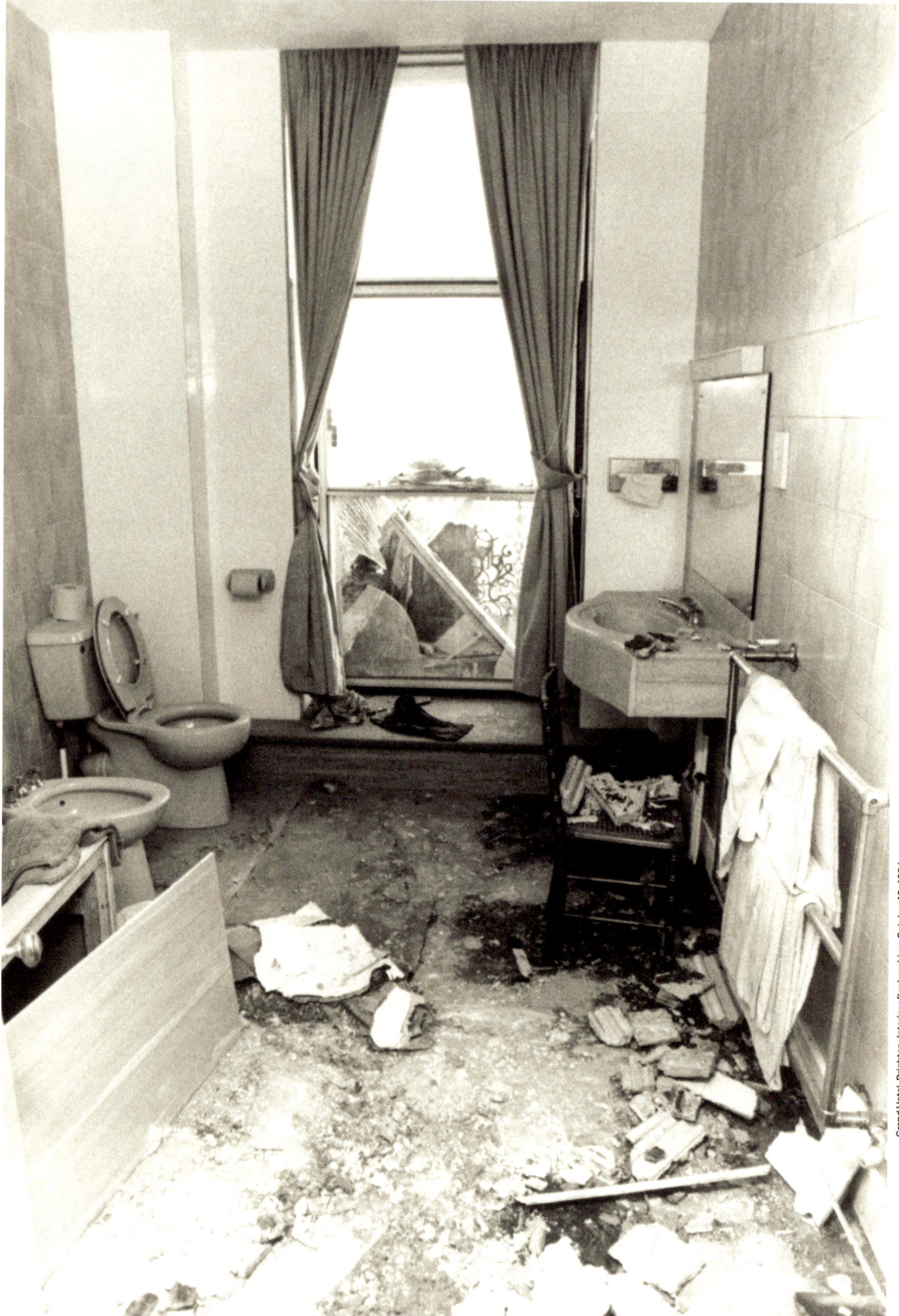

Grand Hotel, Brighton. Interior after bombing, October 12, 1984

12
Ibid.

13
Which Morrissey obligingly sources
(well, at least partially) in the 1972 Cajun
song "Saturday Nite Special" recorded
by The Sundown Playboys, which he heard
a few times on the radio as a youth but was
never able to identify until the late eighties.
It appears as the first selection on *Under
the Influence*, a Morrissey-compiled CD
of the music that has shaped his sensibility.
The Sundown Playboys sang in Acadian
French, rendered further unintelligible to
Morrissey's infant ears ("I can't understand
a single word," he recalls of that baptismal
hearing) by the astonishing coyote-keening
style of the lead vocalist. In the CD's sleeve
note Morrissey writes of the Cajun vocal
style, "the singers (usually male) had to
sing high and loud in order to be heard above
the instruments. . . . Vocals would be belted
out without restraint . . . and overstretched
to an almost feminine tonality." Beyond
being electrified by his encounter with this
androgynized vocal, it seems significant
that one of Morrissey's primal pop moments
involved an experience similar to witnessing
speaking in tongues. He further notes
that the first time he appeared in front
of a microphone in a recording studio he
used "the melody of this mystery song as
my guide."

There's a sense in which pop music is what Western youth had instead of revolution. Pop is where our most charismatic leaders, our poet-rebels went; rock culture, all its upheavals and internal dissensions, is our equivalent to the Cultural Revolution. When actually revolutionary countries, such as Iran, restrict or ban rock, do they do so because it's disruptive, decadent, corrupting? Or because it is a rival recruiter, competing for youth's hearts and minds?

Antti Nylén, an acute Morrissey analyst (and devout fan) argues that "when you say yes to Morrissey in a radical way, you say no to the world and its requirements."[12] That's what the suicide ballad "Asleep" says, in its way: "There is a better world / Well, there must be . . . ." The world that won't listen must be negated or replaced. But this uncompromising message, as voiced by Morrissey, has an extraordinary ability to traverse the world. Morrissey sets huge store by his lyrics, and they are undeniably a major part of his claim to greatness. But in some ways the words are beside the point, as can be seen from the range and often loopiness of lyric interpretations put forth by fans on the Web. It's a quality of the voice itself that connects and that opens up something inside even outwardly bluff and manly types (the cult of Morrissey does skew remarkably male, and heterosexual male too). Morrissey's popularity among those for whom English is a second language is striking. These are fans for whom the subtleties of the lyrics — oblique and fragmentary much of the time, riddled with English archaisms, inflected with varying degrees of archness and irony — are necessarily lost.

Perhaps Morrissey's eloquence reaches its peak during his wordless flights of falsetto, keening and plangent — the yodeling gyrations of self-raptured flutters[13] at the close of "The Boy With The Thorn In His Side," for instance. Here Morrissey's singing most closely resembles his extraordinary dancing, its alchemy of awkwardness into grace itself constituting an eloquent protest against the Normal and the Real. Emulated with poignant gawkiness by the Turkish boy who shimmies and twirls to the instrumental "Oscillate Wildly" in Phil Collins's *dünya dinlemiyor*, it's a ballet of yearning and violence. A war dance.

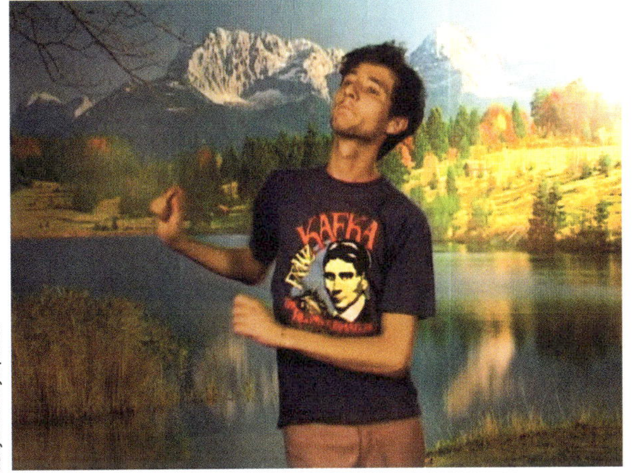

dünya dinlemiyor, 2005

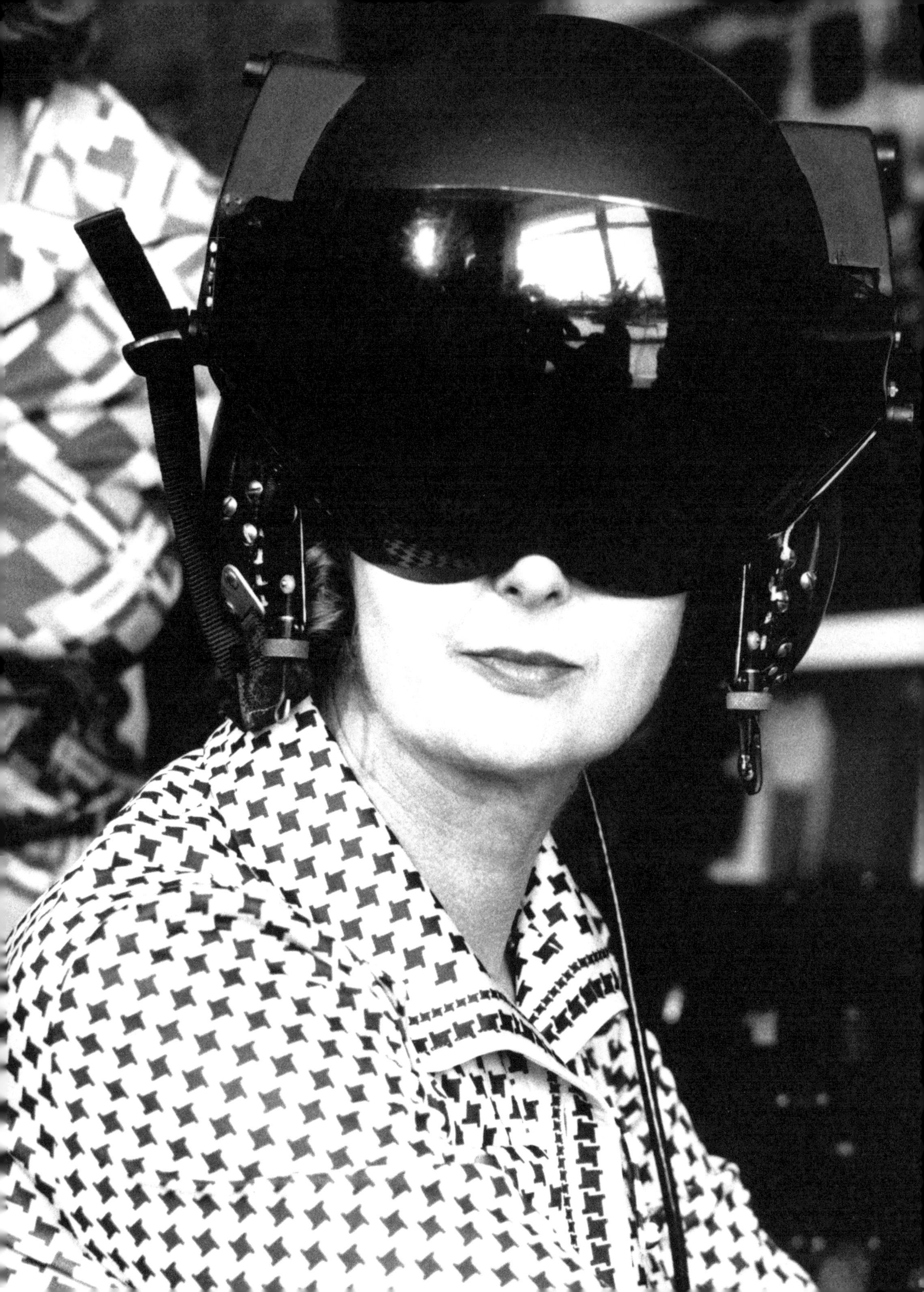

EL MUNDO NO ESCUCHARÁ

EL KARAOKE DE LOS SMITHS

PARA LOS TIMIDOS, LOS INSATISFECHOS, LOS NARCISOS, LAS ESTRELLAS DE LA DUCHA Y TODOS AQUELLOS QUE QUIERAN SER OTRO(A) POR UNA NOCHE.

Un Nuevo Karaoke Video que se Grabará Durante Noviembre con Fans de los Smiths en Bogotá

¡TU OPORTUNIDAD DE BRILLAR!

LLAMA A: 245 10 40

email: ilovethesmiths@michica.org

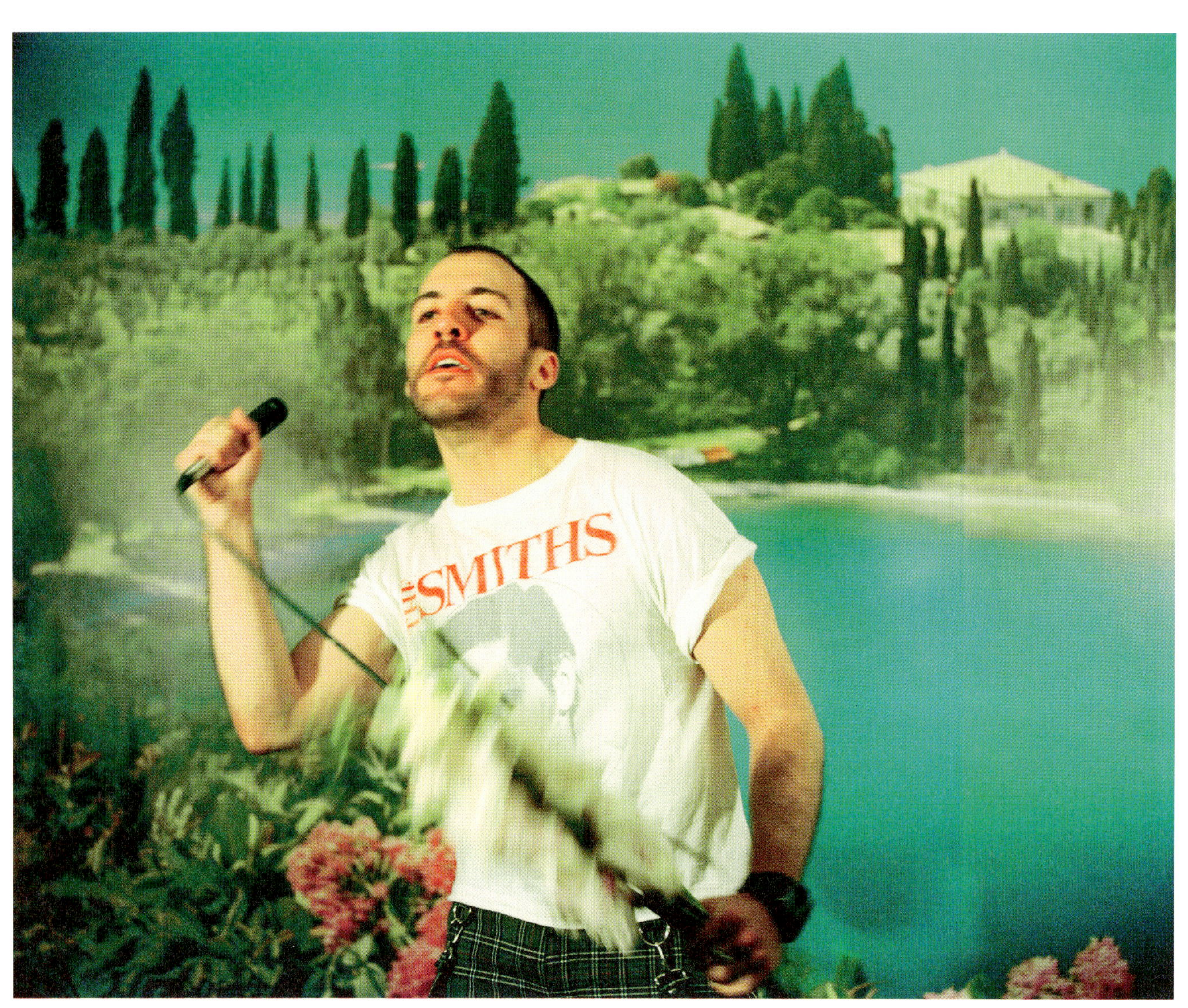

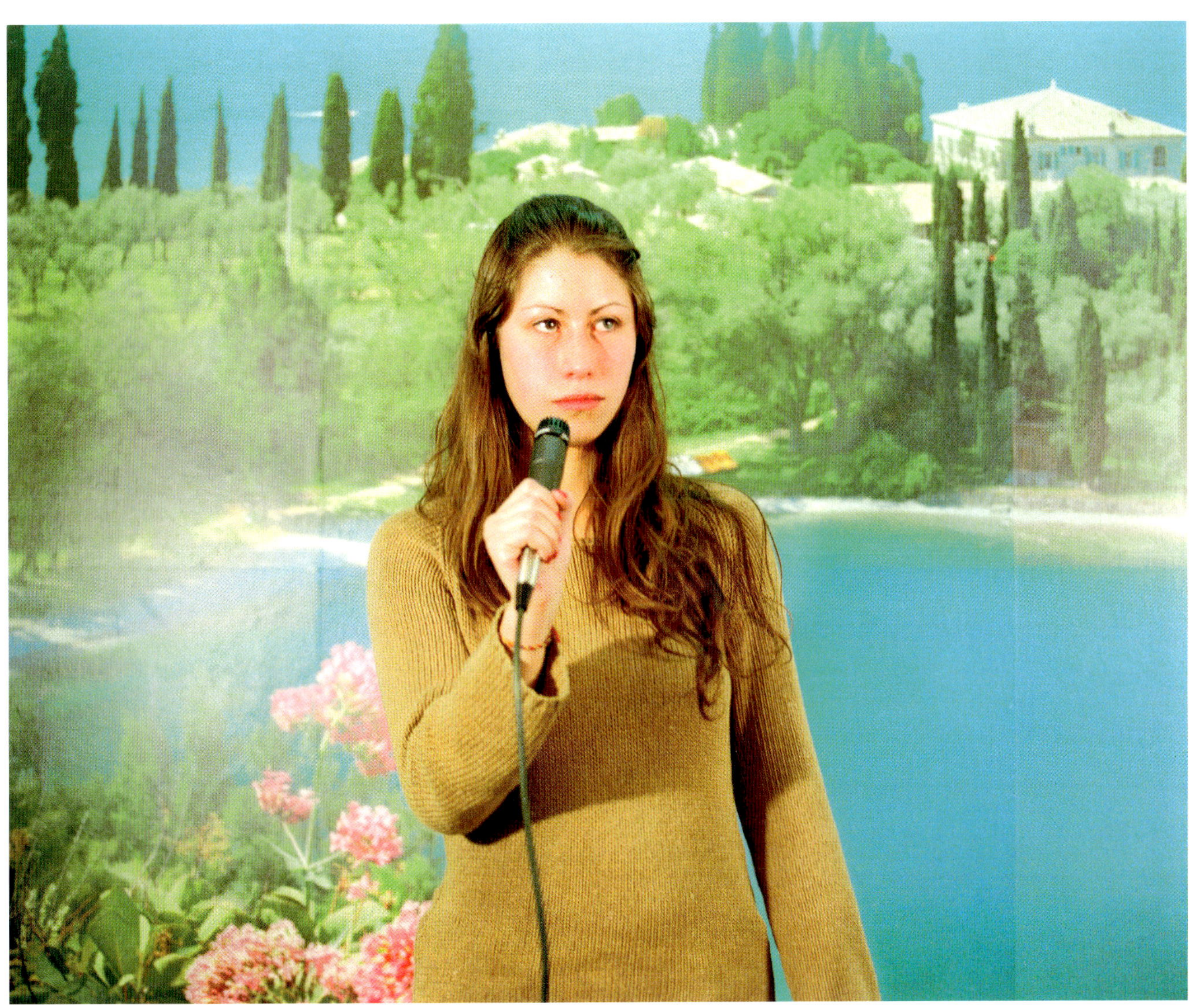

el mundo no escuchará

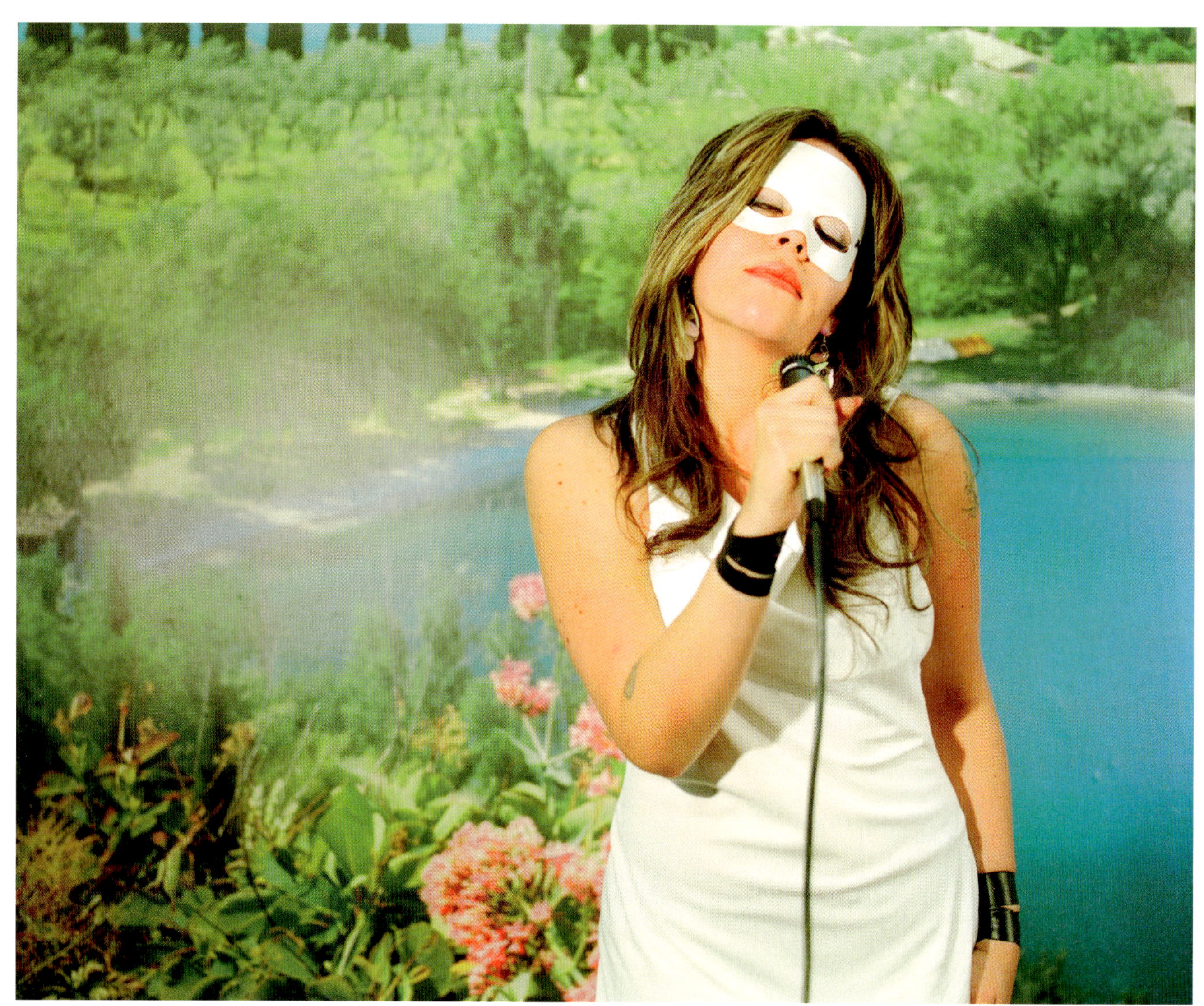

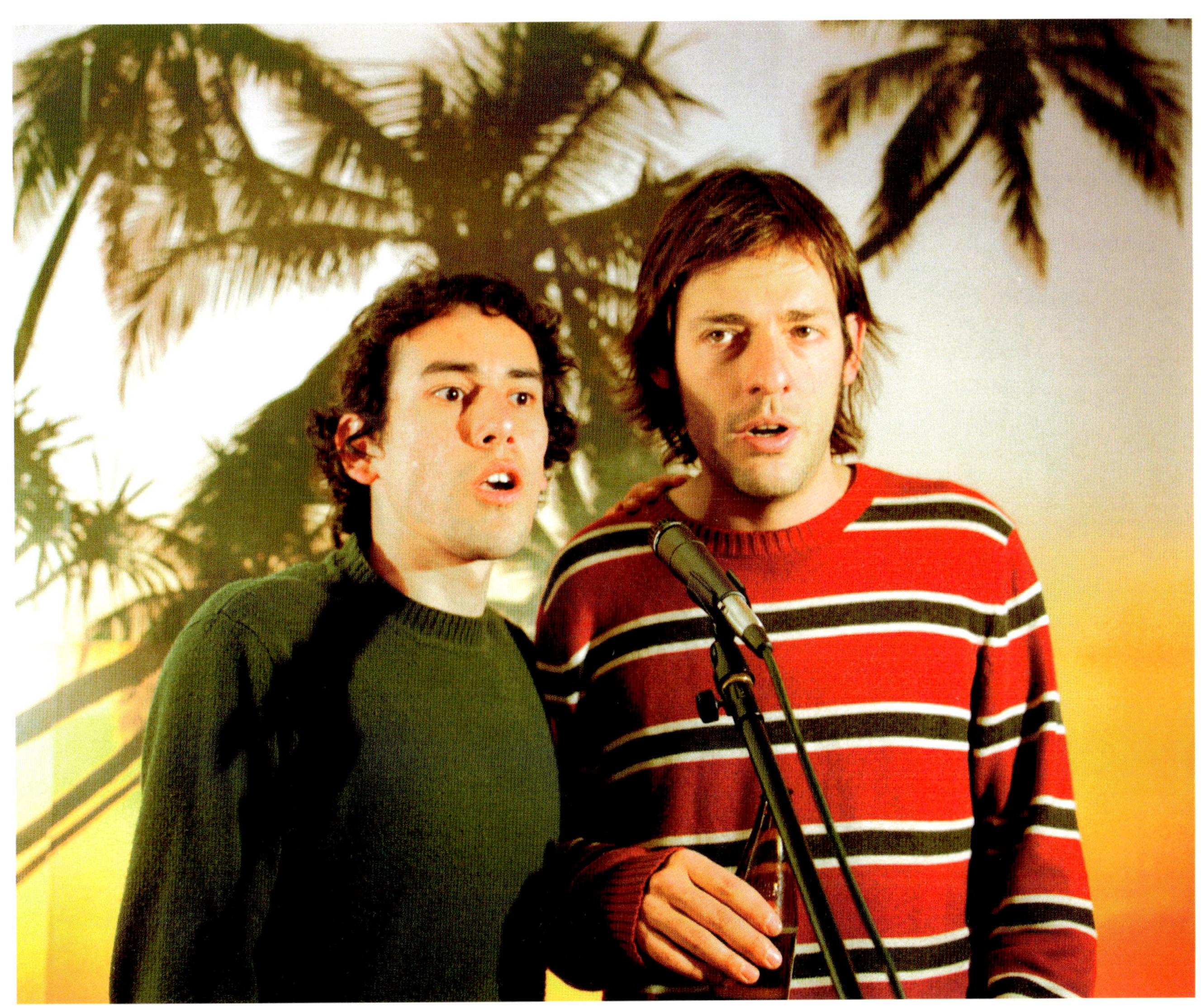

el mundo no escuchará

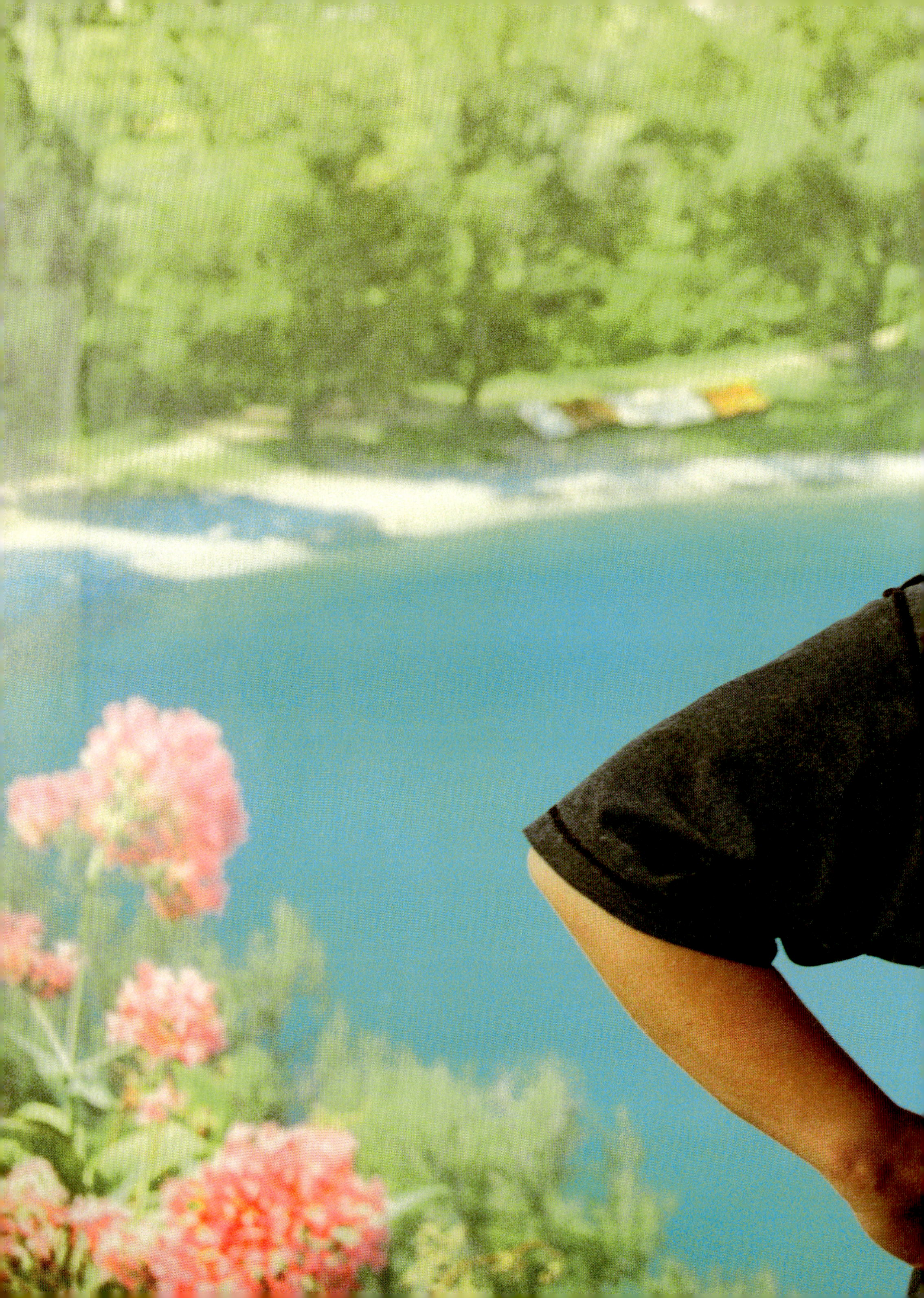

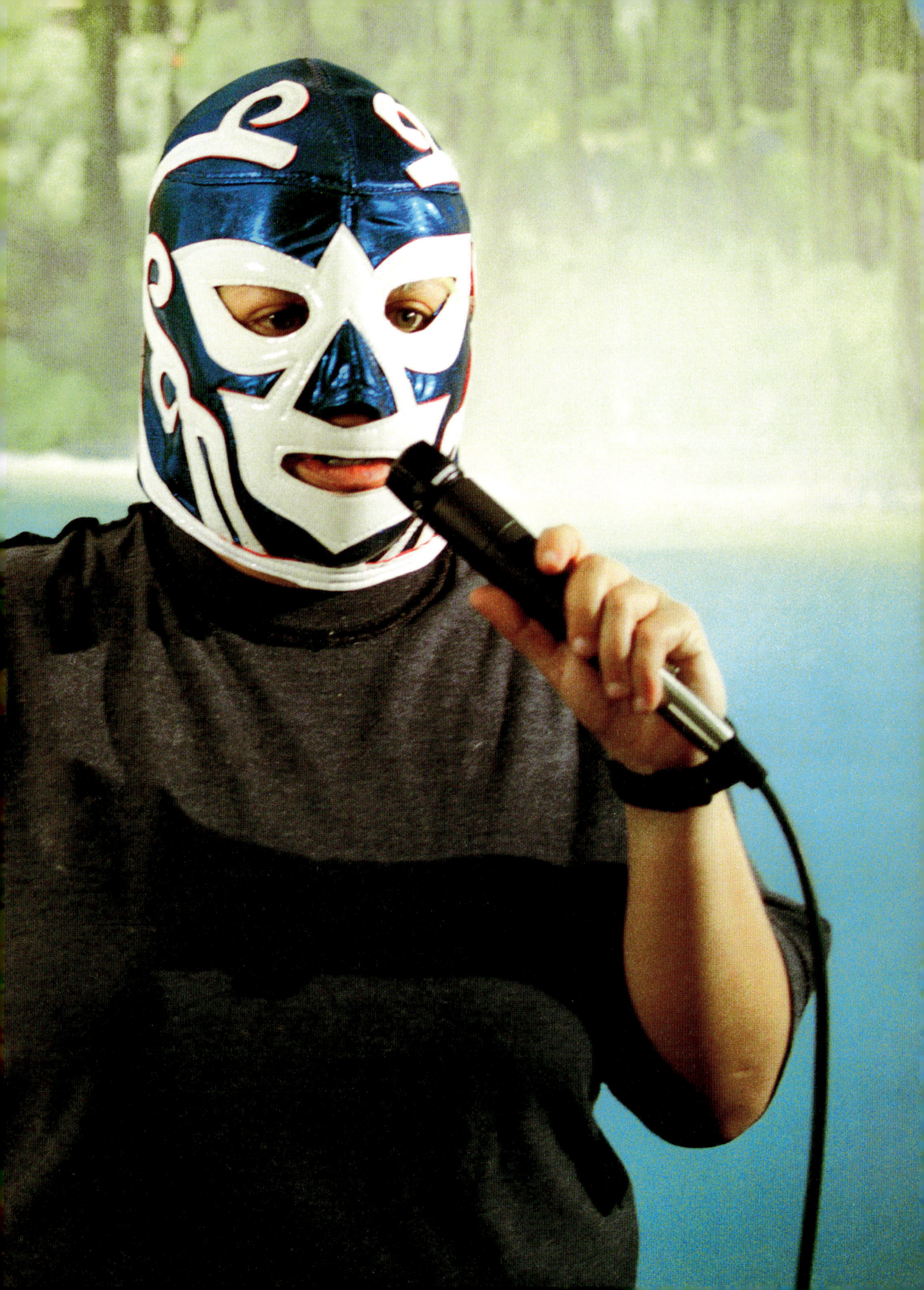

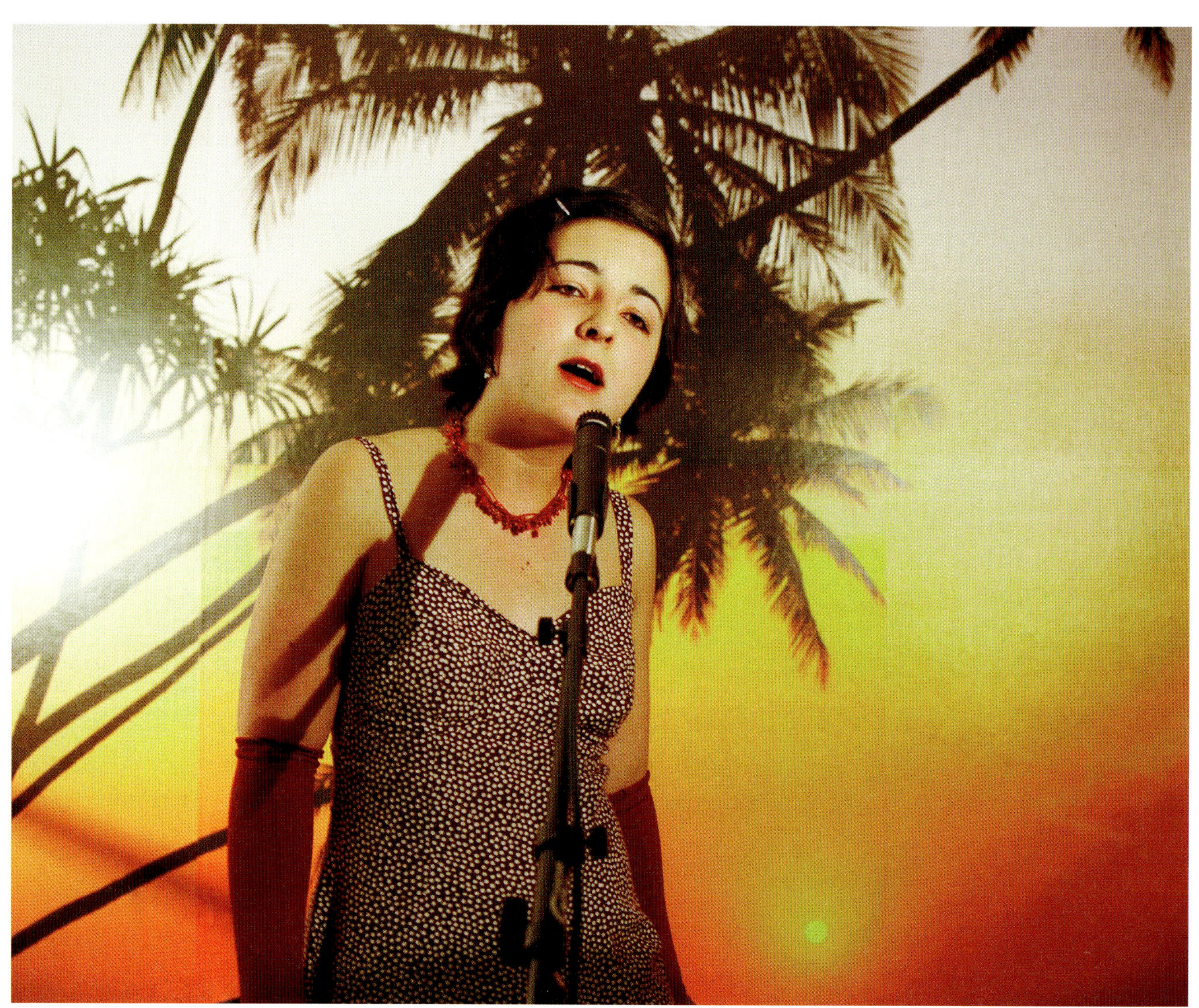

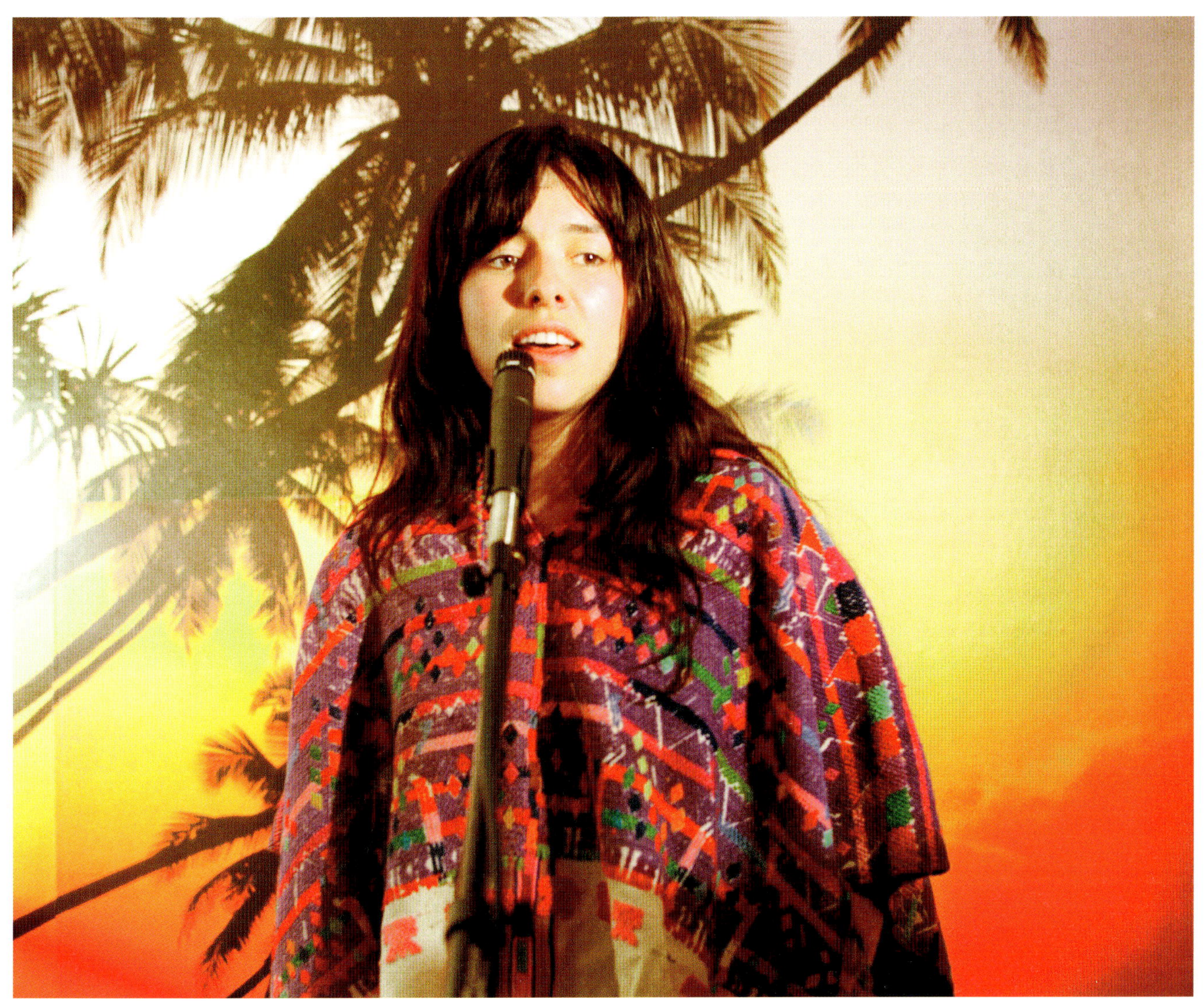

el mundo no escuchará

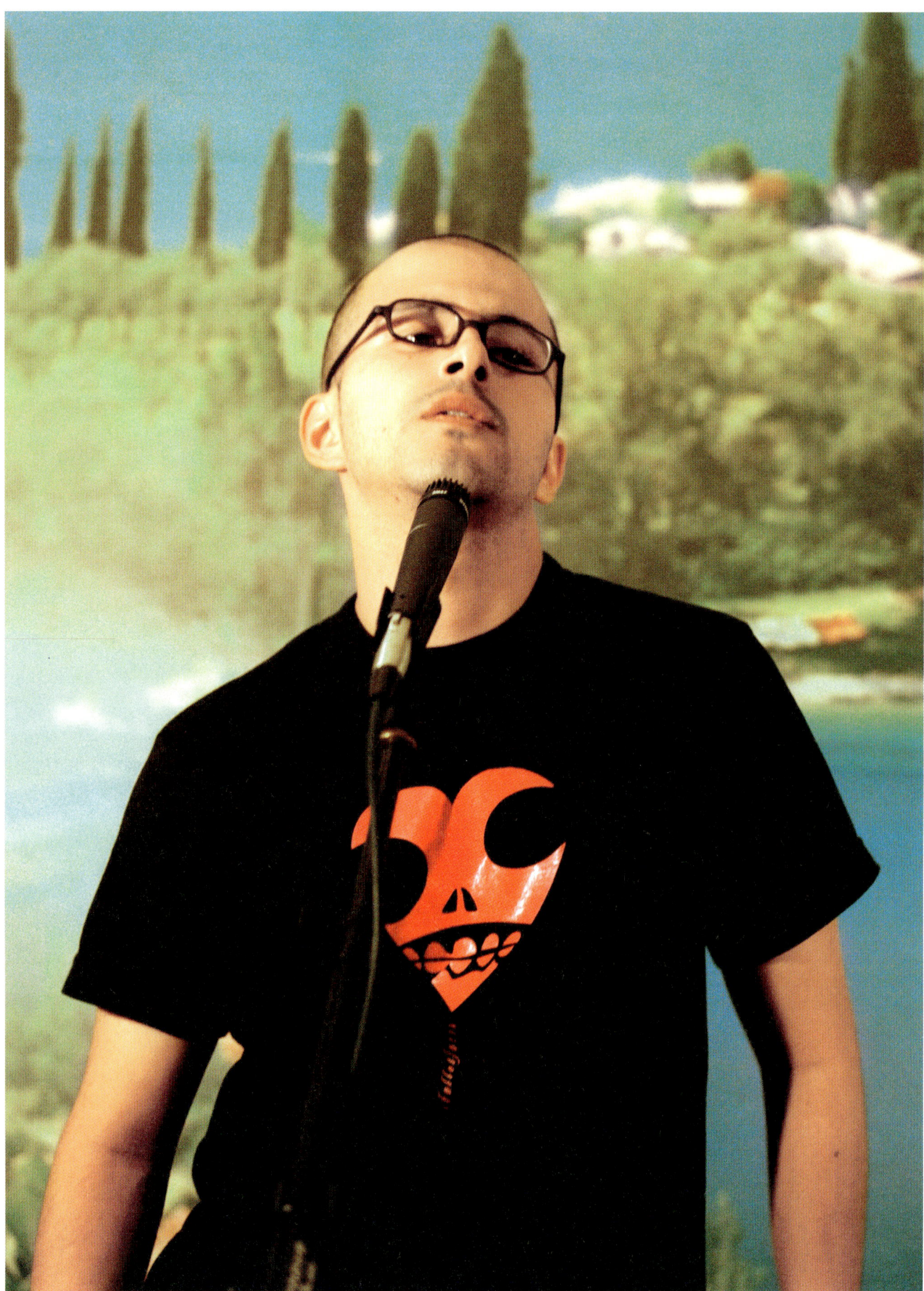

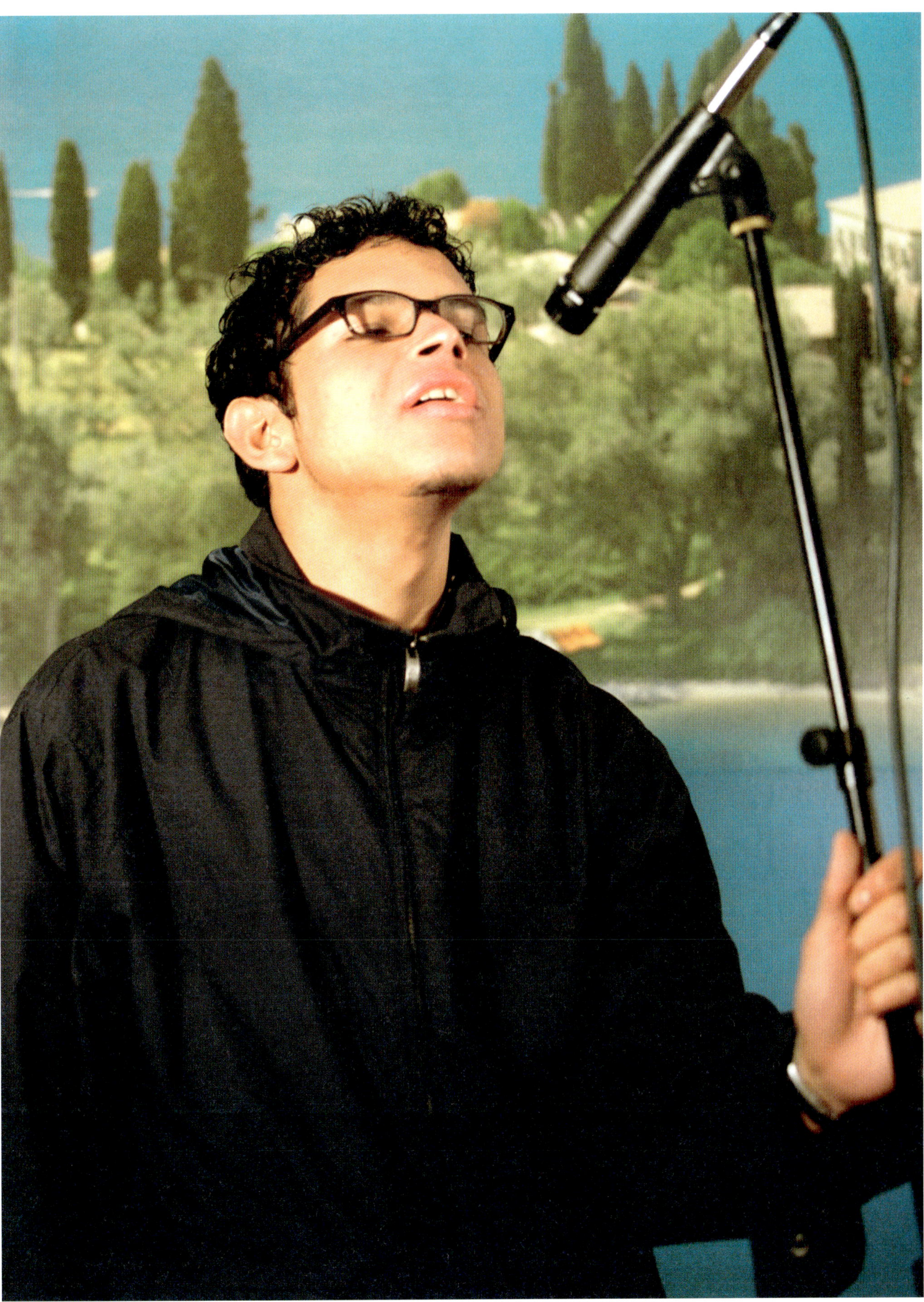

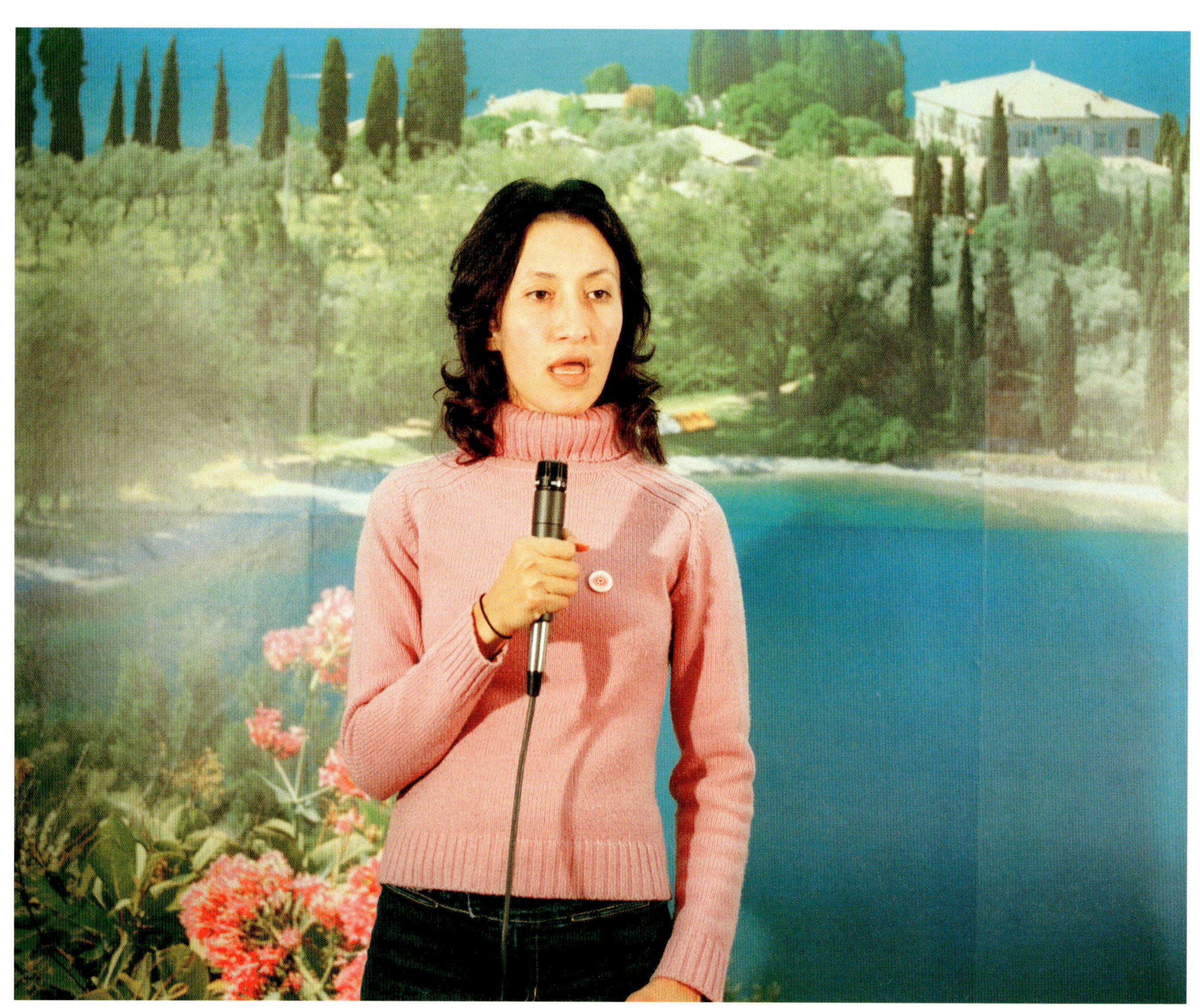

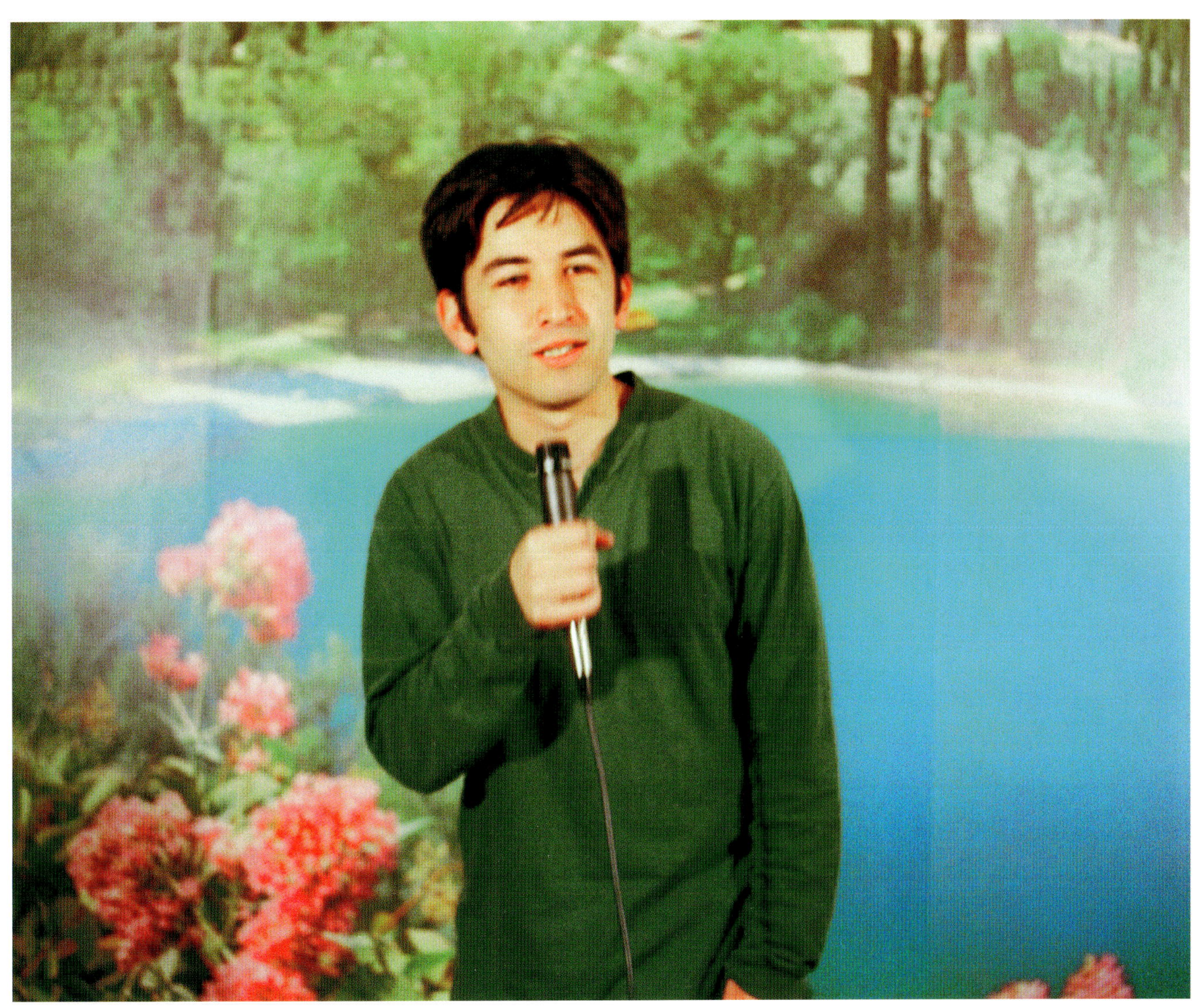

el mundo no escuchará

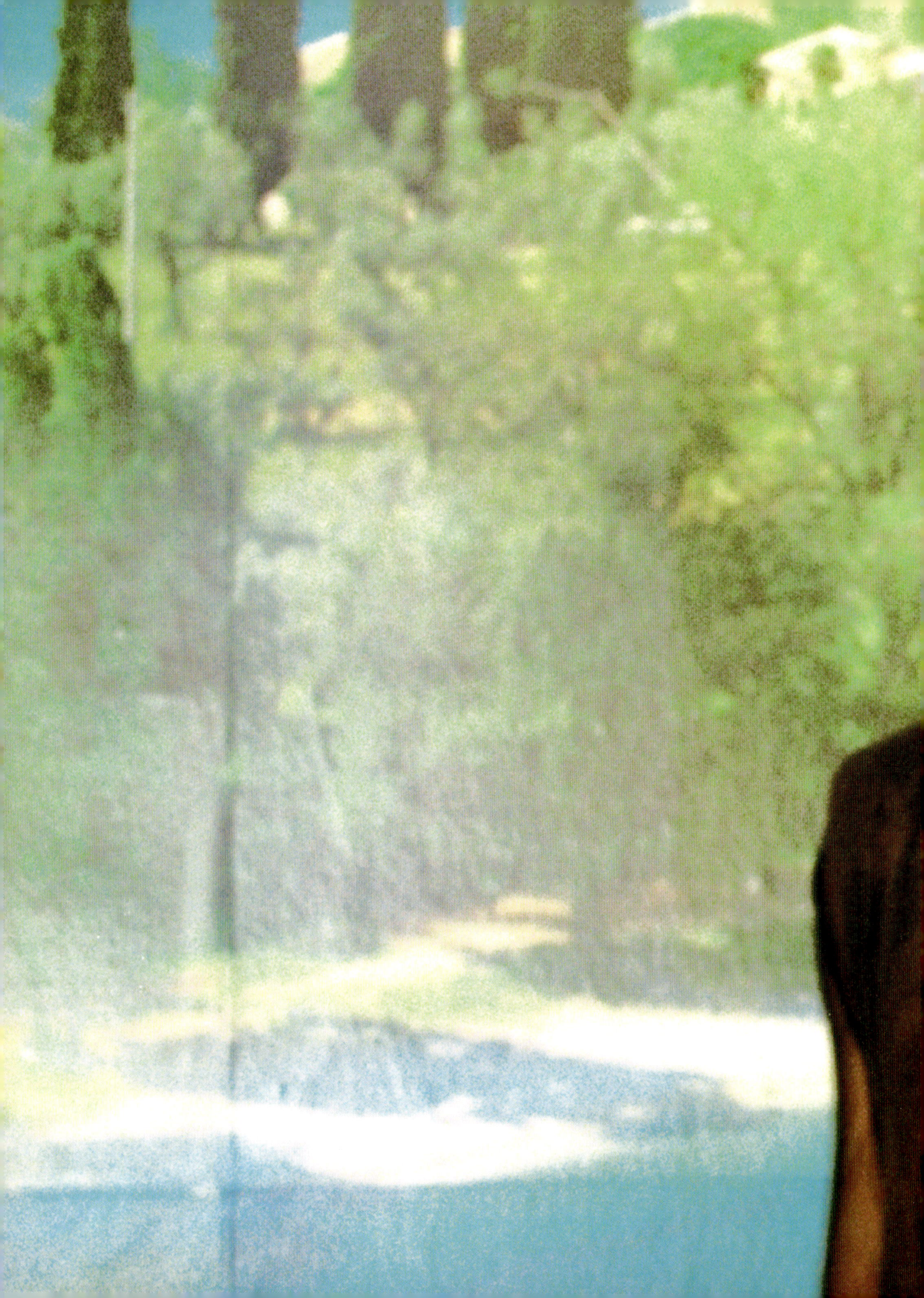

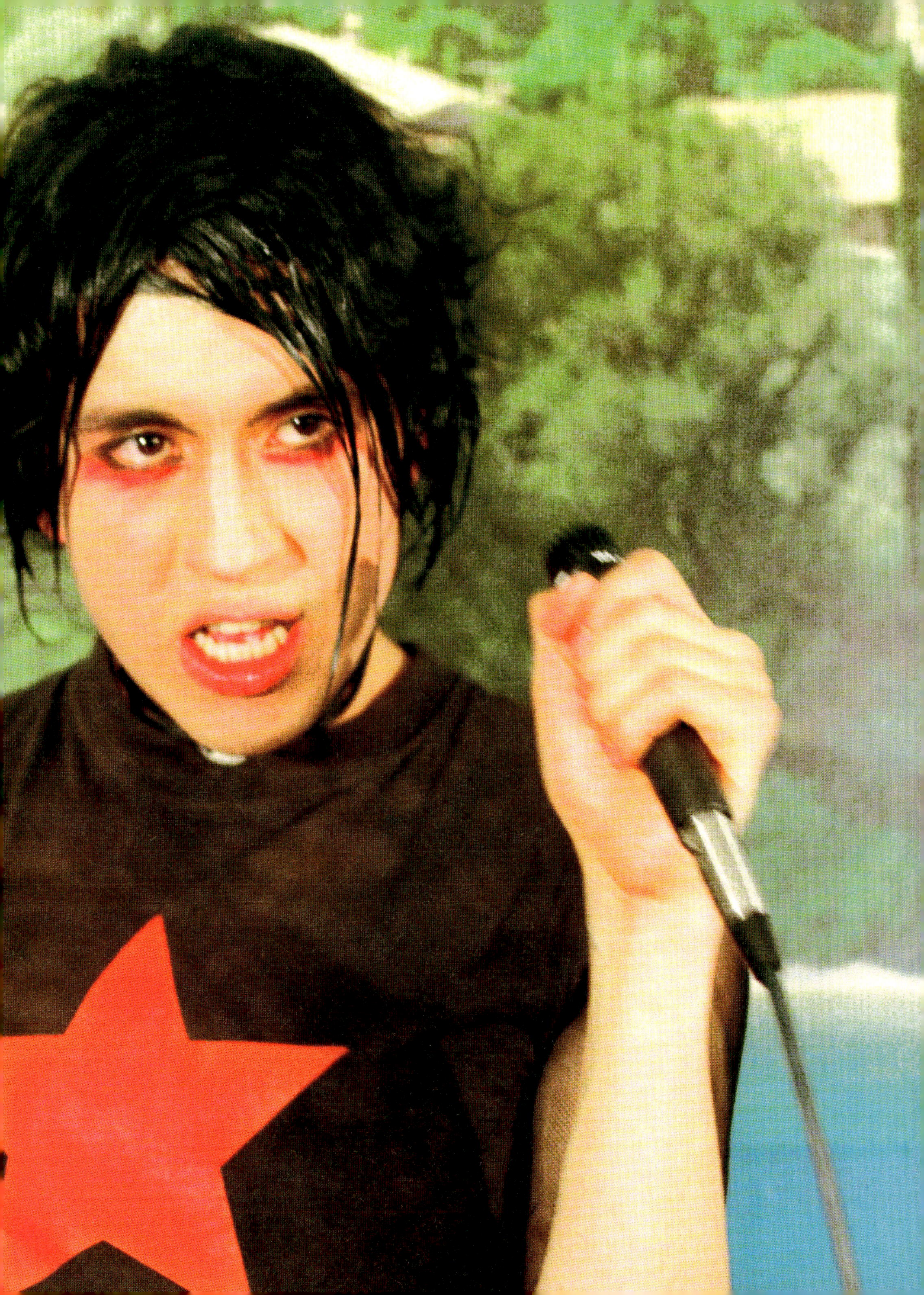

Pero no olvides las canciones
que te hicieron llorar
y las canciones que salvaron tu vida
sí, ahora estas más viejo
y eres un verraco astuto
pero esas canciones fueron las únicas
que siempre estuvieron a tu lado

EL KARAOKE DE LOS SMITHS

PARA LOS TIMIDOS, LOS INSATISFECHOS,
LOS NARCISOS, LAS ESTRELLAS DE LA
DUCHA Y TODOS AQUELLOS QUE
QUIERAN SER OTRO(A) POR UNA NOCHE.

Un Nuevo Karaoke Video que se Grabará
Durante Noviembre con Fans de los Smiths en Bogotá

¡ TU OPORTUNIDAD DE BRILLAR !
LLAMA A: 245 10 40
email: ilovethesmiths@michica.org

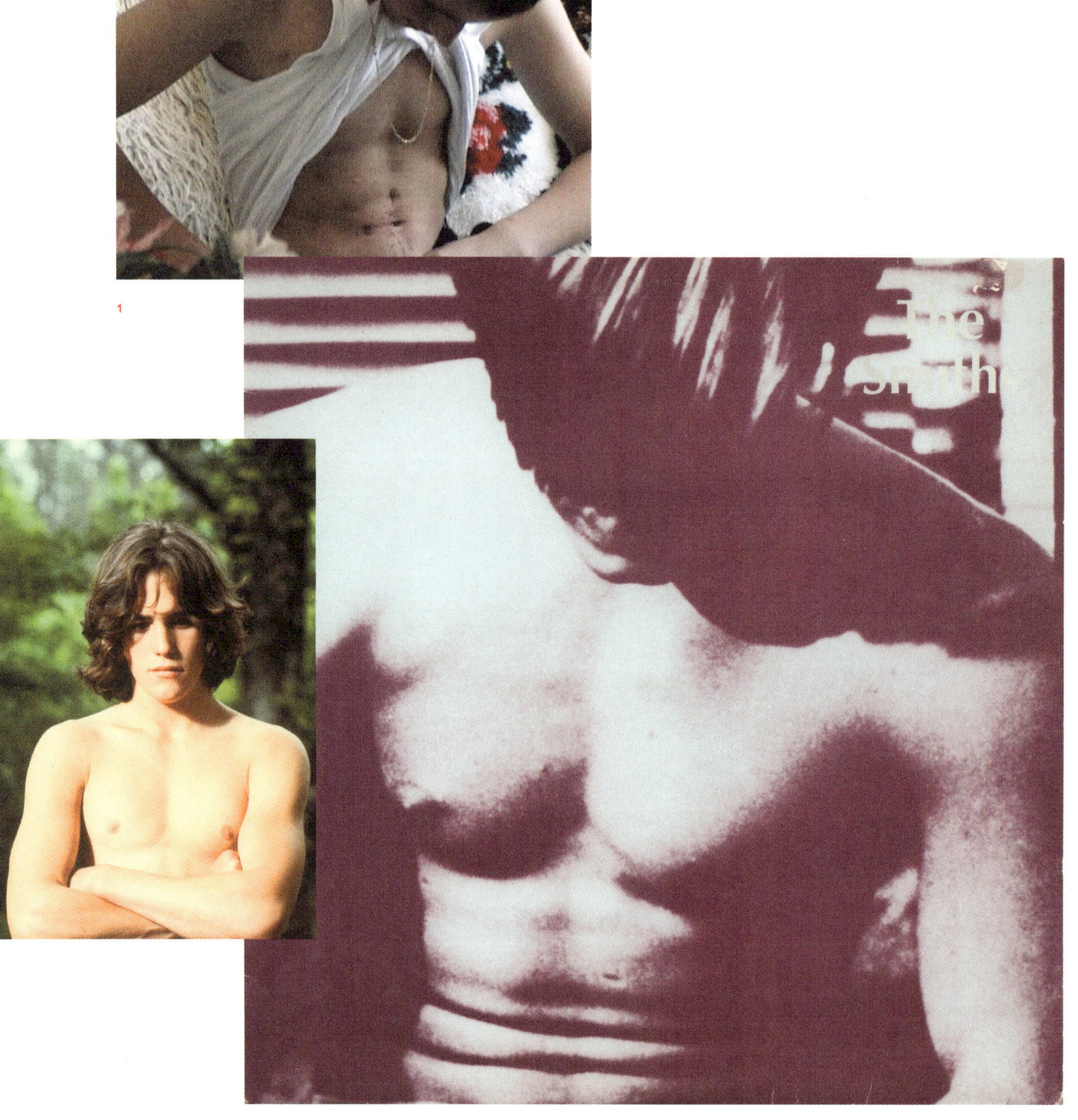

1

2

3

The Maenads
Bruce Hainley

It's difficult not to raise a somewhat obvious question: Why not Genesis karaoke?
I mean, the artist's name's Phil Collins.

—

When I first listened to The Smiths, Stephin Merritt had not yet coined the term
unboyfriendable, although it was how I often felt. I don't remember how I learned about
The Smiths, but I imagine it was by seeing a poster or an ad for their first album rather
than hearing "Hand In Glove" or "This Charming Man" or "What Difference Does
It Make?" Freshman year of college, I was just beginning to have little more than no
available language that would allow me to discuss the radioactivity of the album's cover
image — Joe Dallesandro, his epic body undressed, head bowed, sitting on the edge of
a bed; a still, tinted (maroon and bluish), from Andy Warhol Presents *Flesh*, directed
by Paul Morrissey, a film it would be years before I could see — or the songs' bittersweet
negotiations of desires I didn't yet fully know what to do with or how to express.
Of course, this is no small part of why the album meant so much to many: pop culture,
pop music, art, these entertainments provide ways to articulate what someone may not
be able to communicate about the feelings one knows one has. I had a few more words
in my vocabulary the summer after my freshman year when I slept with my first boyfriend
for the first time, the first time I'd slept with any man, in my attic bedroom, my parents
a floor below. It seemed they had no idea, but I was equally clueless. Afterward, Boyfriend
took me to New York City, where he held my hand walking down the street, summer
1984. A DJ at the college radio station, he had the softest skin, took me to see Pina Bausch
at BAM, and taught me what the acronym AIDS conveyed. I was or, more accurately,
thought I was in love with him until he somehow managed to send me postcards, a single
one arriving each day, from Europe (where he was spending the summer, celebrating
his graduation), blowing what I considered the secure cover of my homeland identity.

—

Before Red T-shirt (or shall I call him Sweetness for the first word he sings?), the fourth
performer in *el mundo no escuchará* , gets his groove on, a man in voiceover, while the screen
is black, between visual but not audio takes, either commenting on the previous performer
or setting the mood for Red T, states: "This is Hollywood." Ironically? Or because
something about Hollywood and what it means and the dreams it sells — home, circa 2004,
before his "return," as Norma Desmond would insist it be called, to a record-contractless
Morrissey — still shadows the proceedings, even if by a British video artist at work in

Bogotá with the locals? In any case, these interstitial, "wild" audio moments of the video, where people laugh or explain that they only want to sing a certain Smiths song because it is the best Smiths song, the best song ever, along with the synched-sound moments, brief as they are revelatory, when the performer waits (for the karaoke backing to start) and relaxes (just after the performance is over), seduce. People become themselves waiting forsomething to happen, before they have to do what they think they're going to do. Red T, or Sweetness, fusses a little with his hair before Marr's guitar line jangles in. He bounces and strums the air before singing, his sweet lips testing the lyrics, silently. Red T thinks about the words he's going to have to sing before he has to sing them, even before (it's my guess) they've begun to scroll on the karaoke monitor. Red T has a little scruff on his chin and above his upper lip; he sports a beaded necklace, the current trend of what would have been puka shells on the guys I envied who could carry off such stylings when I was a teen. Red T's necklace is a little too long, only making it more charming, and maybe someone he cares about gave it to him, which has more to do with why he wears it than aesthetics. He flubs the lyrics about "Joan of Arc" — jumping the gun and singing "hearing aid" rather than "Walkman" (Joan's hearing aid, melting in the conflagration, isn't mentioned until a later verse) — and corrects himself. The mistakes don't matter: they only make him more winning. Skinny Red T, eyes bright, smiles a lot while he's singing; he dances and swings his arm and air guitars key bridges rousingly. He laughs after his rendition, covering his mouth, eyes aglow, then raises his arm — *song conquered!* — when the assembled crew present at the filming cheers his efforts. Joy is beautiful and rarer than anyone might think in contemporary art. Red T is a joyologist and his joy, an apotropaic force, spreads. Red T's the reason Warhol thought people were so beautiful that you couldn't take a bad picture, but Bogotá and its turmoil are why he didn't understand it when some people, even intelligent people, say that violence can be beautiful. For him beautiful is some moments, and those moments are never violent.

—

What's being performed in Collins's trilogy isn't The Smiths. Rather, it's The Smiths who are performing, over a sixty-minute duration, these various and (to most viewers) anonymous individuals, men and women, their particular way of expressing themselves, moods, quirks, gazes, intensities, meaningful-nesses, flaunting and/or revealing what they themselves don't know they're going to display. Karaoke as a form — formal properties emphasized by the seamless backdrop images of palm trees, mountaintops, sunlit meadows, or tropical landscapes reiterating those that would normally appear on the karaoke monitor — removed from its usual context of booze and humiliation, takes away certain decisions and motivations, allowing some unrehearsed piece of the immediate to oscillate wildly and, like life, to no conclusiveness. It should be noted that what we're watching, in no small part, is people *reading*, following a teleprompting that paradoxically reveals their being and not The Smiths' or Morrissey's.

—

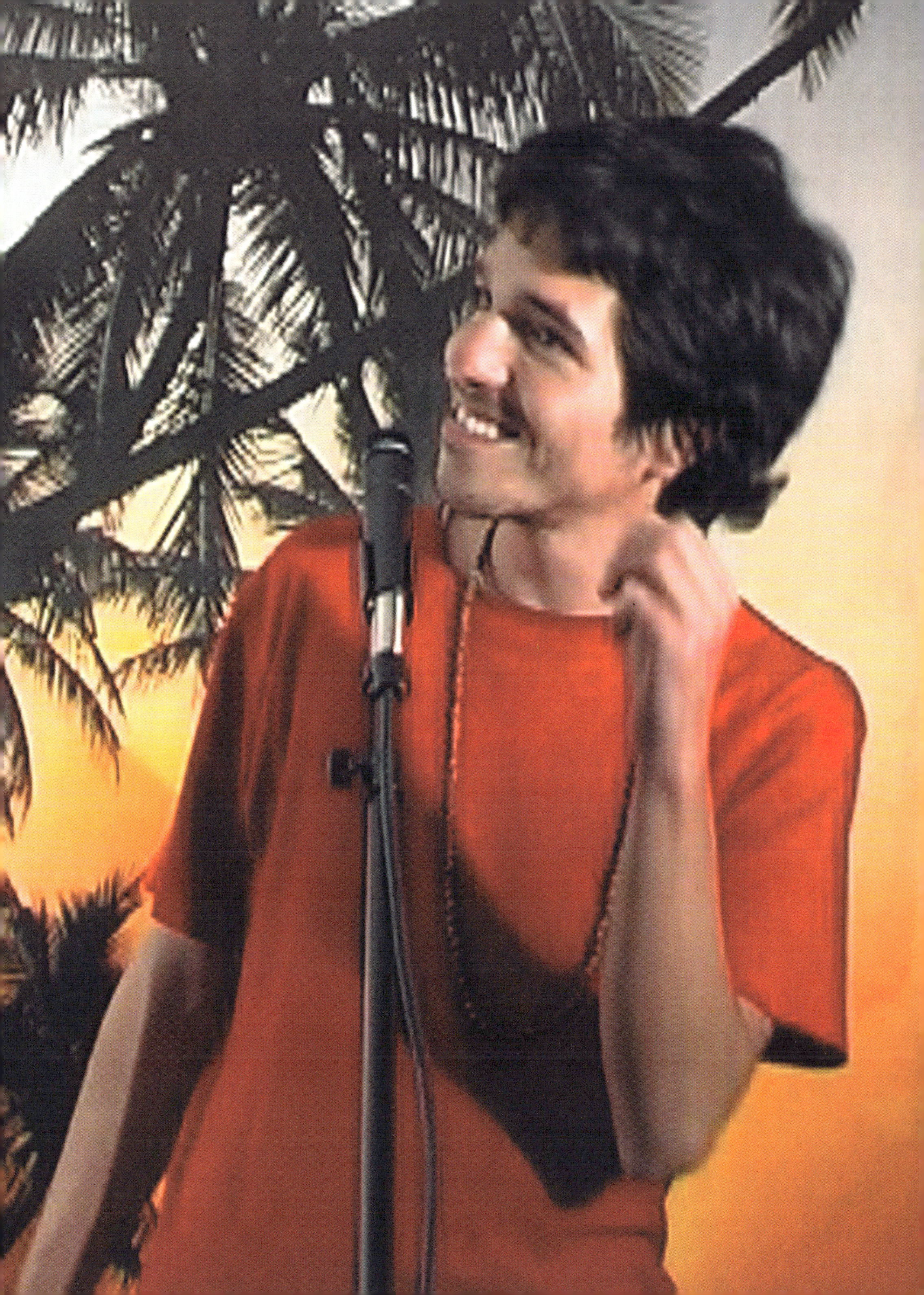

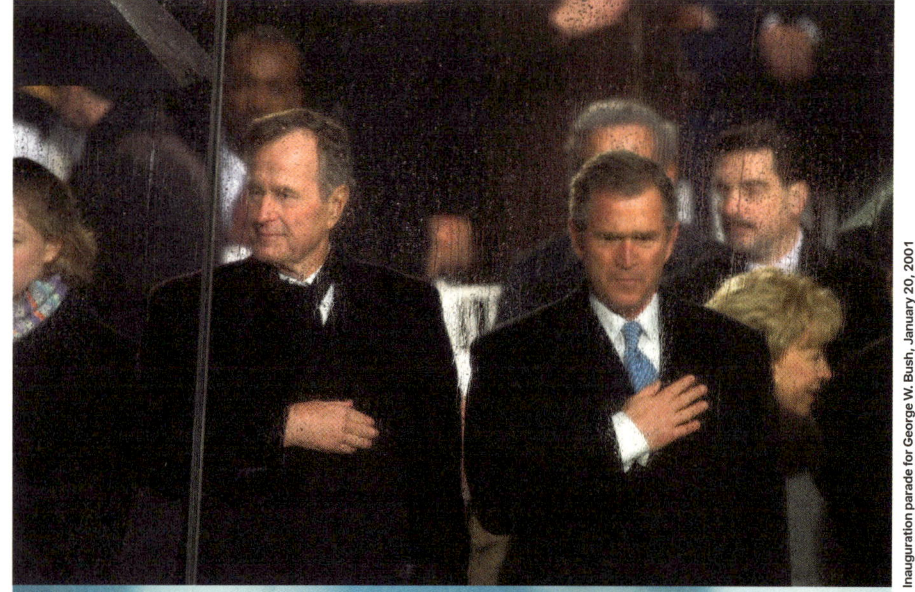

Inauguration parade for George W. Bush, January 20, 2001

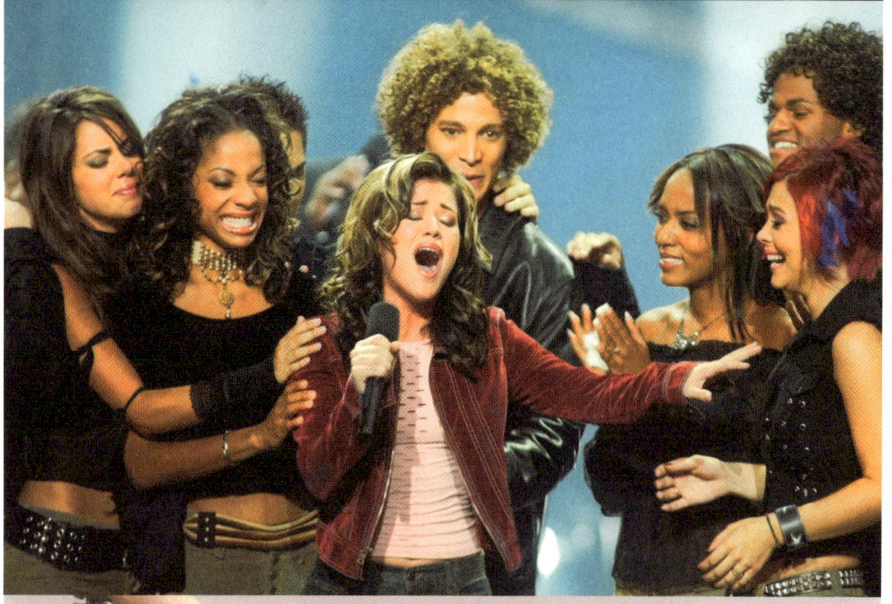

American Idol finale, September 4, 2002

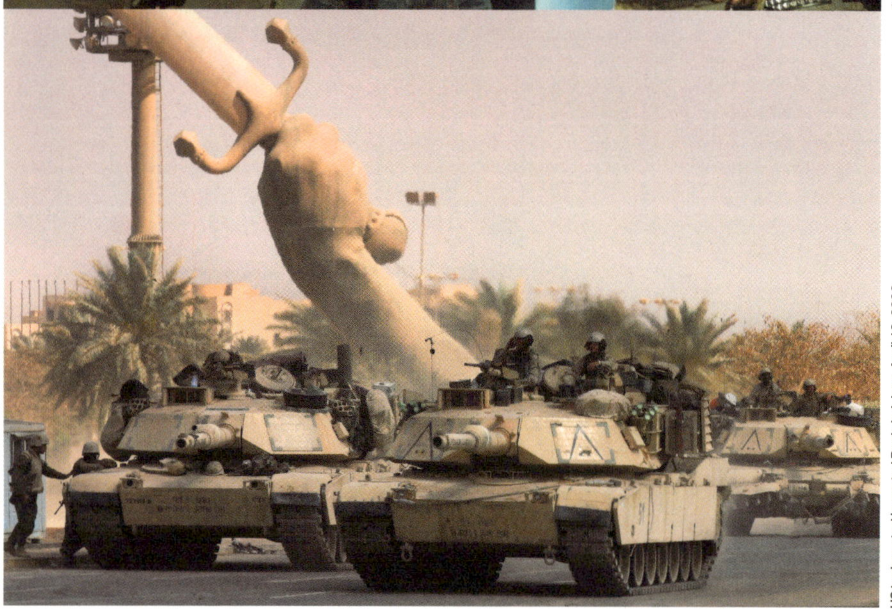

US tanks patrol in central Baghdad, Iraq, April 16, 2003

I am skeptical about the political efficacy of any artwork, especially those vaunted as "political." When I hear the word *politics*, I usually ask, how does it look? I start to consider the aesthetic situation at hand. The politics of *the world won't listen* trilogy are, crucially, obscure, which, perhaps, allows them to be potentially active. Most art called "political" is only art *about* politics and the signs of the political, so-called. Setting up a situation — anywhere, not just in a war or strife zone — in which people might find relief from the onslaught called "contemporary life" requires some dynamic political maneuvering. I am not sure any of this is discernible in watching someone singing "Panic" or "Stretch Out And Wait," although the performance is frequently moving. Honestly, I'm not sure what I'm supposed to be looking at, and this uncertainty demands, if I am a thinking person, that I question the reasons for someone's orchestrating such a production in the name of art.

—

That Collins chose The Smiths to provide the score of his work lends a certain proletarian energy to the goings-on, not to mention a complicated sexual and/or queer resonance always hovering around the band, due, despite his dandy flagrance, to Morrissey's always brilliantly cagey elusiveness about the definition of such issues and his own participation in or performance of them. But at this particular moment, especially in America, karaoke and its offspring have their own political burdens. Consider the joyless circumstance — coincidence? fate? — of this chronology:

> G. W.'s inauguration: 20 January 2001
> First season of *American Idol* begins: 11 June 2002
> Invasion of Iraq: 18 March 2003

The contestants, the winners, the marketing orgy of *American Idol* — let's be clear: it is *only* about hawking product and the corporate evisceration of what had been the loving beauty of amateurism — are all an aesthetic effect and affect (backdraft as much as backwash) of war time and of the Bush administration, with the world relegated to Brian Dunkelmans. (Remember Dunkelman?) *AI* (artificial intelligence in every sense) is a burlesque of the numbing, vacuous, incompetent, and contrived raison d'être of it all — and just because this may be a failed logic doesn't mean it couldn't still resonate, bleakly, especially since G. W. and Laura appeared *live via videotape* on the show, ostensibly to thank *Idol*'s charity branch and not, with the president's low approval ratings idling, to rally support. *AI* is just karaoke with a bigger budget, karaoke almost literally on steroids, producing their equivalent sham ("Mission Accomplished"). What does it take to be a celebrity (not a star), circa 2007? Twelve weeks and consumers voting with more gusto than they have voted in any recent American presidential election.

—

Having had an effect on popular culture not unlike the effects the current administration's policies have had on Baghdad, *AI*'s political and aesthetic structures "Las Vegas" the most vicious aspects of conservatism, all in the name of a buck — and putting it that way is deeply unfair to Las Vegas, which is, at least, honest about its cons. That Collins has been able to turn the karaoke form against its dominant mode of sheer commodification to convey something desperate, because human, about the stake of the individual in the current world, gives me hope. Contestants for *AI* sign up with dollar signs in their eyes, and the corporate honchos behind *AI* are happy to capitalize on the desire; the musical capabilities of all those involved, even the winners — I'm tempted to say, especially the winners — is nil, their every note ventriloquizing only greed. Collins's performers, most of them, sign up for much more complicated and vague reasons. With their flubs and off-key and out-of-tune vocalizations, they become a contemporary incarnation of the maenads, those worshippers and celebrants of myth who wreaked havoc as a consequence of what they loved, indecorously risking self and sanity in the name of honor.

—

When Red T appears again, it's on another day and in another outfit (jeans jacket, mustard pullover), helping a friend or countryman show off his record collection and Smiths memorabilia. Red T looks somber and unsure. Was it filmed *before* his earlier joy session or has someone broken his heart in the meantime?

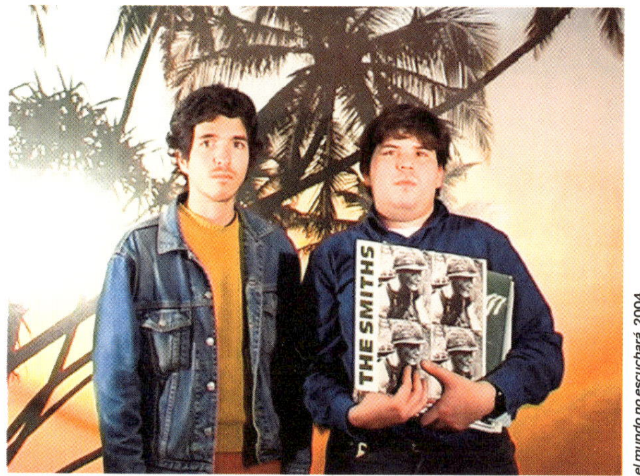

el mundo no escuchará, 2004

DÜNYA
DİNLEMİYOR

THE SMITHS KARAOKE

Dünyanın tüm
çekingen tatminsiz güzel
kaybedenleri için
18-19-20-21 Ağustos´ta
İstanbul´da yeni bir film çekiliyor.

İLETİŞİM: thesmithskaraoke@yahoo.com.tr
TEL   : 0538 459 3064

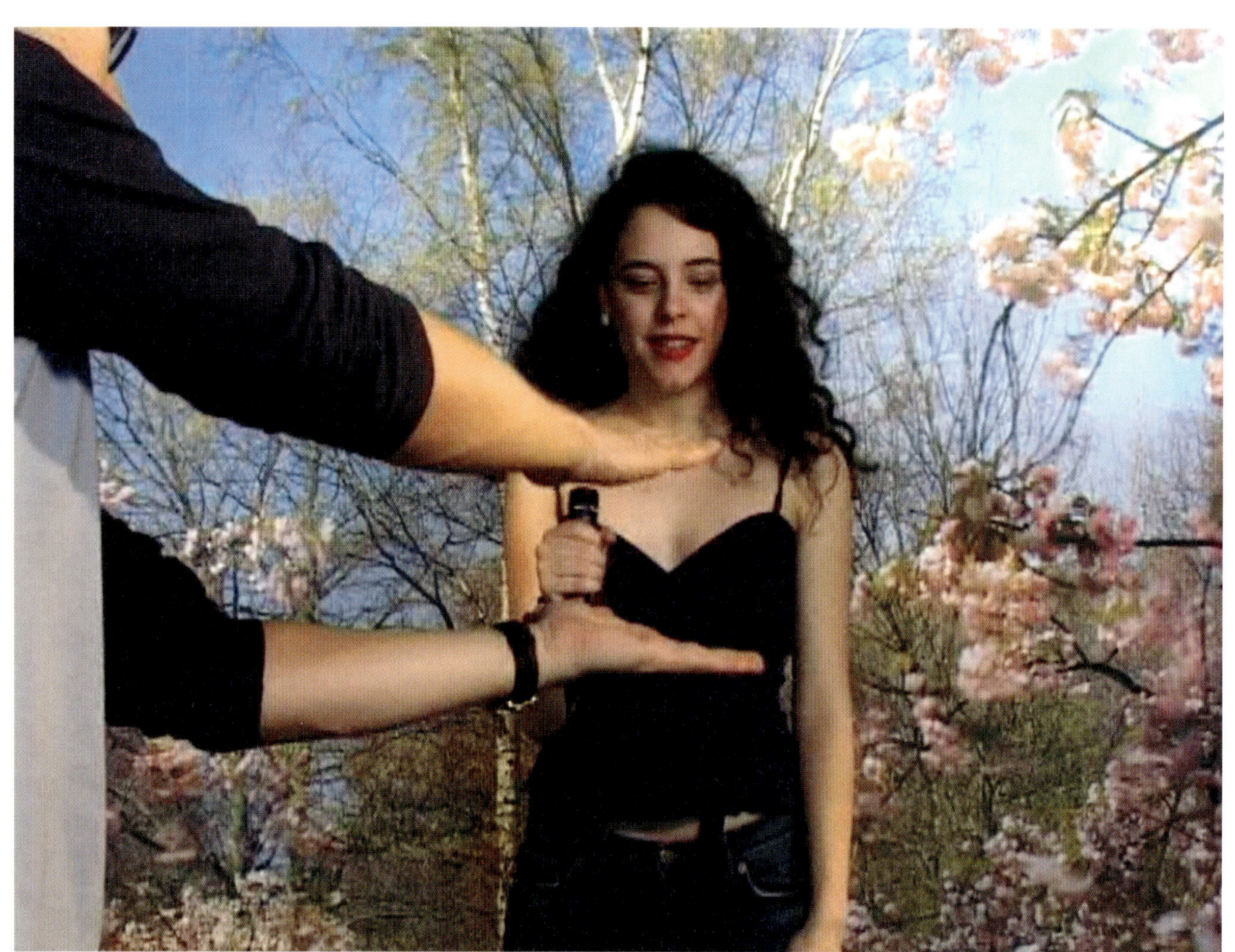

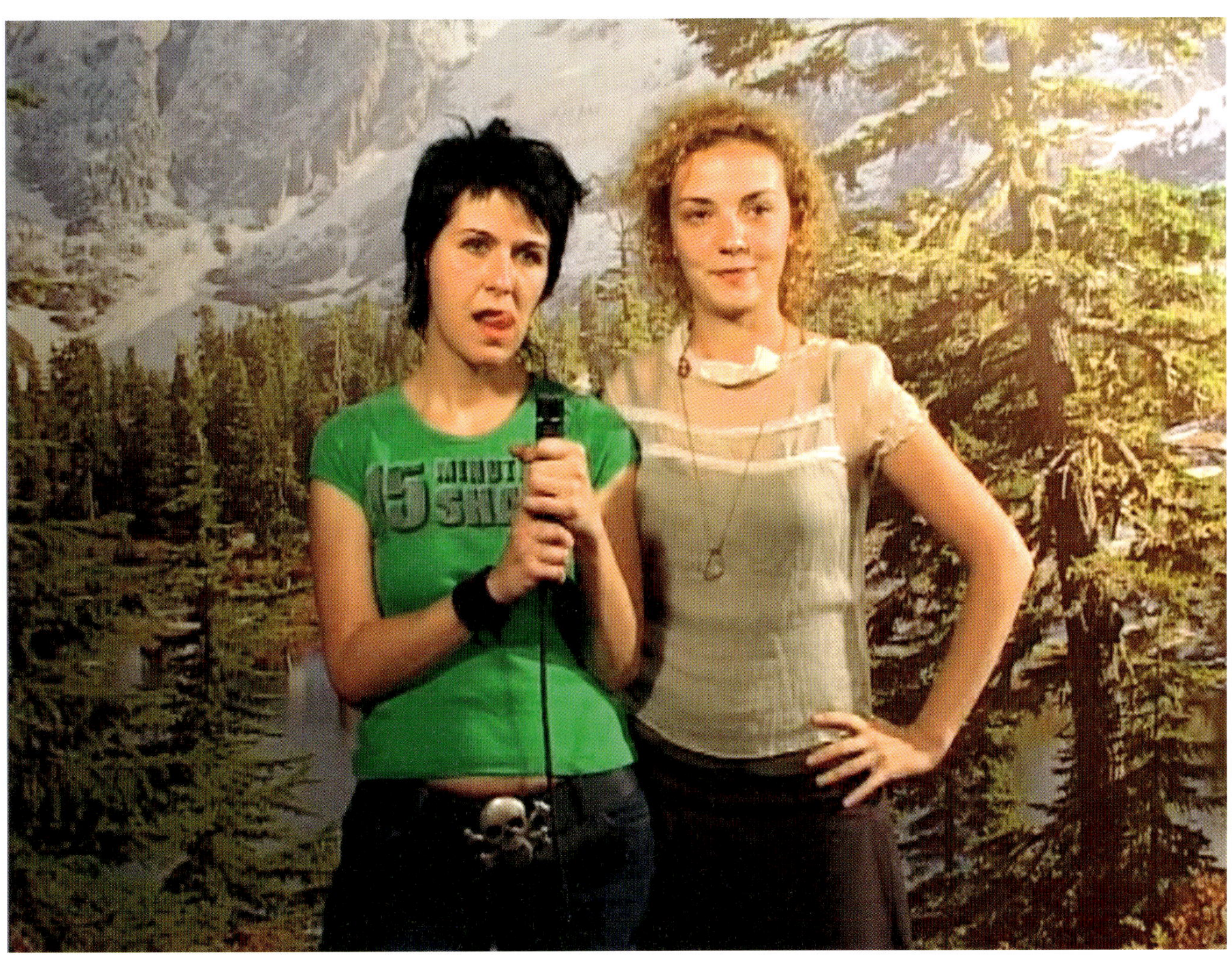

dünya dinlemiyor

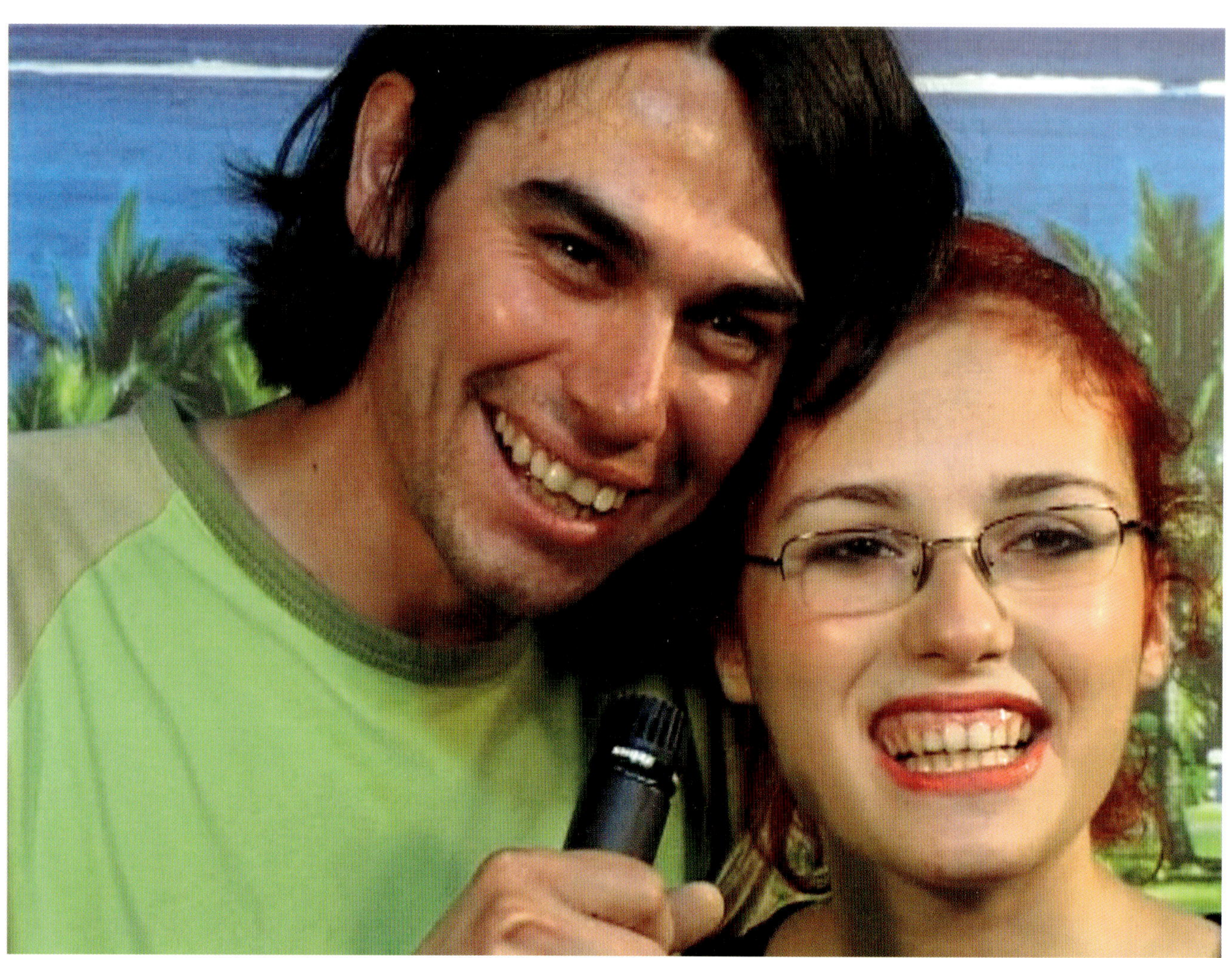

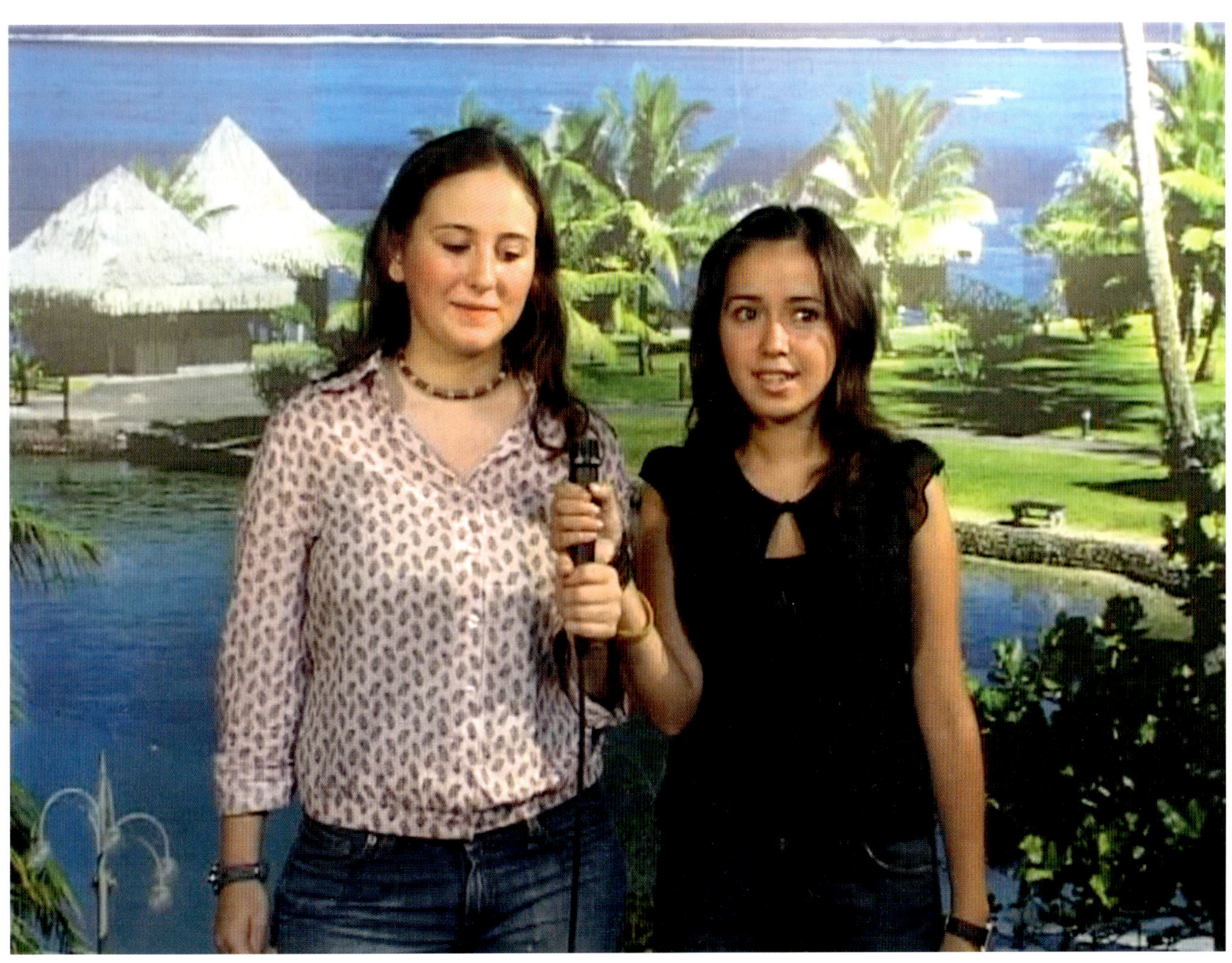

dünya dinlemiyor

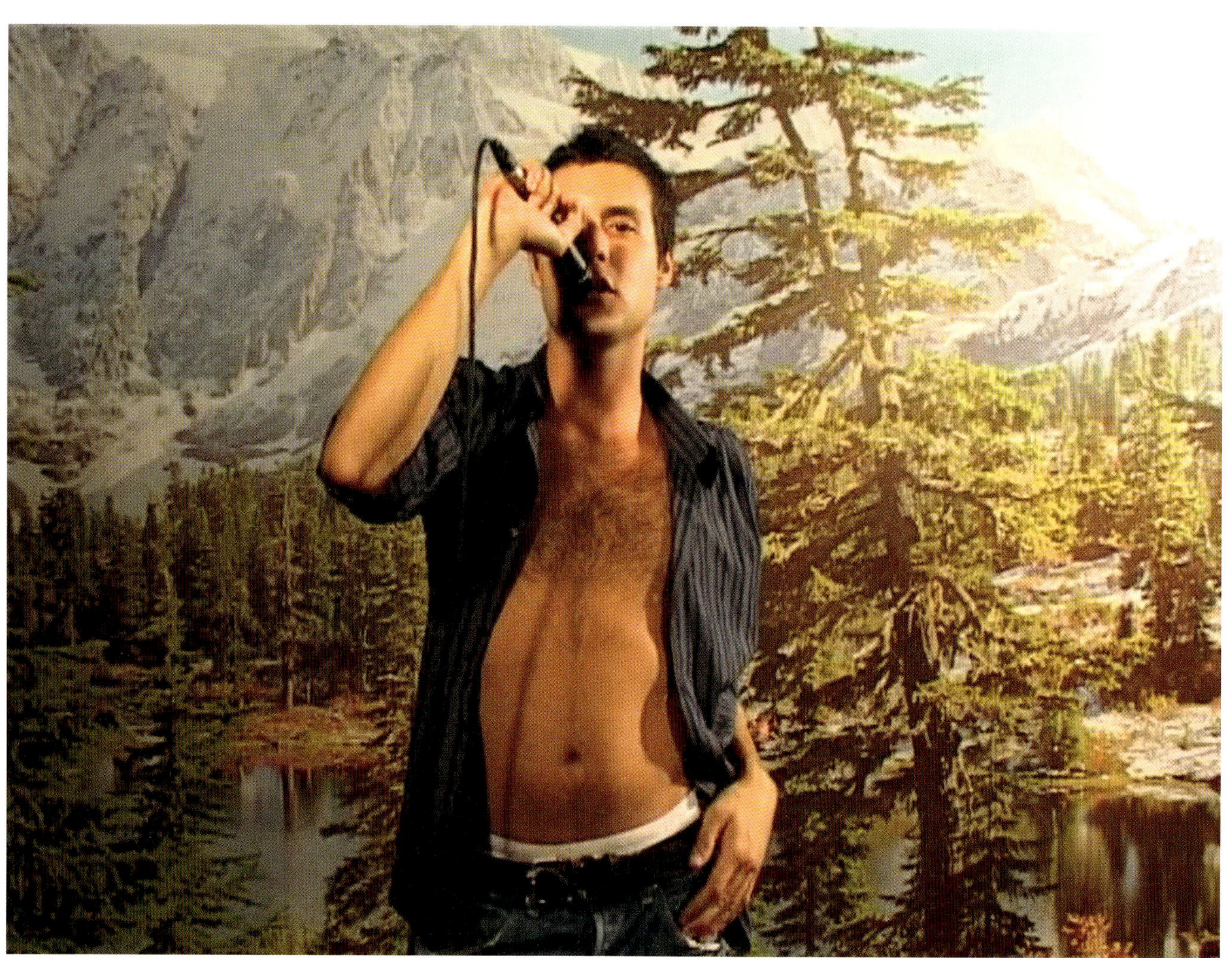

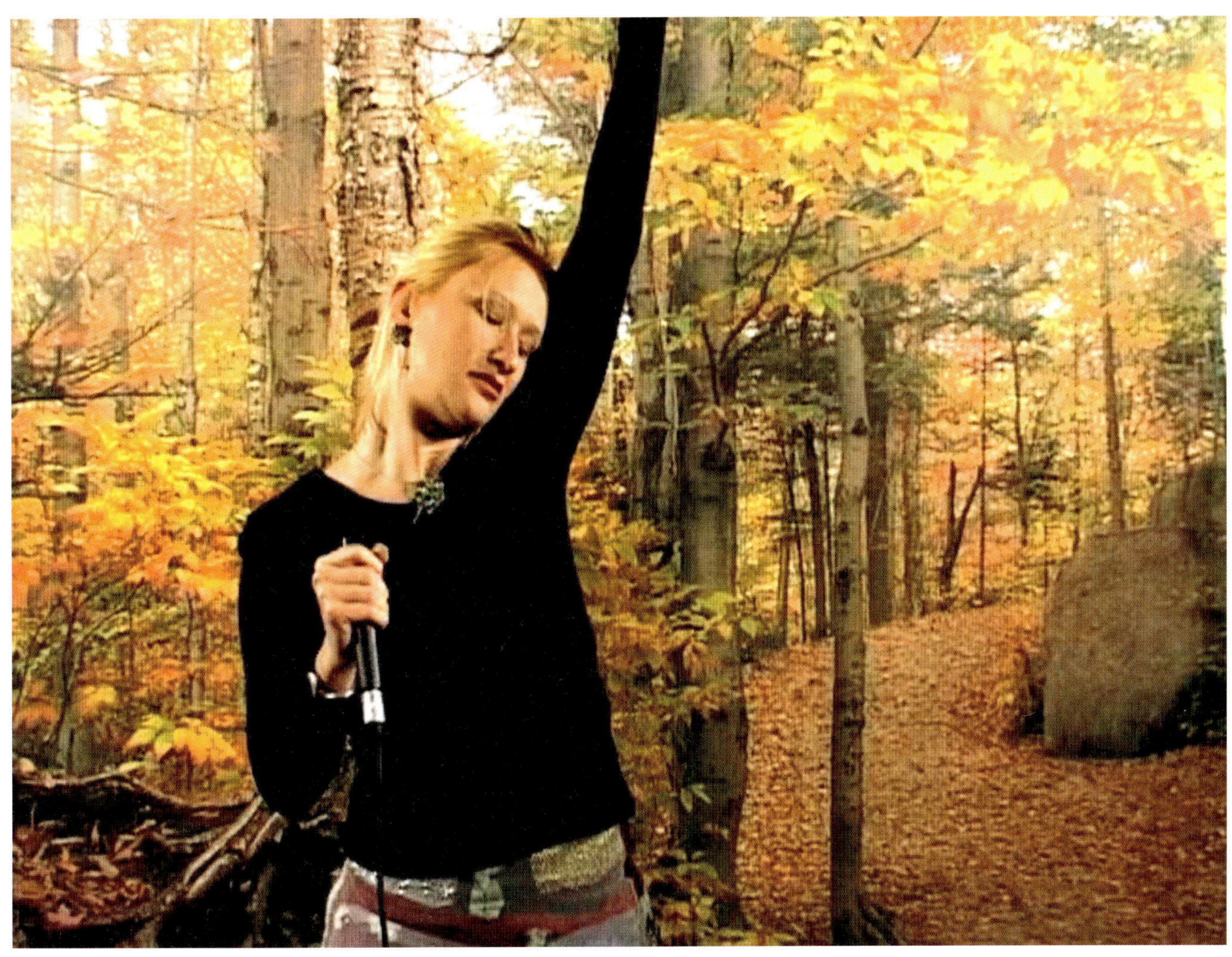

dünya dinlemiyor

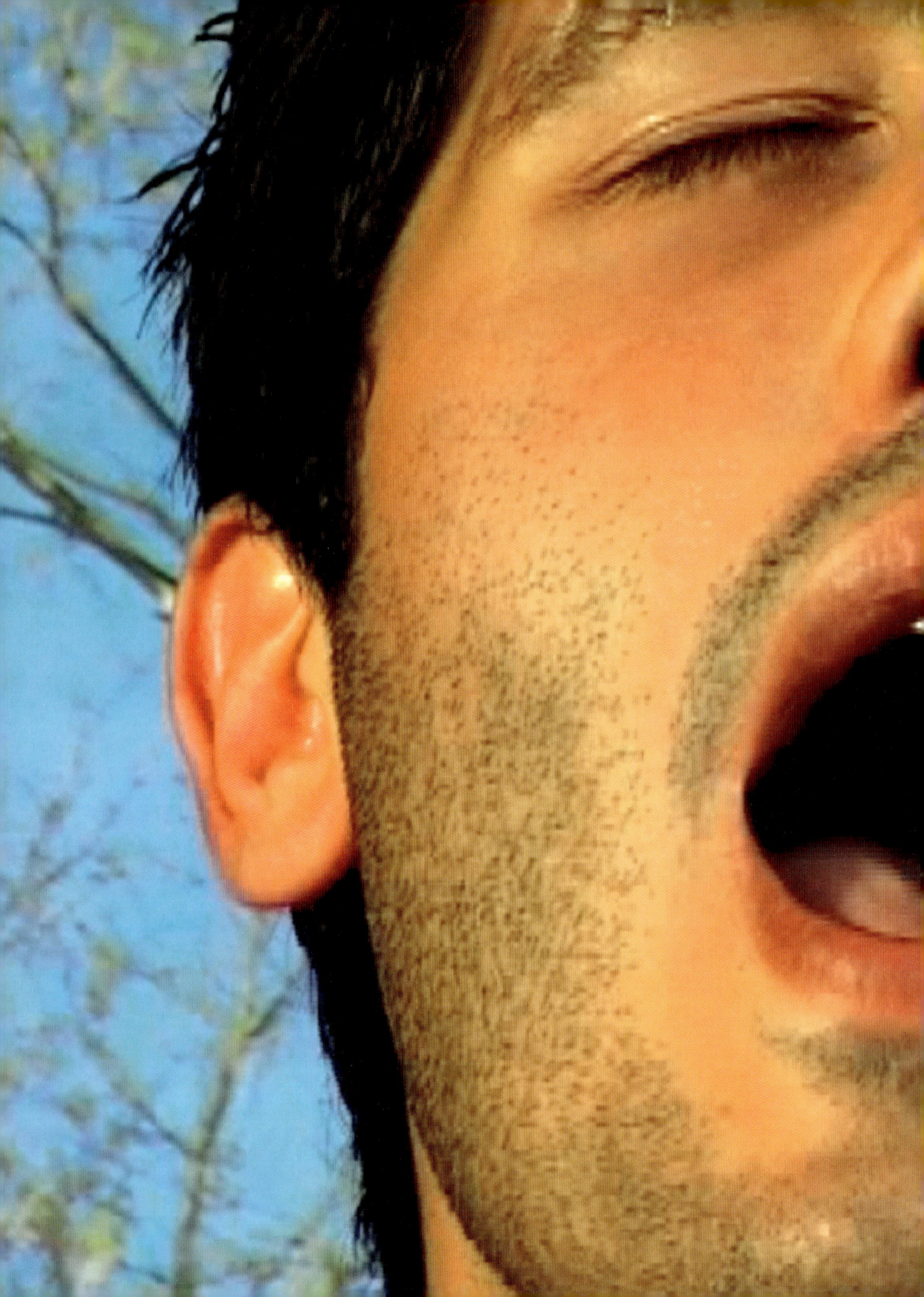

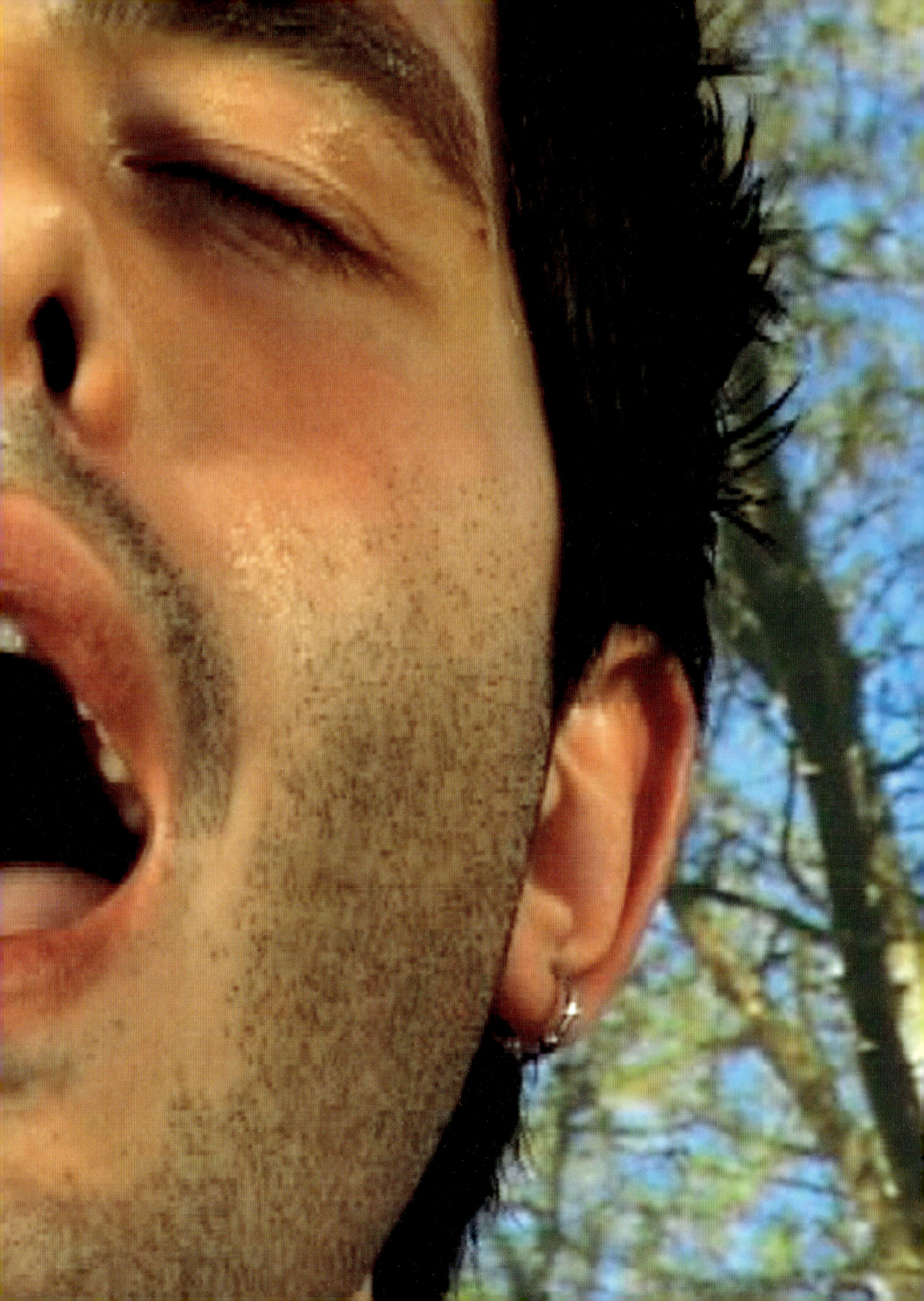

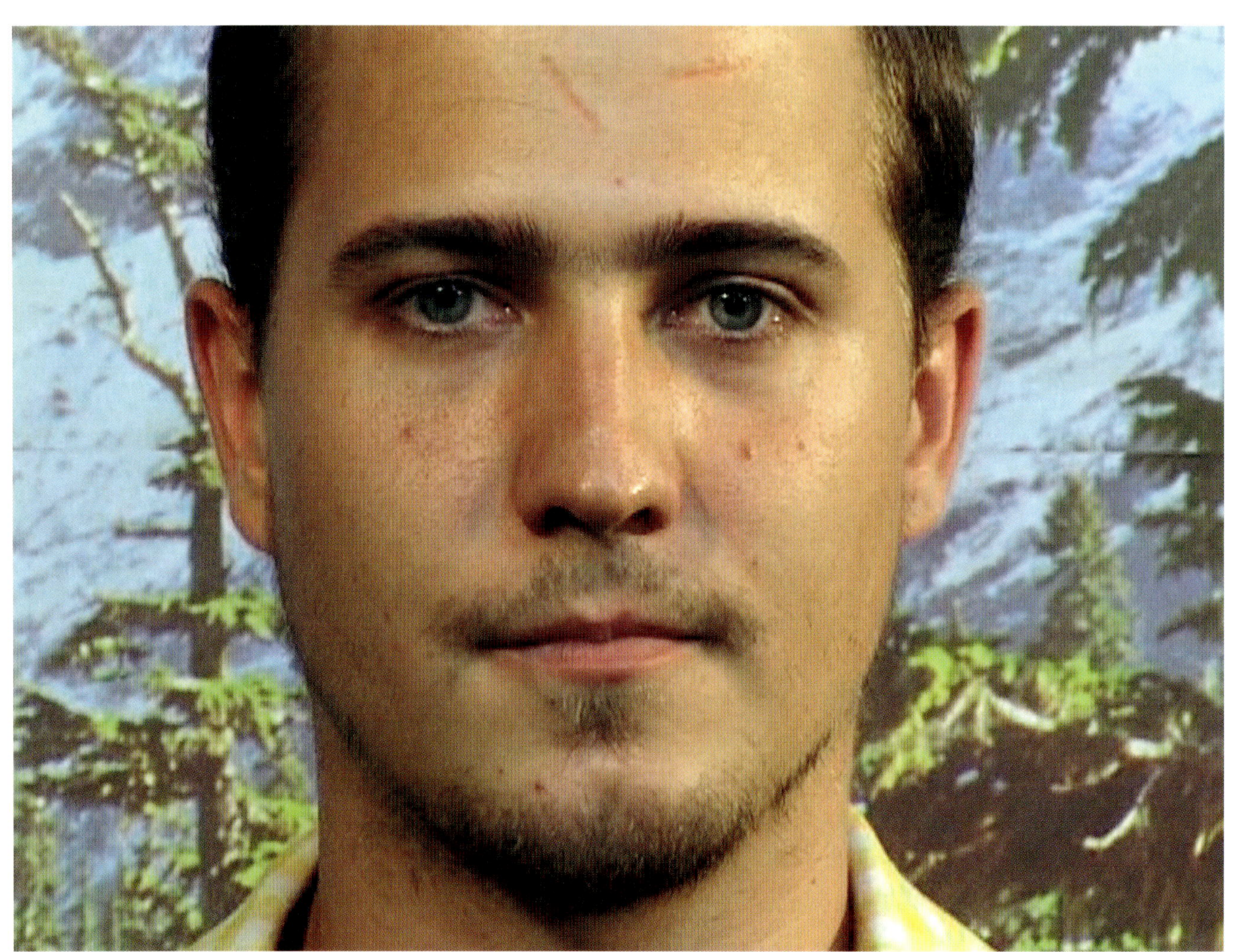

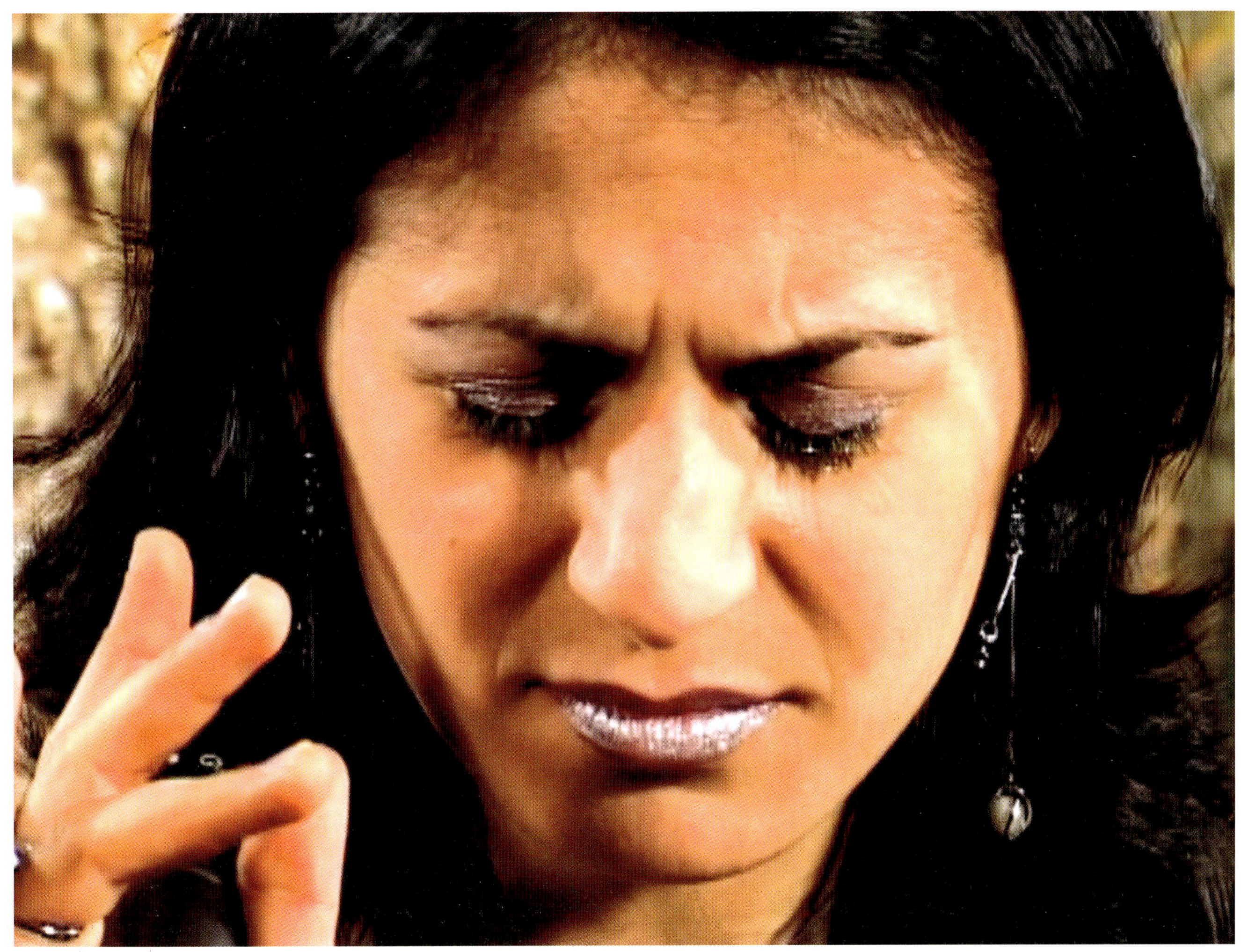

dünya dinlemiyor

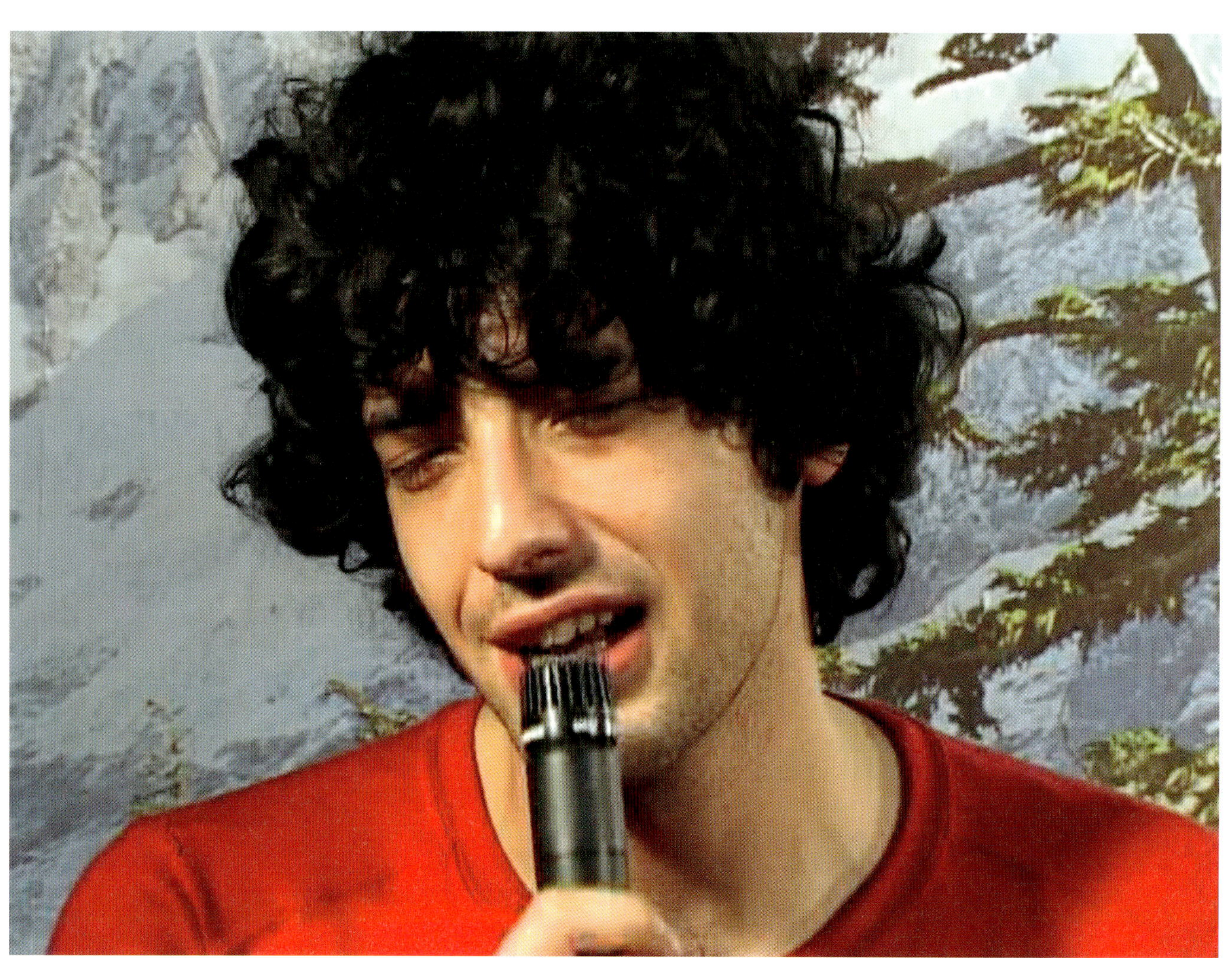

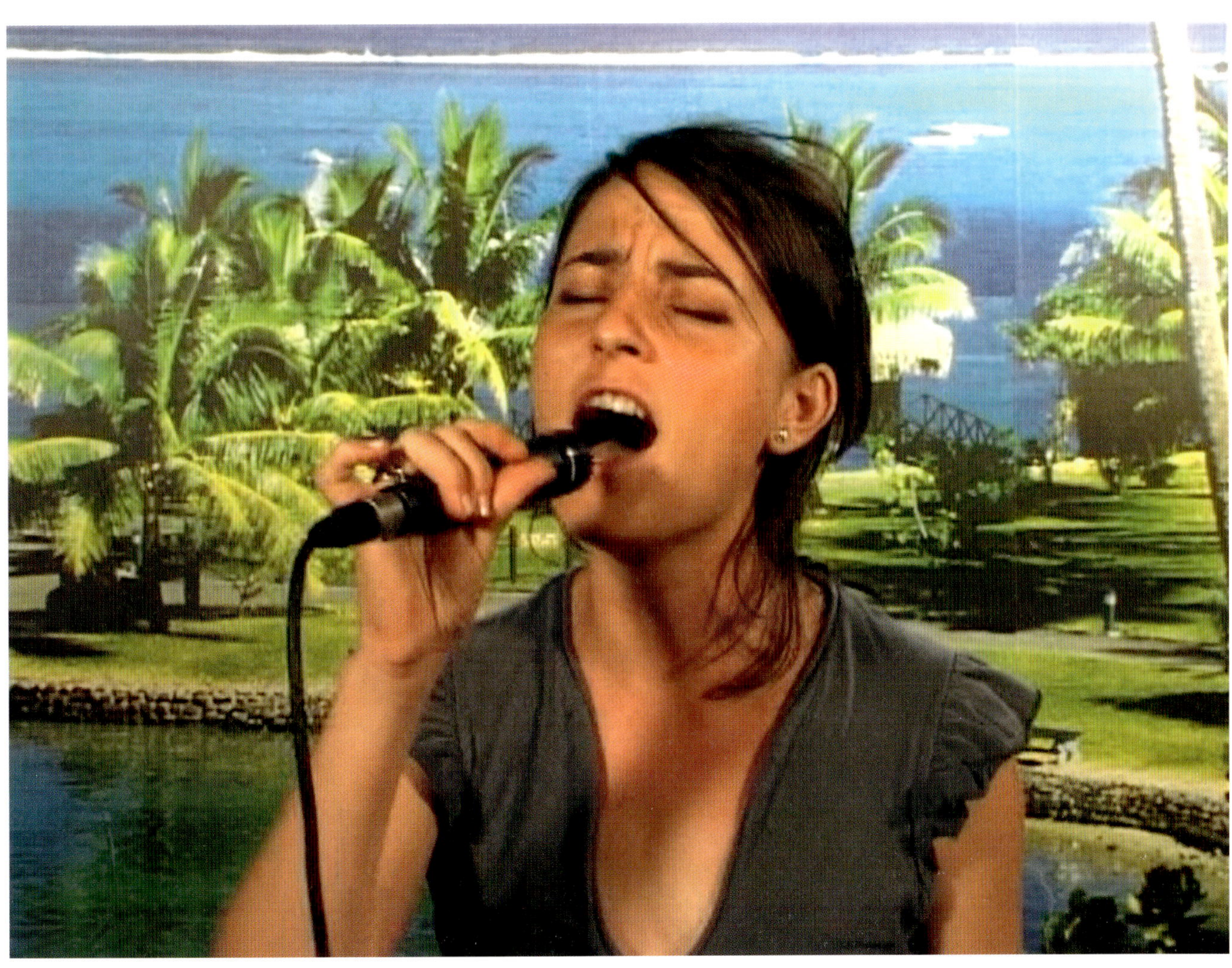

dünya dinlemiyor

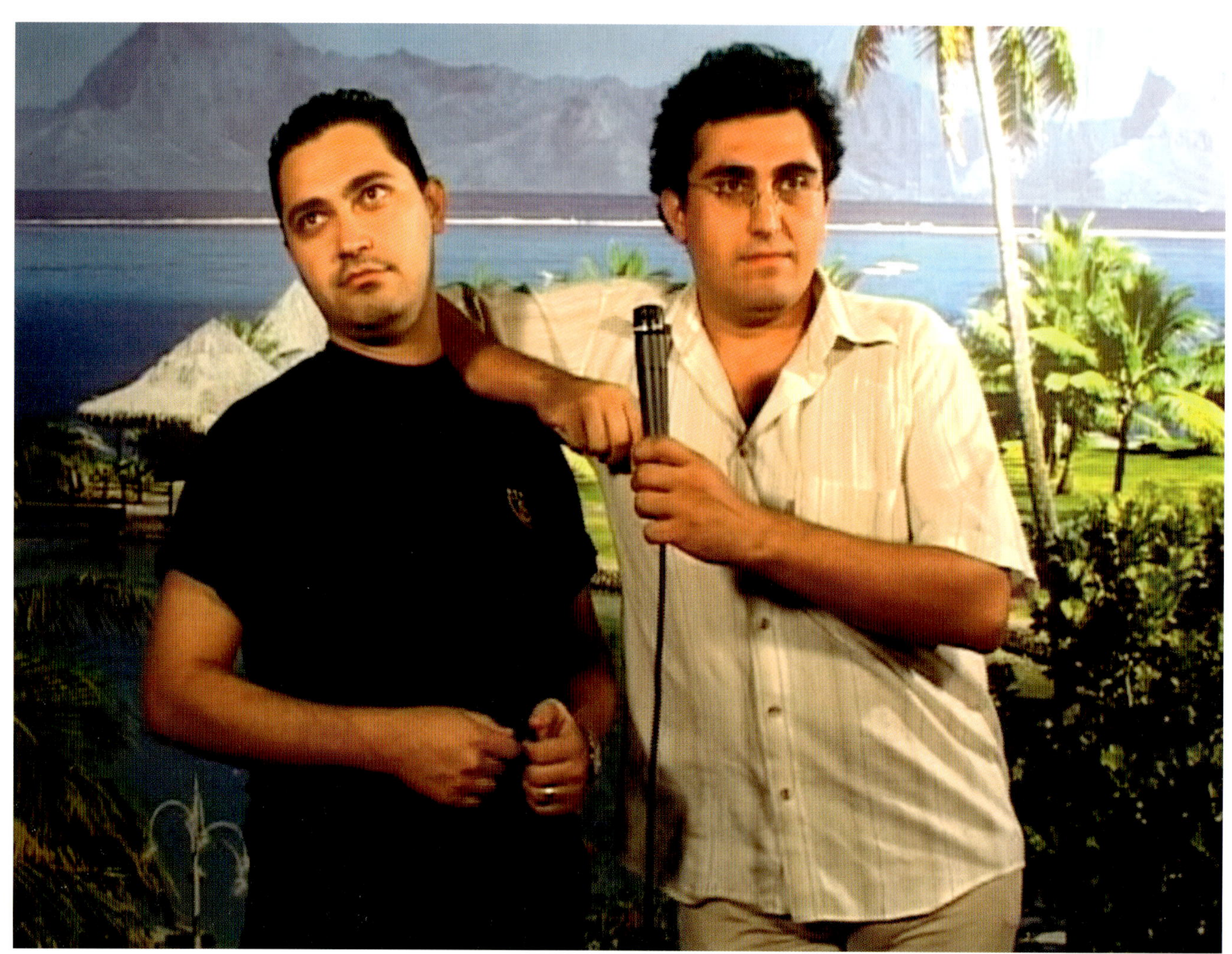

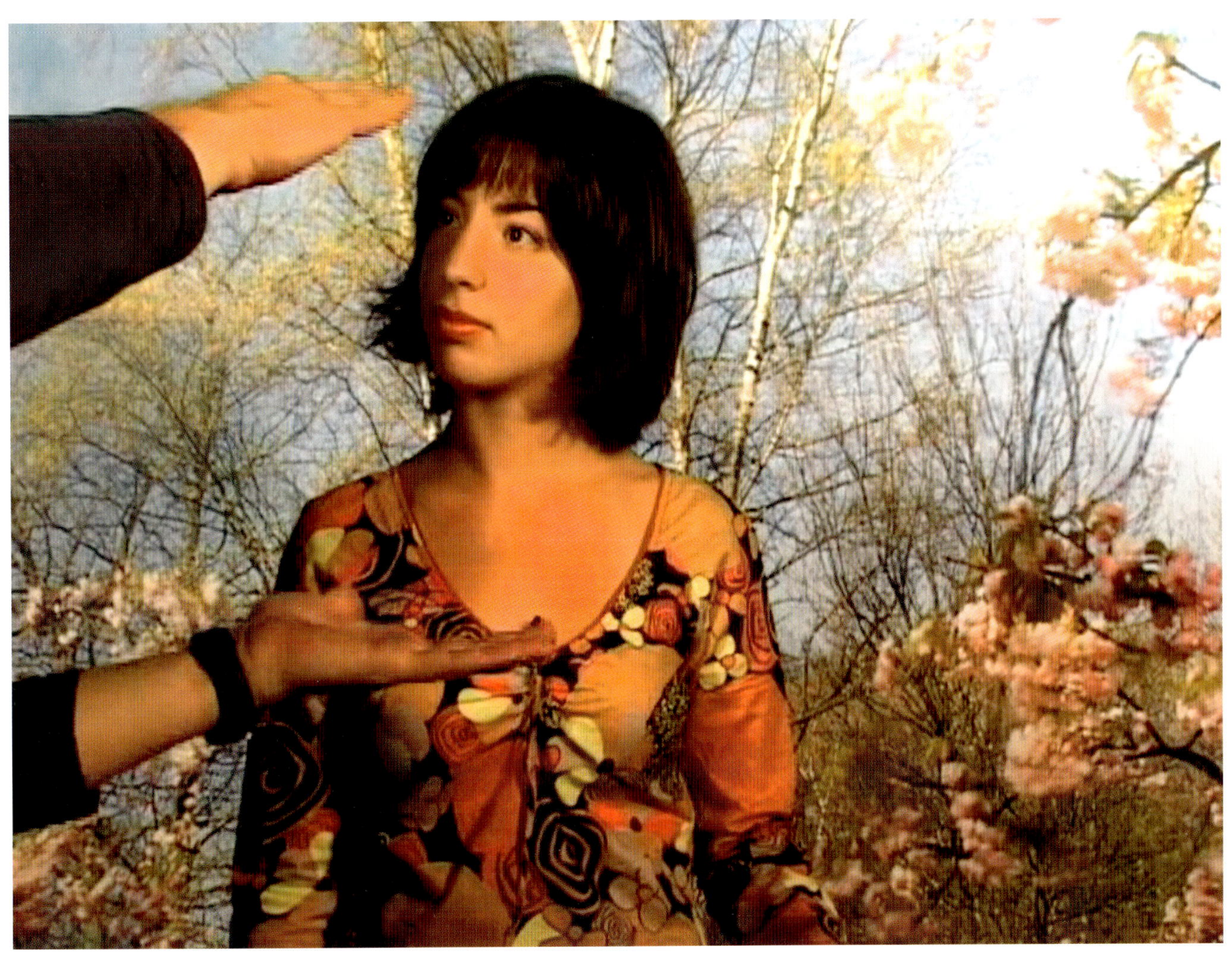

dünya dinlemiyor

Ama şarkıları unutma
Seni ağlatan
Ve hayatını kurtaran şarkıları
Evet, artık büyüdün
Ve zeki bir domuzsun
Ama sadece onlardı hep yanında olan

THE SMITHS KARAOKE

Dünyanın tüm
çekingen tatminsiz güzel
kaybedenleri için
18-19-20-21 Ağustos'ta
İstanbul'da yeni bir film çekiliyor.

İLETİŞİM: thesmithskaraoke@yahoo.com.tr
TEL : 0538 459 3064

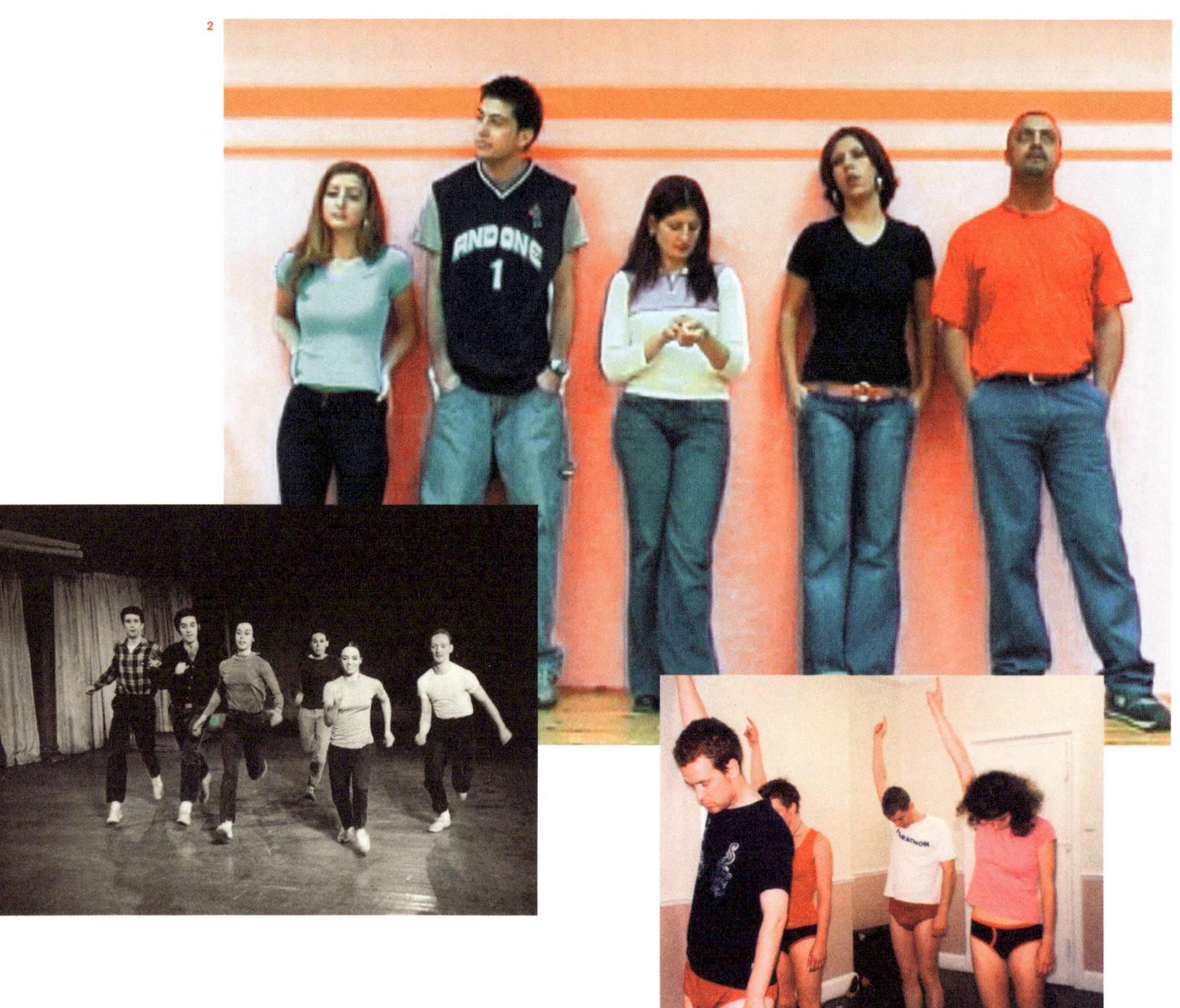

1

2

3

1
Rosalind Krauss, "Video: The Aesthetics
of Narcissism," *October*, no. 1
(Spring 1976): 55.

2
See my essay, "Video Projection: The Space
Between Screens," in *ContemporaryArt
in Theory*, ed. Simon Leung and Zoya Kocur
(London: Basil Blackwell, 2004); reprinted
in Tanya Leighton, ed., *Art and the Moving
Image: A Critical Reader* (London: Afterall/
Tate Publishing, 2007).

Live Through This

Liz Kotz

Over thirty years ago, the art historian Rosalind Krauss famously diagnosed the then-new medium of video art as structured by an "aesthetics of narcissism." Viewing artists' tapes of the early 1970s by Vito Acconci, Bruce Nauman, and Lynda Benglis, among others, Krauss focused on the insistent moments of self-mirroring and self-regard in these works, to propose that the medium of video art was "the psychological condition of the self split and doubled by the mirror-reflection of synchronous feedback."[1]

Krauss's essay has been criticized for its seeming antipathy to video art, but its fundamental insights are still sound. They alert us to the ways that the very infrastructure or structuring principles of moving-image media consist not merely of the physical, material apparatus — the stuff of camera, monitor, screen, pixels, and so on — but the peculiar personal and psychological relations that these technologies become embedded in and help generate. For well over a century now, the creation of selves and the production of images, moving and still, have existed in a strange symbiosis. Many of the most compelling psychoanalytic models have come to focus on the displaced moments of self-mirroring that occur when we look at images and on all the strange interplays of love and aggression, envy and desire that occur when we see ourselves in the image of another and see another in ourselves.

Even more than photography, the durational nature of film and video allows on-camera subjects to expose themselves in ways that provoke an unstable transference between viewer and viewed. Since the 1970s, the closed-circuit and self-referential systems that Krauss saw as pointing to an incessant and self-enclosed now have been partly supplanted by projects that use found and recorded materials to probe structures of cinematic and televisual viewing. Each mutating setup, from closed-circuit monitor to handheld gadget to large-scale projection, potentially creates vastly different ways of addressing, engaging, and involving a viewer. These differences — in scale, in the bodily position and activity of the viewer — generate a nuanced array of phenomenological, experienced and spectatorial effects, yet our deeply rooted capacities to involve ourselves in a face or a story migrate surprisingly well from platform to platform.

Over the past several years, Phil Collins's work in video has investigated the complex, unpredictable, and often fraught relationships among those who watch, shoot, and appear on video and TV. Although positioned within the art world, Collins's project has emerged from the margins of recent visual art practice. Since the 1990s, countless artists have pushed the medium toward spectacular and pictorial uses that divorce it from its roots in amateur video and TV — often adopting video technology to contrive quasi-cinematic narratives or create giant luminous tableaux that decorate buildings.[2] In the artfully constructed world of high-end gallery-based video, irruptions of the real are rare; almost no one talks.

3

In, for example, *hero* (2002), which records the drunken reminiscences of a journalist who witnessed the 9/11 World Trade Center collapse, and *gercegin geri donusu* (2005), which features the stories of people who "felt their lives had been ruined" by appearing on reality TV.

4

"Who Said an Artwork Shouldn't Be an Imposition? A Conversation between Phil Collins and Jeremy Millar," in *Deutsche Börse Photography Prize 2006*, ed. Stefanie Braun (London: Photographers' Gallery, 2006), 77.

5

Claire Bishop and Francesco Manacorda, "The Producer as Artist," in *yeah . . . . . you, baby you*, ed. Siniša Mitrović (Milton Keynes and Hove, England: Milton Keynes Gallery and Shady Lane Publications, 2005), 24.

Collins's work insistently pushes back, into the psychic entrapment, confessional moments, and the troubling power relations occasioned by vernacular uses of video. In it, people do sing and also talk and tell stories.[3] Part of the reason video so often fails as a device for self-mirroring is that many of us don't feel comfortable with what we see on the monitor — the selves that appear from without are not always ones we recognize, much less identify with. Collins's videos explore the danger and awkwardness of such exposure. Yet from within the violence of representation, he nonetheless extracts moments of extraordinary beauty, even ecstatic bliss. And even if a number of his tapes are shot in adamantly low-fi, improvised conditions, his gallery presentations are often seamless and highly crafted, self-consciously aware of the validation and drama that media presentation accords everyday life.

As his oddly awkward photographs suggest, Collins isn't interested in making pretty pictures. Instead, his turn to video seems to have begun with pain. The artist has discussed how he came to make his first video, *how to make a refugee* (1999), while recording photo shoots by journalists working in a Kosovar refugee camp across the border in Macedonia. In *how to make a refugee*, we look on as a crew of British photojournalists pose and photograph a Kosovar family, focusing on a petulant, bored-looking fifteen-year-old boy. In one charged moment, he is asked to raise his undershirt to reveal a long scar across his stomach; in another, the extended family is arranged on the couch as in an ersatz portrait session. As crew members chatter mindlessly in the background and issue terse

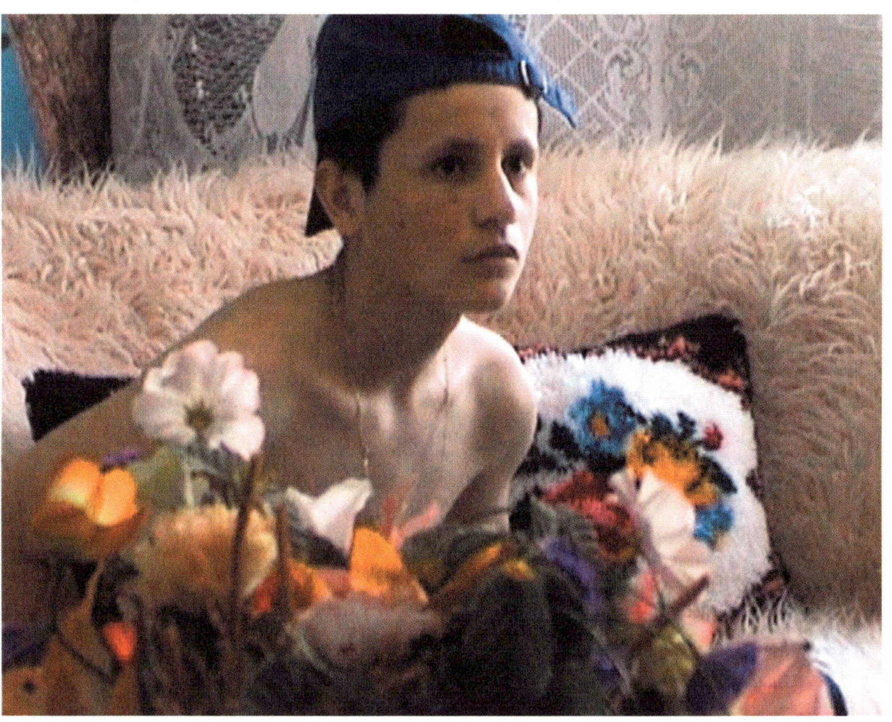

how to make a refugee, 1999

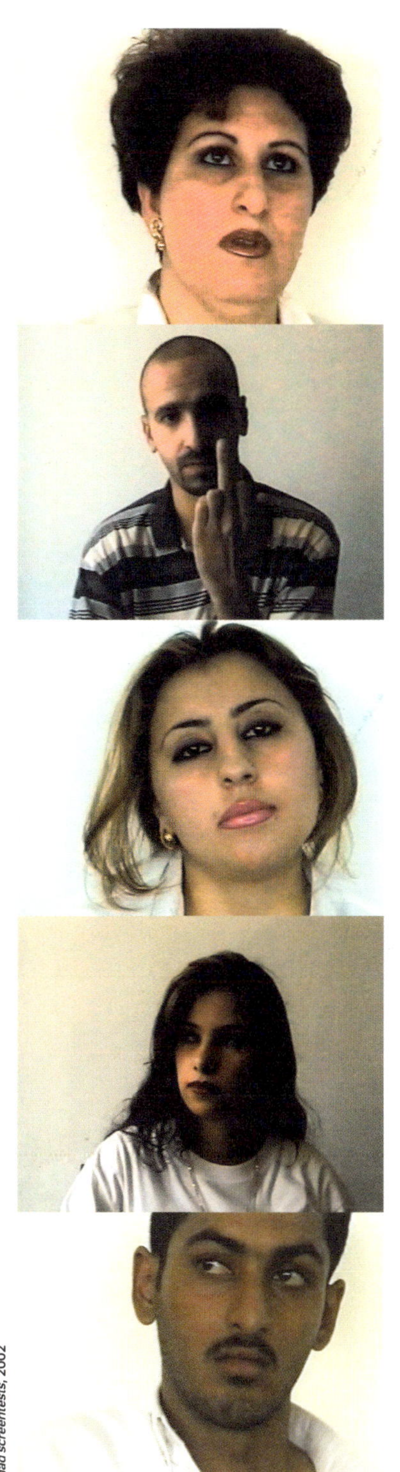

commands, the scene takes on a casual brutality. Commenting on the experience, Collins recalls that there was "something very ugly and brutal about the total disregard for the subject, and a complete lack of understanding of the reasons why he won't expose his wounds. . . . "[4]

For us, in watching *how to make a refugee*, this discomfort is replicated. The tape is a document of a chance encounter between Collins and routine practices of photojournalism in war-torn locales. It's like a shard, a found object. The tape starts abruptly and cuts off abruptly; its eleven minutes contain enough garbled dialogue, blocked views, and off-kilter shots to strain the patience of a Warhol fan. Yet it contains seeds of Collins's subsequent work in video — from the intense fascination with the interior performances that distressed subjects provide for the camera to the artificial backdrops and incongruous props that emphasize the sense of placelessness. Although his videos are often shot in intense, conflict-ridden places — Baghdad, Bogotá, Ramallah, among others — Collins's shooting style deliberately dislocates us, in ways that obliterate any direct reference to their immediate circumstances.

Clad in a dark blue T-shirt and baseball cap, the boy who is the main subject of *how to make a refugee* is pretty average looking — at first glance, he could be a skinny kid from anywhere. In watching the tape, our attention lingers on odd props and details— the thin gold chain around the boy's neck, his Western teen attire, and the large bouquet of fake flowers that sits on an end table, partly blocking our view. Against the world-historical register of ethnic conflict and catastrophe, Collins is clearly drawn to these sorts of details and the glimpses they give us of private fantasies and desires. As Claire Bishop and Francesco Manacorda note, Collins's work evidences what may seem to be "a politically-incorrect or frivolous attitude toward his subject-matter." His works avoid direct references to the political situations they nonetheless record, preferring "generic globalized teenagers" to the overtly located subjects of most documentary work. As Bishop and Manacorda suggest, by "voiding the work of direct political narrative,"[5] Collins's videos open spaces to be filled by our own fantasies and projections.

Elements that seem to have occurred accidentally in *how to make a refugee* are then explored as strategies in Collins's subsequent works. In *baghdad screentests* (2002), Collins adopts the format and serial structure that Warhol used in his *Screen Tests* (1963–66). In Warhol's films of the mid-1960s, visitors to the Factory were seated in front of a camera mounted on a tripod and were told not to move or blink for the duration of the approximately three-minute-long camera rolls. In Collins's work, the effect is arguably different: shot in video, against a white background, the sequences mostly sidestep the confrontational, testlike quality of Warhol's starkly lit portrait films. Is it the softer focus of the video camera or a different relation between viewer and viewed? Some of the subjects perform for the camera; others just sit there, quite formal, quietly staring. One man restlessly smokes onscreen and appears to talk to the camera. He looks irritated and bored, gives the camera the finger, then starts reading a magazine. If Warhol's

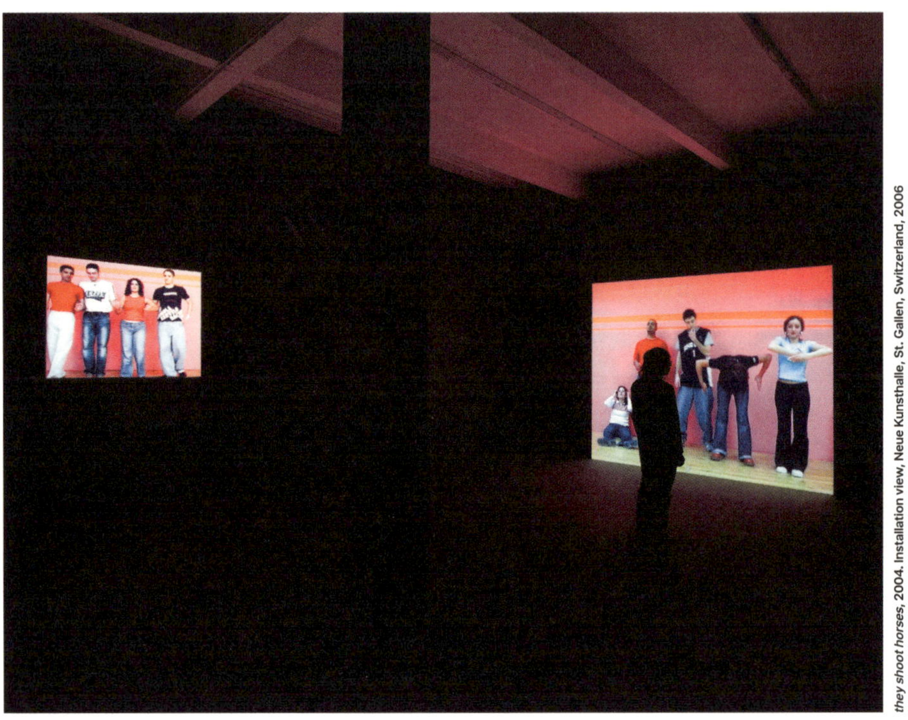

they shoot horses, 2004. Installation view, Neue Kunsthalle, St. Gallen, Switzerland, 2006

would-be stars mostly were held transfixed by the camera, Collins's subjects are far more difficult to read. In the absence of contextual information, we look all the harder for the small signs and details that might allow us to read these faces, to bring them closer to us.

The serial form, presenting one thing after another, is not only a debt to Warhol but also a classic strategy of 1960s minimal art and structural film. Collins's videos tend to employ one of a handful of minimalist devices — task structures, extended durations, serial presentations. Unlike the classic minimal and conceptual projects of the 1960s and 1970s, however, the activities and materials are loosely drawn from popular culture. In some of the videos pop music is firmly integrated into the fabric of the work. Thus the karaoke project compiles an album of performances based on The Smiths' 1987 compilation album, *The World Won't Listen*, and *they shoot horses* (2004) lines two groups of young people against a wall to perform a seven-hour dance marathon to a selection of music from the past three decades.[6]

they shoot horses is Collins's most sculptural work. In it, his involvement with early video and performance art becomes most visible. In his projects of the past several years, Collins has adopted sculptural and performance-based approaches to video, using process, duration, and repetition to create a complex relationship with the viewer, one in which positions of subject and object are usually far from stable. Taking its cue from the use of scale and "theatricality" in minimalist art, early work in video (and structural

6

Both groups danced for eight hours, but the work contains only seven hours as one of the hour-long tapes was inexplicably lost in transit at the Israeli border.

60

film, as well) created performative situations that forced viewers not only to respond to the work but also, in a sense to "complete" it. Drawing from these models, Collins's videos set up rule-based structures and then see how they play out.

The opening moments of *they shoot horses* are a beautiful transition from stillness to movement, as the two groups of dancers start to move to the rhythm of the song. In each projection, several young people are lined up against a bright pink wall that has two horizontal stripes painted at about head height. The strict spatial arrangement allows permutations and variations to reveal themselves vividly. The dancers are confined to a shallow stage-like set, so their bodies bounce around all the corners of their narrow box much like pictorial elements trapped in a frame. When they are projected nearly life-sized on adjacent walls of the gallery, we encounter these figures in an almost one-to-one bodily relation. As the two groups of dancers keep trying to dance, song after song, hour after hour, their energy flags and then rallies and then flags again. One or two individuals sit out for a while, and then someone gets them going again. We have never met these young people, but after a while we feel as if we know them intimately: the cheerleadery girl with the long earrings and athletic clothes, the tired girl, the handsome aloof guy. As fatigue takes its toll, their efforts appear alternately tragic and comic, heroic and heartbreaking.

This type of task-based performance, recorded on video, inevitably recalls the studio films and videos that Bruce Nauman made in the late 1960s, in which he would perform a simple action for an extended period — for instance, *Bouncing Two Balls between the Floor and Ceiling with Changing Rhythms* or *Walking in an Exaggerated Manner around the Perimeter of a Square* (both 1967–68). Nauman's actions were not random but highly structured and rehearsed, but over time the execution of these actions became disrupted by the operations of chance and human fatigue. We watch him get tired, get angry, lose focus, and lose control. In Nauman's work the permeable line between everyday movement and choreographed task, between practice and performance, was inspired by Merce Cunningham's transformations of everyday activities into dance and by the Judson Dance Theater's experiments with task structures and repetition.[7] The discipline with which he carries out these seemingly pointless tasks gives the tapes a black humor and pathos.

Like that of a number of artists of the late 1960s and early 1970s, Nauman's address to his audience is physical. Through his use of endurance and real time — the actual time it takes to perform the action — he performs a transfer onto the body of the viewer: through duration, one undergoes the experience with him, one, in a sense, becomes him. As Nauman noted in an interview in 1970, the durational aspect of the performance, along with the concentration of the performer, is crucial for creating a sense of physical sympathy in the viewer: "If you really believe in what you're doing and do it as well as you can, then there will be a certain amount of tension — if you are honestly tired or if you are honestly trying to balance on one foot for a long time, there has to be a certain

7

For the Judson dancers' use of task structures and repetition, see Yvonne Rainer, *Works, 1961–73* (Halifax: Nova Scotia College of Art and Design, 1974); and Sally Banes, *Terpsichore in Sneakers: Postmodern Dance* (Middletown, Conn.: Wesleyan University Press, 1987).

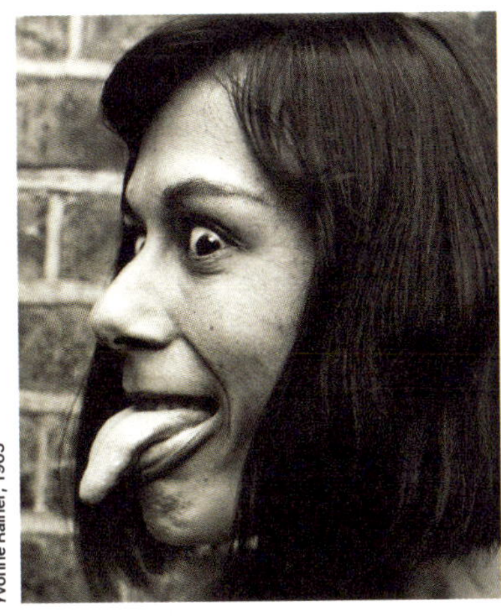

Yvonne Rainer, 1965

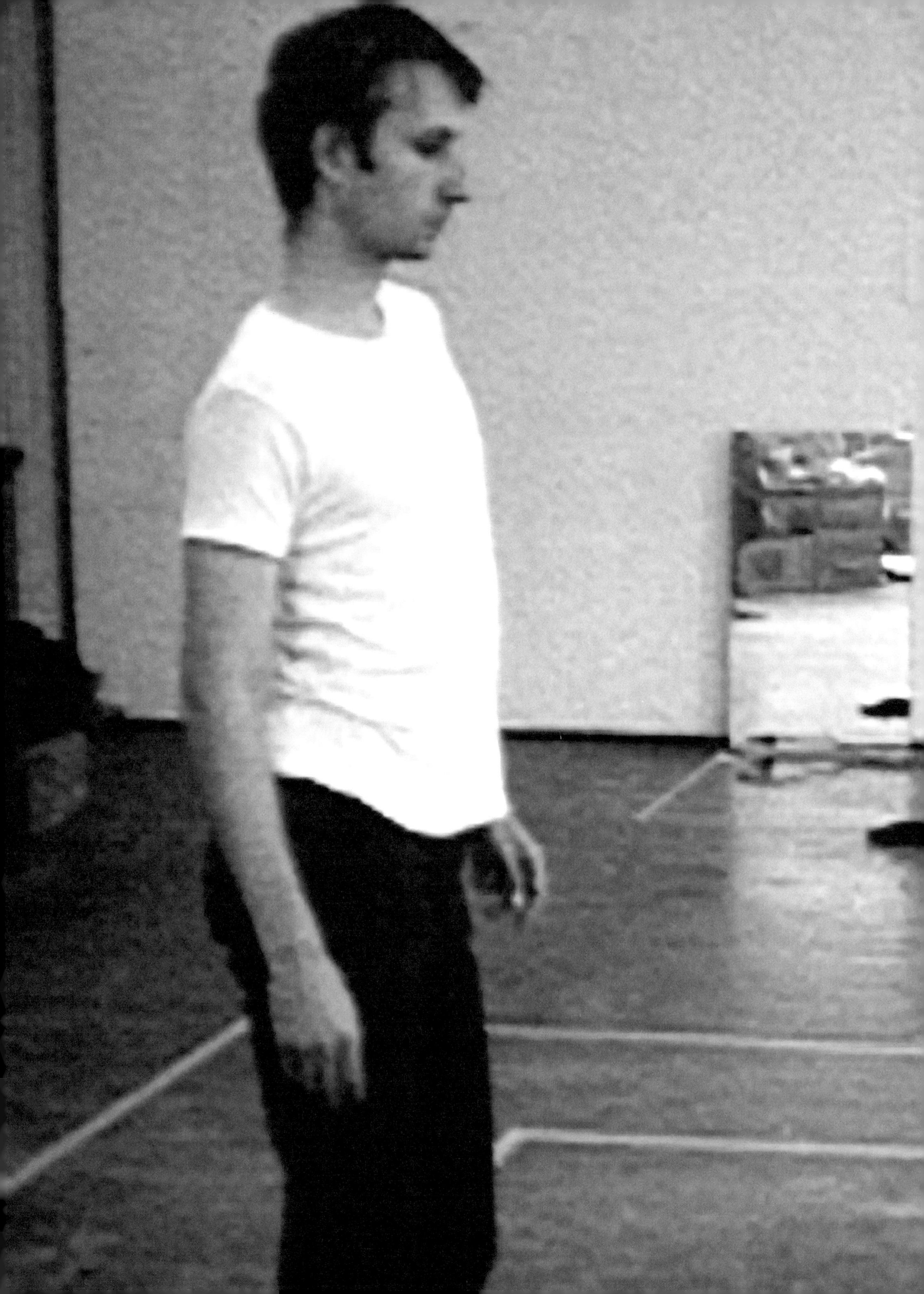

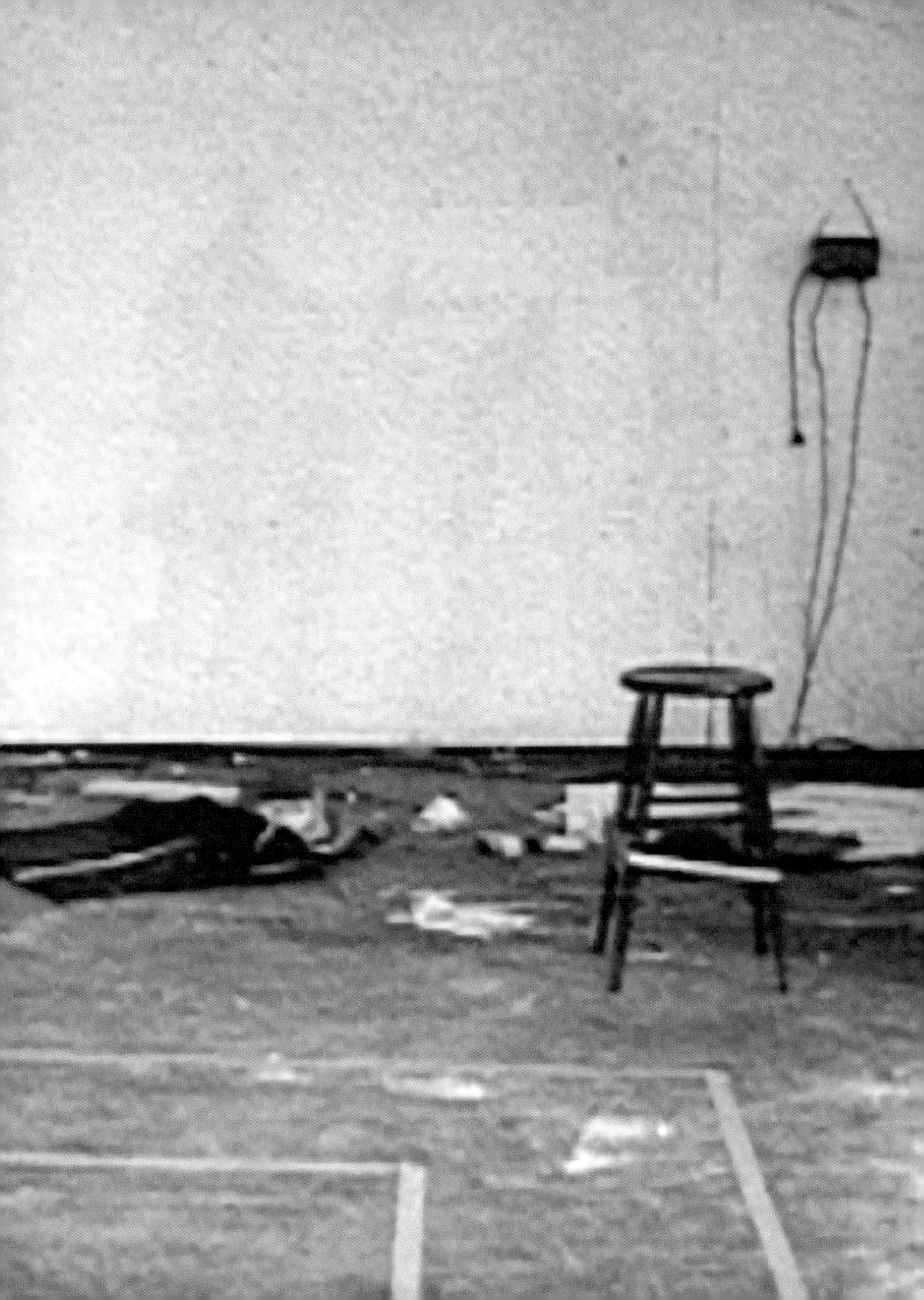

8
Willoughby Sharp, "Bruce Nauman,"
Avalanche, 1971; republished in *The New
Sculpture 1965–75: Between Geometry
and Gesture*, ed. Richard Armstrong and
Richard Marshall, exh. cat. (New York:
Whitney Museum of American Art, 1990),
241, 240.

9
The Turner Prize 2006 audio guide,
Phil Collins, Audio Guide Transcript,
Tate Britain, 2006; http://www.tate.org.
uk/britain/turnerprize/2006/philcollins_
transcript.htm.

10
Phil Collins, "Why Can't I Be You?"
in *Now What? Artists Write!*,
ed. Annie Fletcher, Marija Havlajova,
and Mark Kremer (Utrecht: BAK basis
voor actuele kunst; Frankfurt: Revolver
Archiv für aktuelle Kunst, 2004),
23–26.

sympathetic response in someone who is watching you. It is a kind of body response, they feel that foot and that tension." Going through such activities, according to Nauman, permits an experiential kind of knowledge not available from mere observation or contemplation: "An awareness of yourself comes from a certain amount of activity and you can't get it from just thinking about yourself. You do exercises, you have certain kinds of awarenesses that you don't have if you read books."[8]

Unlike the early artists who made performance videos, such as Vito Acconci and Nauman, Collins does not perform in his own works (except for a brief appearance at the end of *baghdad screentests*, where he is seen smoking). Instead, his videos operate through a kind of delegated performance as he finds subjects to perform for him — to be his surrogates and ours. His own desire for our attention is triangulated off another subject, who presumably wants his attention — and who is, therefore, willing to do intense things on camera. "I approach the construction of every work from a position of envy," he comments, " . . . this is the thing I wish I could do."[9] A durational work such as *they shoot horses* makes particular demands on the spectator. As viewers we have to make a commitment to the piece and although watching it is far less demanding than performing in it must be, we don't just observe the dancers' joy and elation, endurance and fatigue, we experience them too.

This triangular structure made up of artist, performer, and audience is quite different from the self-enclosed mirroring that Krauss diagnosed in early video. Watching another, we are constantly pulled into and back out of ourselves. One might try to describe this as an aesthetics of transference or projection: we become Phil become the performers become us. Yet for all their intimacy, the works preserve a distance. Collins speaks of working with an almost romantic ideal: "to offer nothing more, nor less, than the imagined presence of another."[10] The videos almost require us to fall in love with the subjects, to respect and admire their fractured moments of triumph and distress and extreme vulnerability.

These qualities all come together in the trio of The Smiths karaoke videos that Collins has made in the past three years. In *el mundo no escuchará* (2004), filmed in Bogotá, an array of youngish Smiths' fans perform in front of incongruously sunny backdrops of lakeside and tropical leisure. Each backdrop is close enough to the camera that light bounces off it and the performers' shadows fall on it, heightening the artificiality of the scene and making it harder to sink into the nightclub ambiance conjured by the singers' clothes and manners. They try on various rock star poses and gestures, with varying degrees of credibility. The mood changes from song to song and from singer to singer. Many of the performances are not conventionally good, but they are all captivating and even moving. As the singers deliver their songs, they open up private worlds they invite us to enter with them, their courage and exposure making them beautiful.

As Collins describes it: "Other people sometimes find karaoke embarrassing, or laughable, or delusional — the idea that someone gets up and thinks they can sing. But I find it moving and incredibly courageous. As a format, karaoke offers a promise of completion — this act will somehow make me whole — but at the same time it's predicated on the idea of vulnerability and failure, with its countless false starts, its blind terror. The way the pub falls away, and you can clearly see the spot where someone stands. The way they find themselves lost in the middle of a song but unable to escape until it finishes. Its like a mild form of heroism."[11]

In *dünya dinlemiyor* (2005), shot in Istanbul, the backdrops change more frequently, a parade of sun-kissed mountain vistas and cheery lakeside scenes. Instead of producing any kind of visual recreation of the world of the songs, the video dislocates us, make us feel the enormous gap between the stage set and the performance — a parable of the alienation the lyrics recount. In Collins's serial works, one or two performers appear to be key, seeming to stand for the whole in some indirect way. Toward the end of *dünya dinlemiyor*, a young man wearing a Kafka T-shirt dances throughout the instrumental "Oscillate Wildly." At the very end, a pretty young woman in glittery lipstick and eye shadow works herself into a frenzy during "Rubber Ring," a fervor that outlasts the song, so that the video closes on her face contorted in agony or bliss.

Because of the song's evocative lyrics and the singer's heightened performance, we imagine that we share her feelings: "The passing of time / And all of its crimes / Is making me sad again. / But don't forget the songs / That made you cry / And the songs that saved your life." Collins stages this unabashed belief in the redemptive power of popular culture, in the perverse idea that the music of The Smiths might unearth secret communities of believers in the most far-flung locales. What video allows him to do is to concretize these human subjects into a form of social sculpture; we observe not only gestures and bodies and faces, but also comprehend at least something of the complex social dynamics that underpin them — and us. *they shoot horses* is, after all, a "real time social system," to use Hans Haacke's words — even if Collins's approach to political art or institutional critique could not be more different from Haacke's. What Collins has done is to find forms that engage and lay bare the social and psychological relations among subjects and viewers that integrally comprise the medium of video. The very minimalist devices he adopts have all been understood as strategies to foreground the perceptual and bodily experiences of viewers encountering an object in time and in a specific place. Unlike the strictly phenomenological concerns of minimal art, Collins understands that these encounters are never just in the here and now, but are also located in the very different temporalities of fantasy and projection.

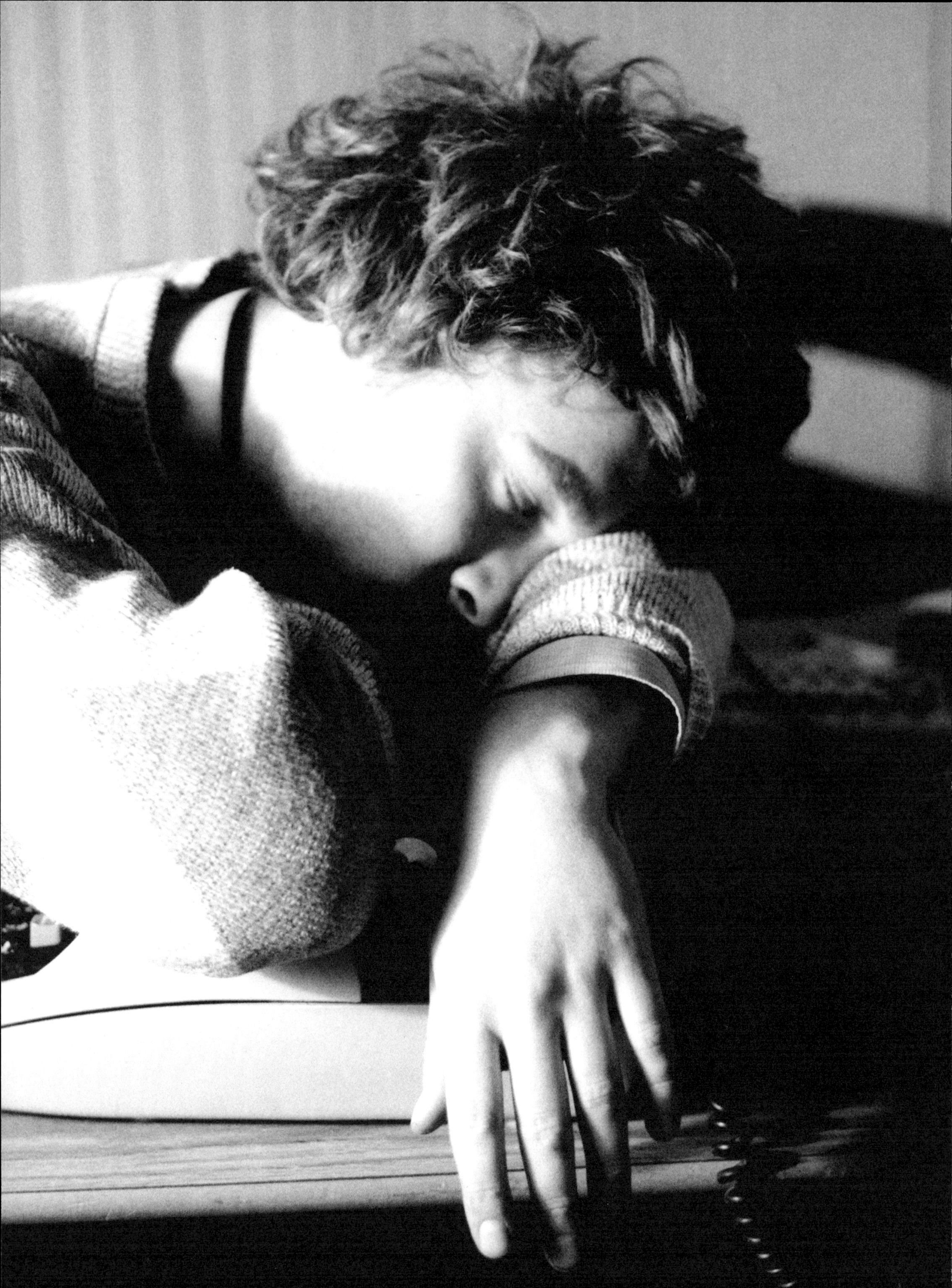

DUNIA TAK AKAN MENDENGAR

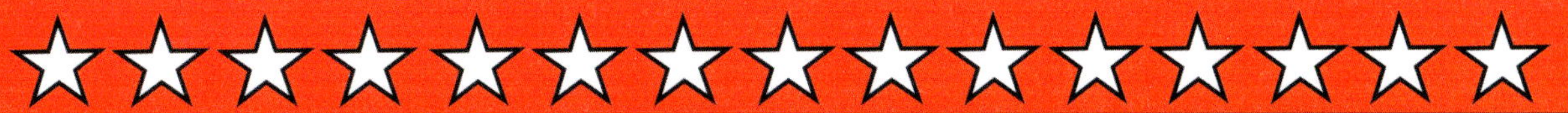

the smiths
KARAOKE

ini kesempatan anda
untuk tunjukkan diri

Untuk si
Pemalu

Untuk Superstar
yang tinggal di rumah saja

Untuk para
Narsis

Sebuah film baru
yang akan di buat di Jakarta dan Bandung pada bulan Maret
bersama para penggemar The Smiths

★ 15, 16, 17, 18 Maret 2007 ★

Bagi yang ingin berpartisipasi di film ini, email ke :

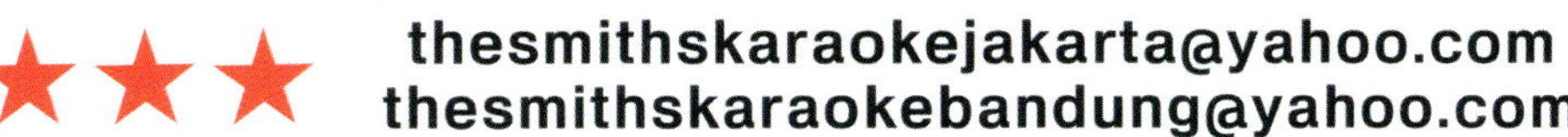

thesmithskaraokejakarta@yahoo.com
thesmithskaraokebandung@yahoo.com

telp / 0811-178-539

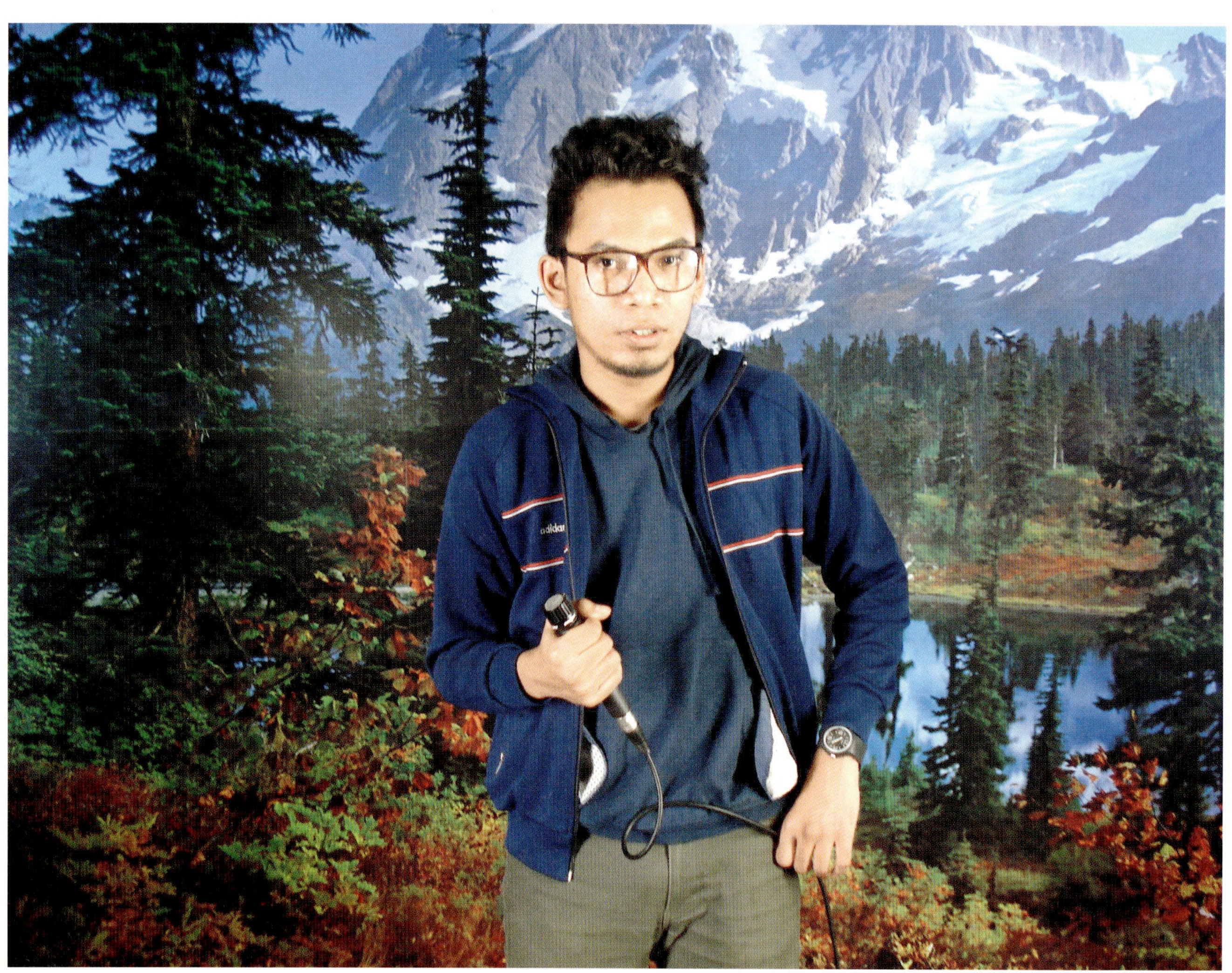

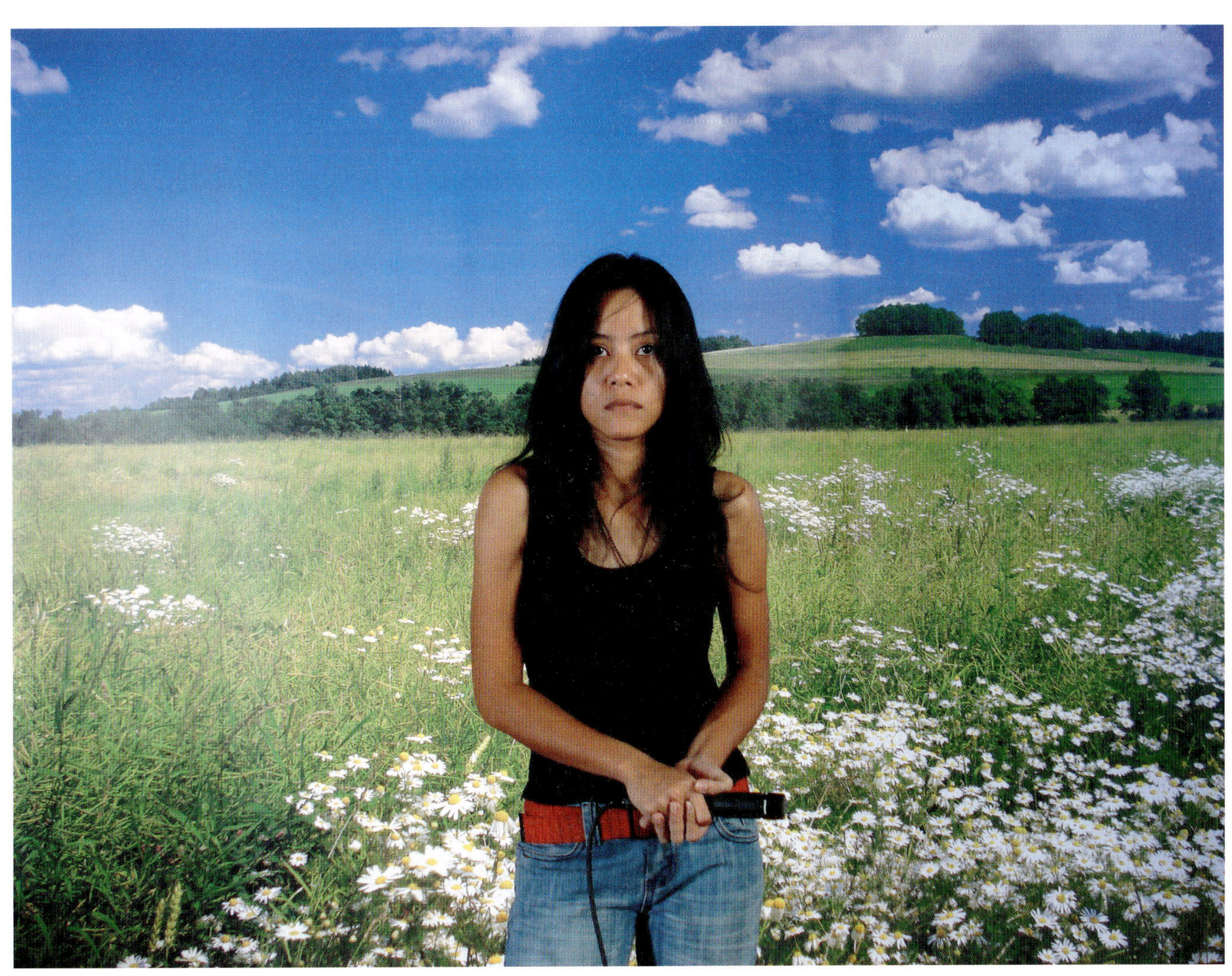

dunia tak akan mendengar

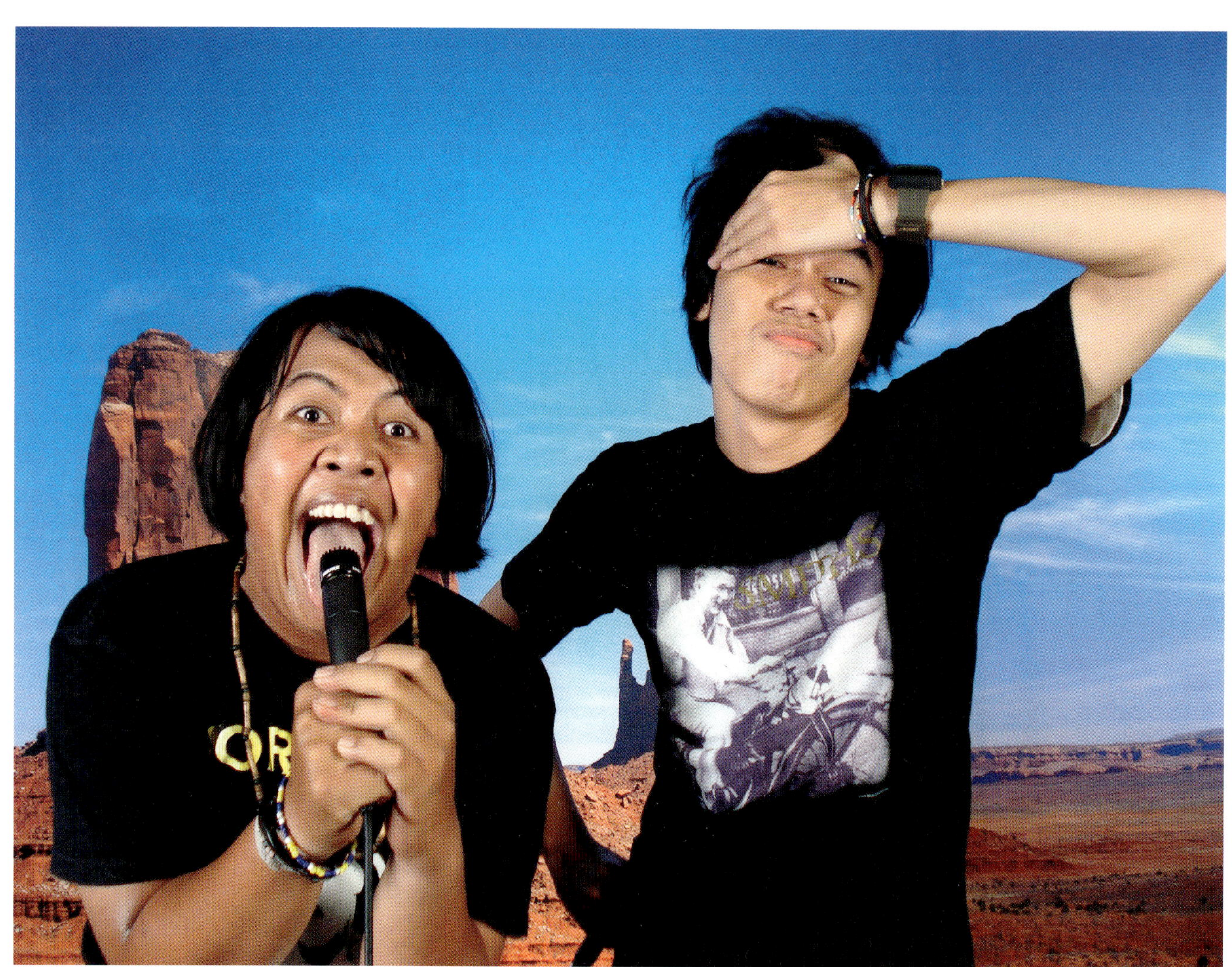

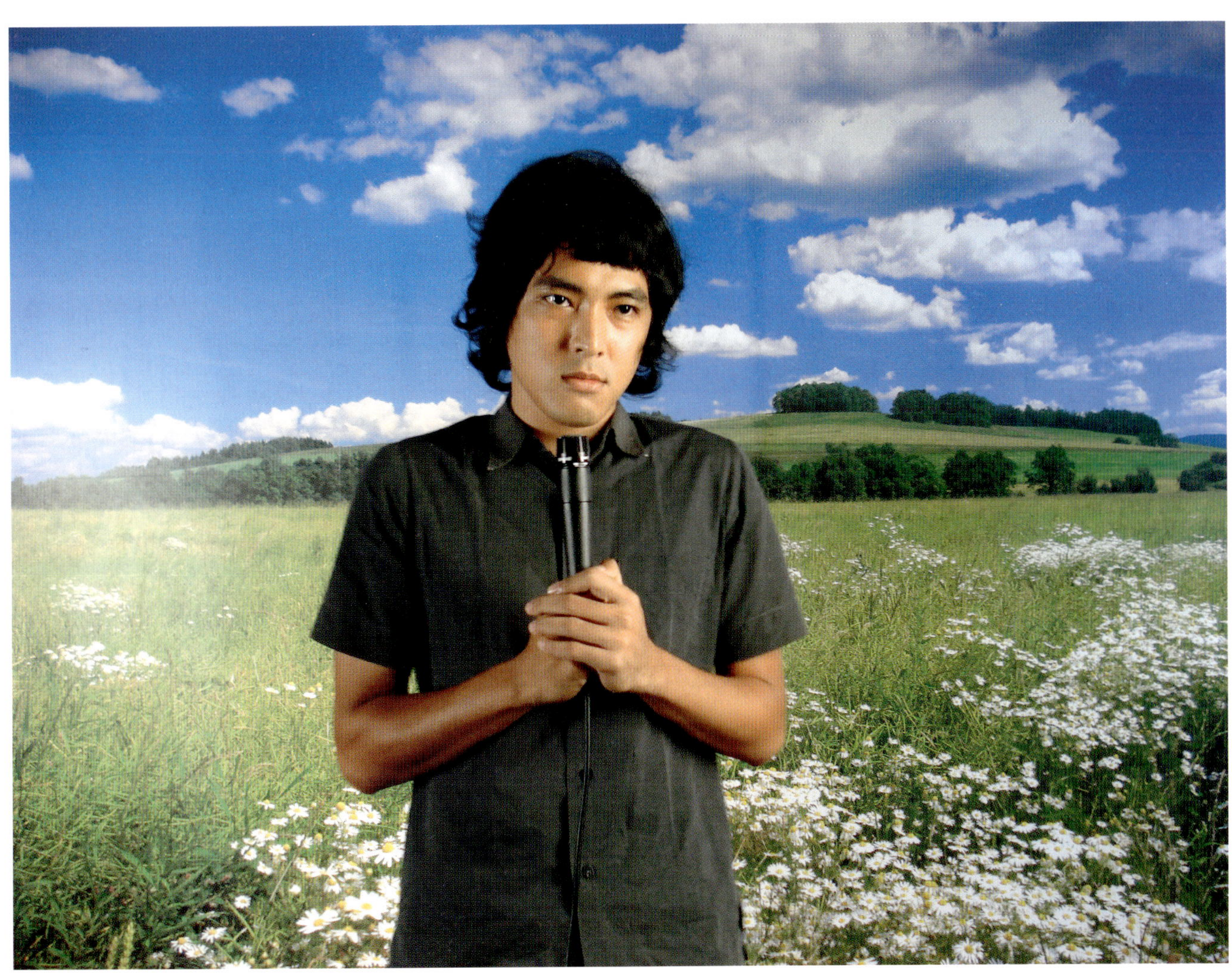

dunia tak akan mendengar

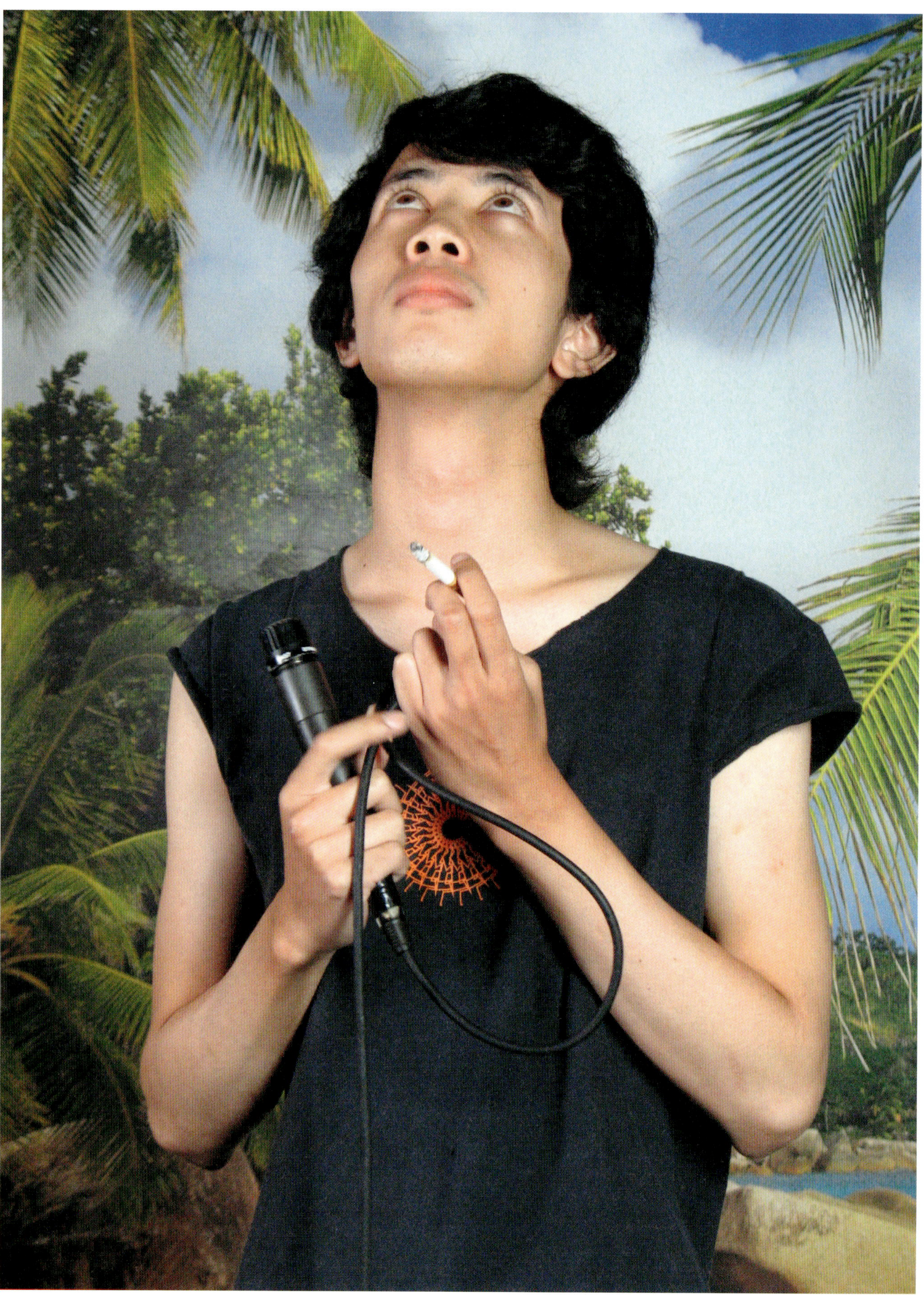

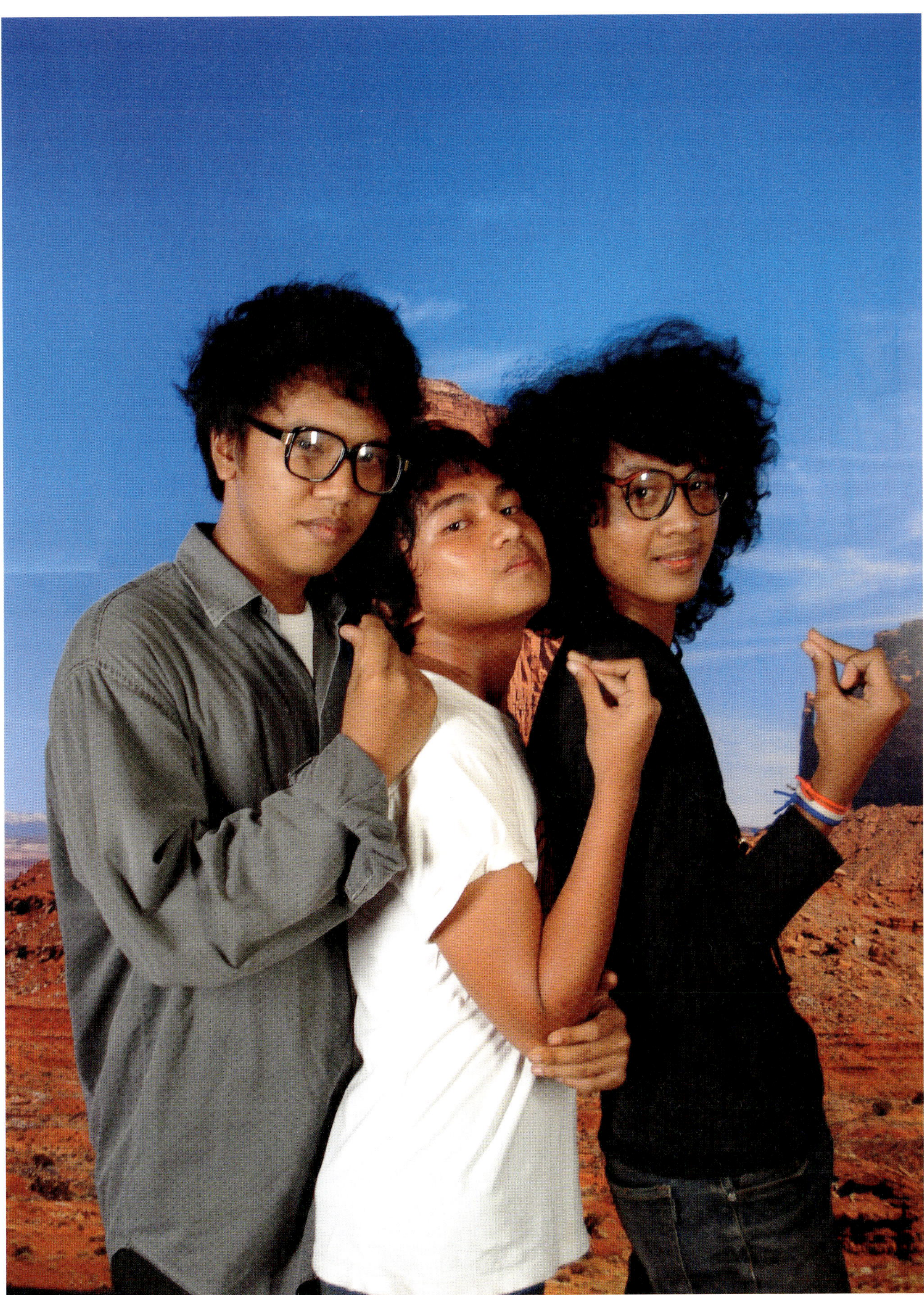

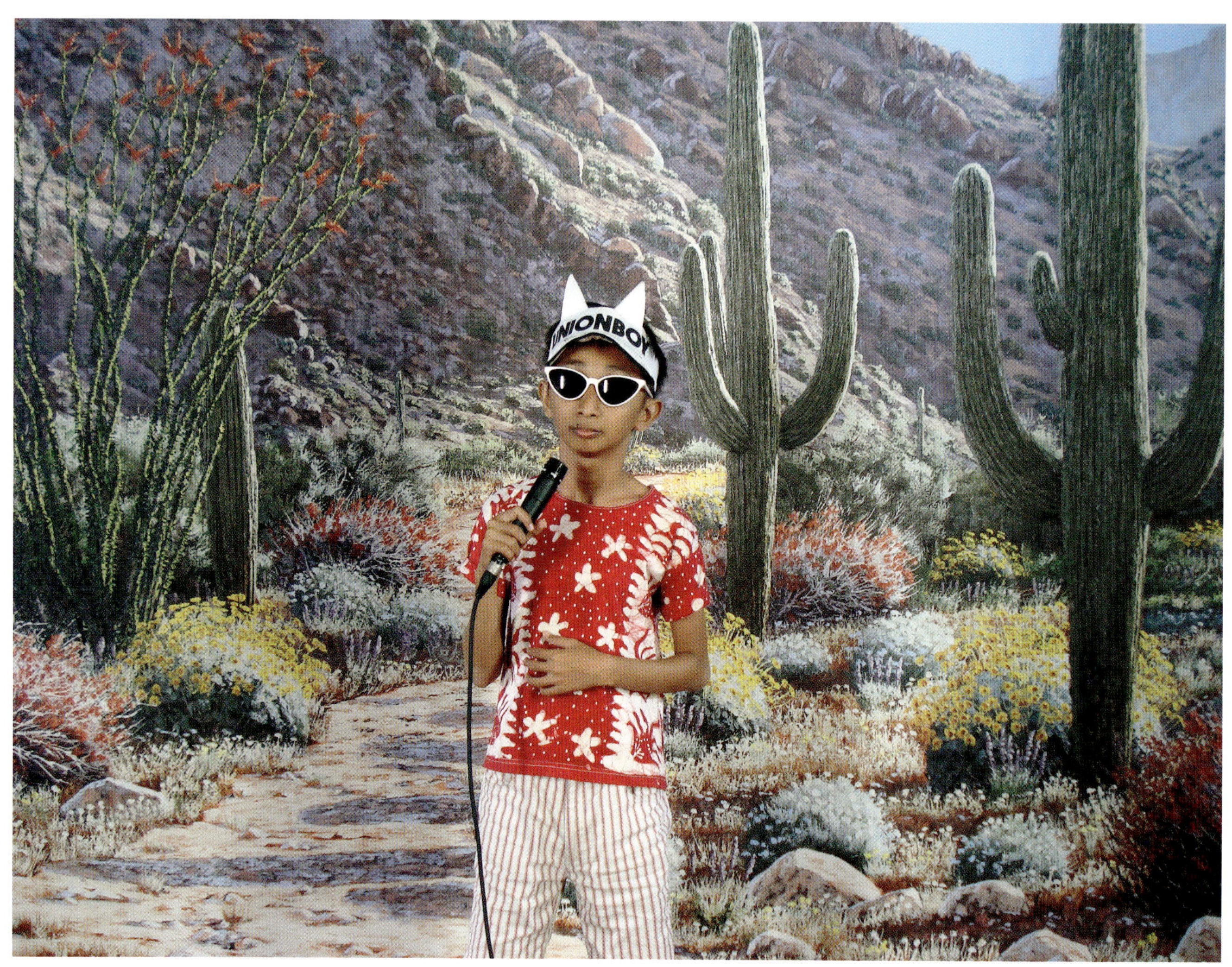

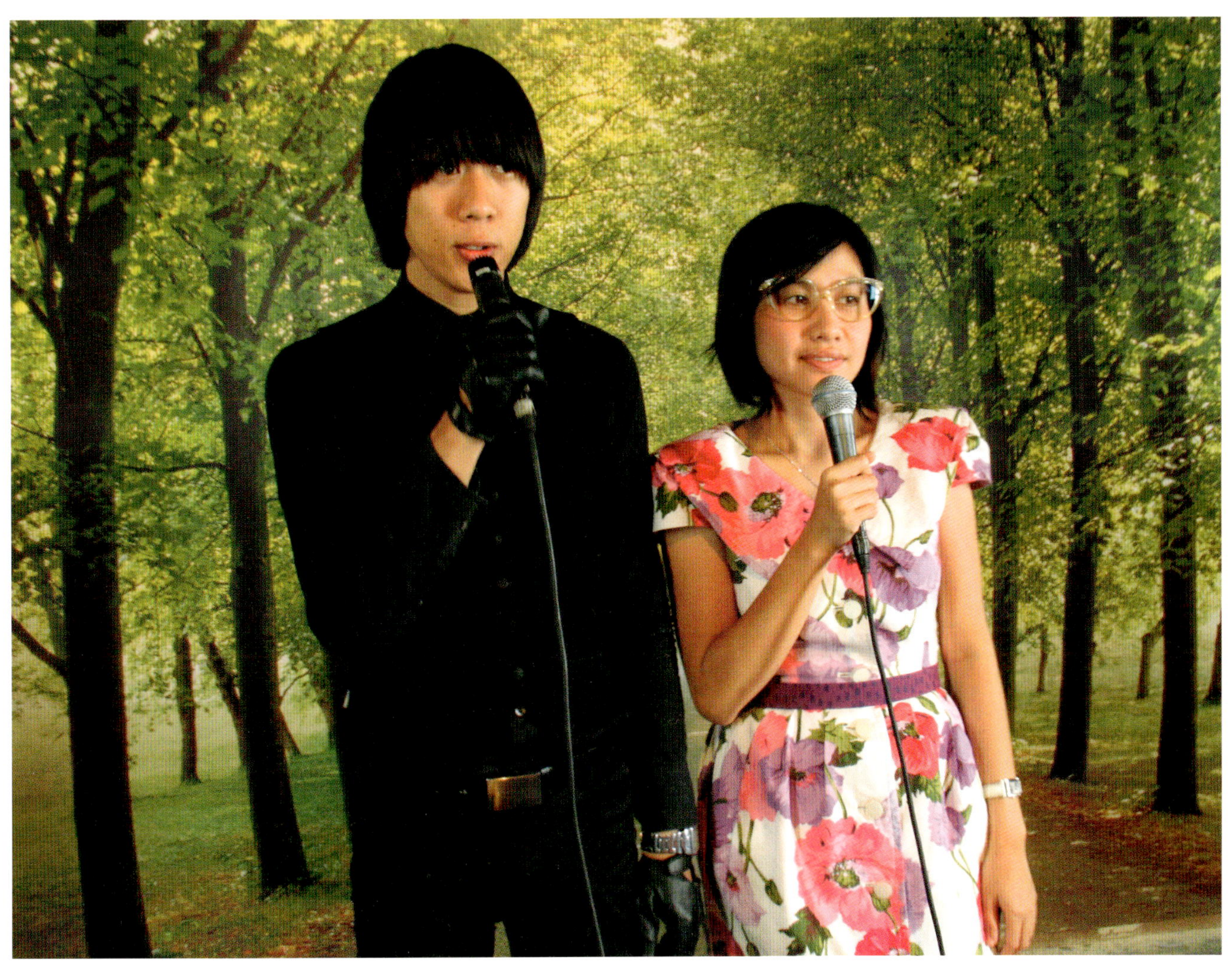

dunia tak akan mendengar

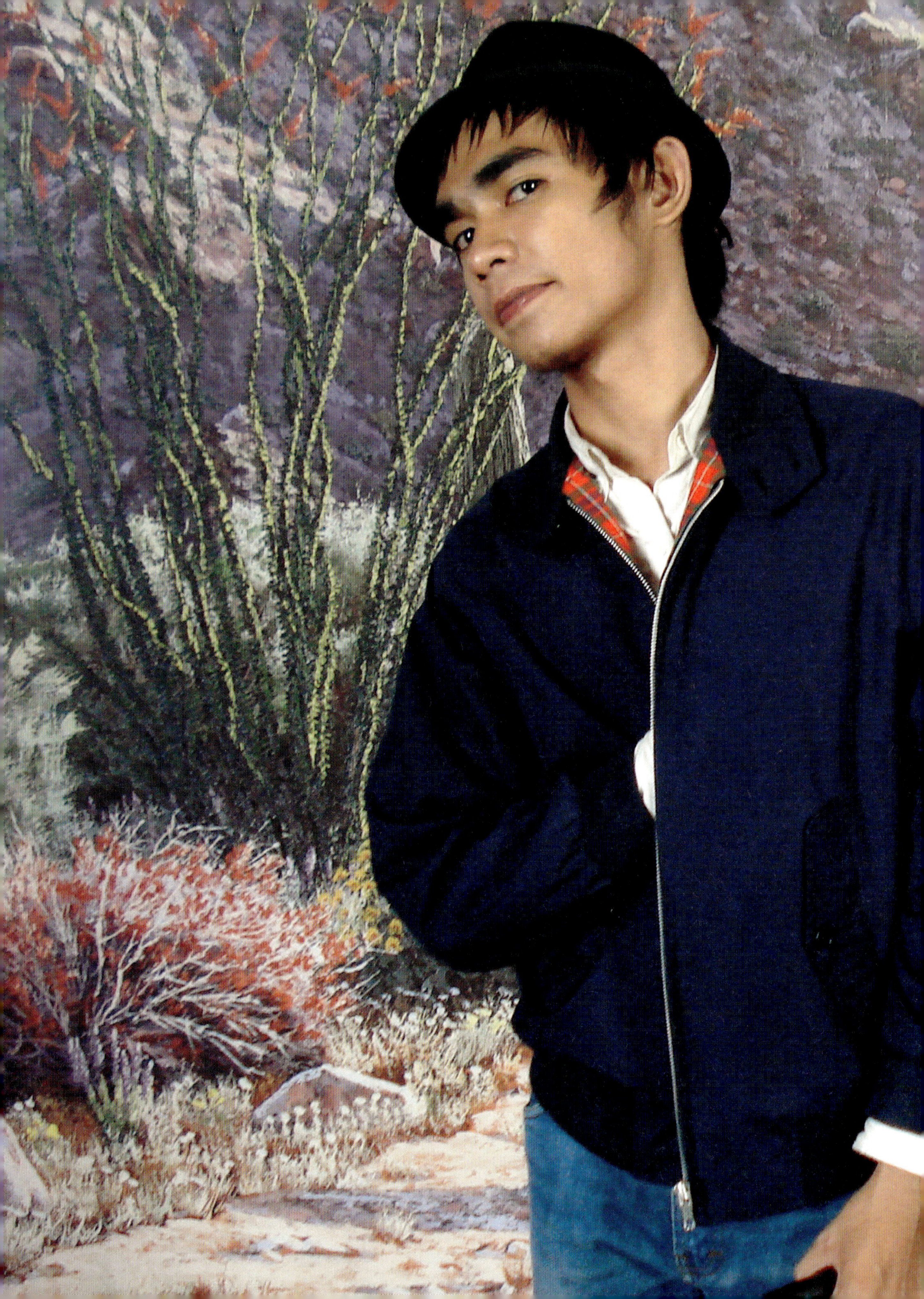

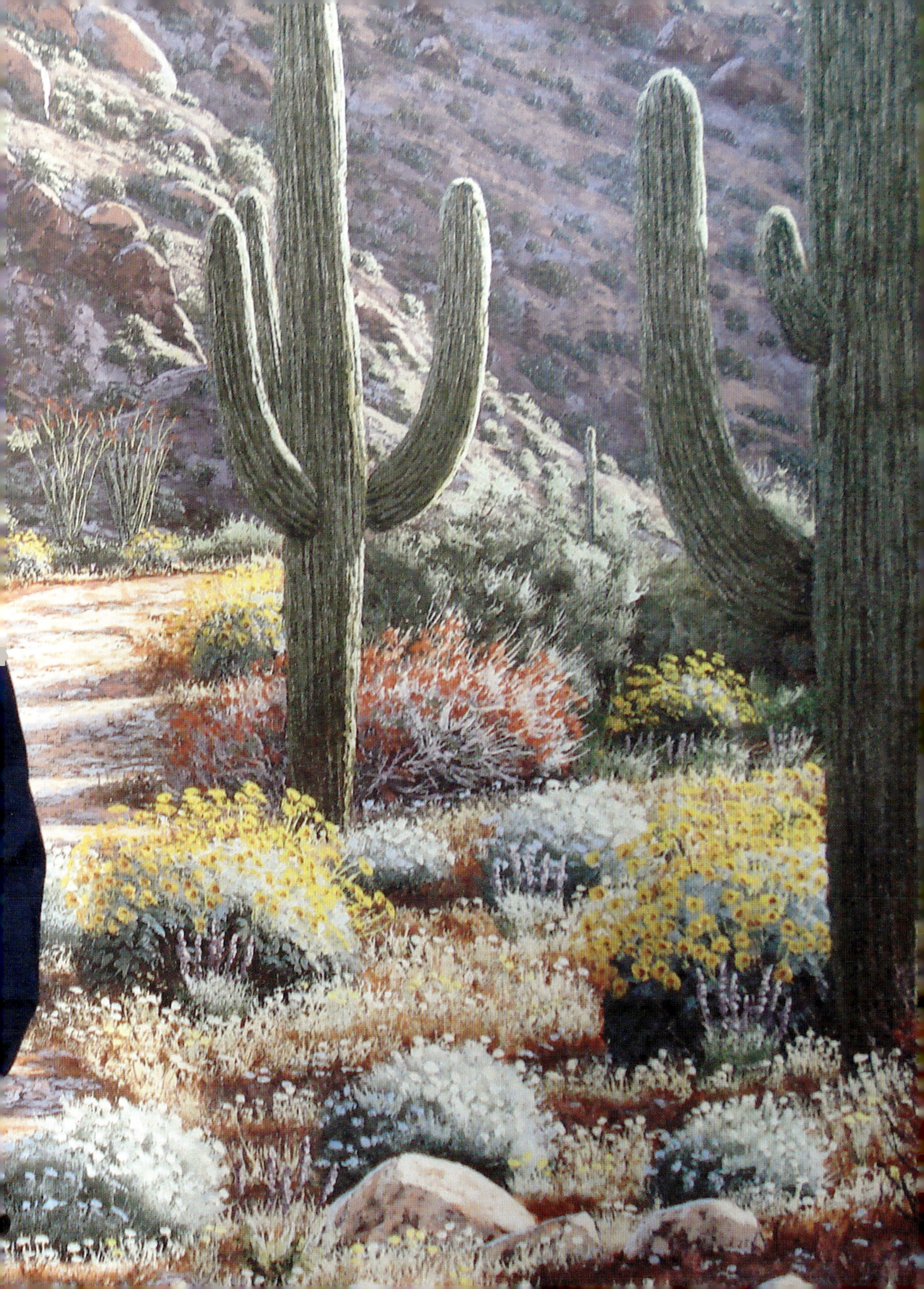

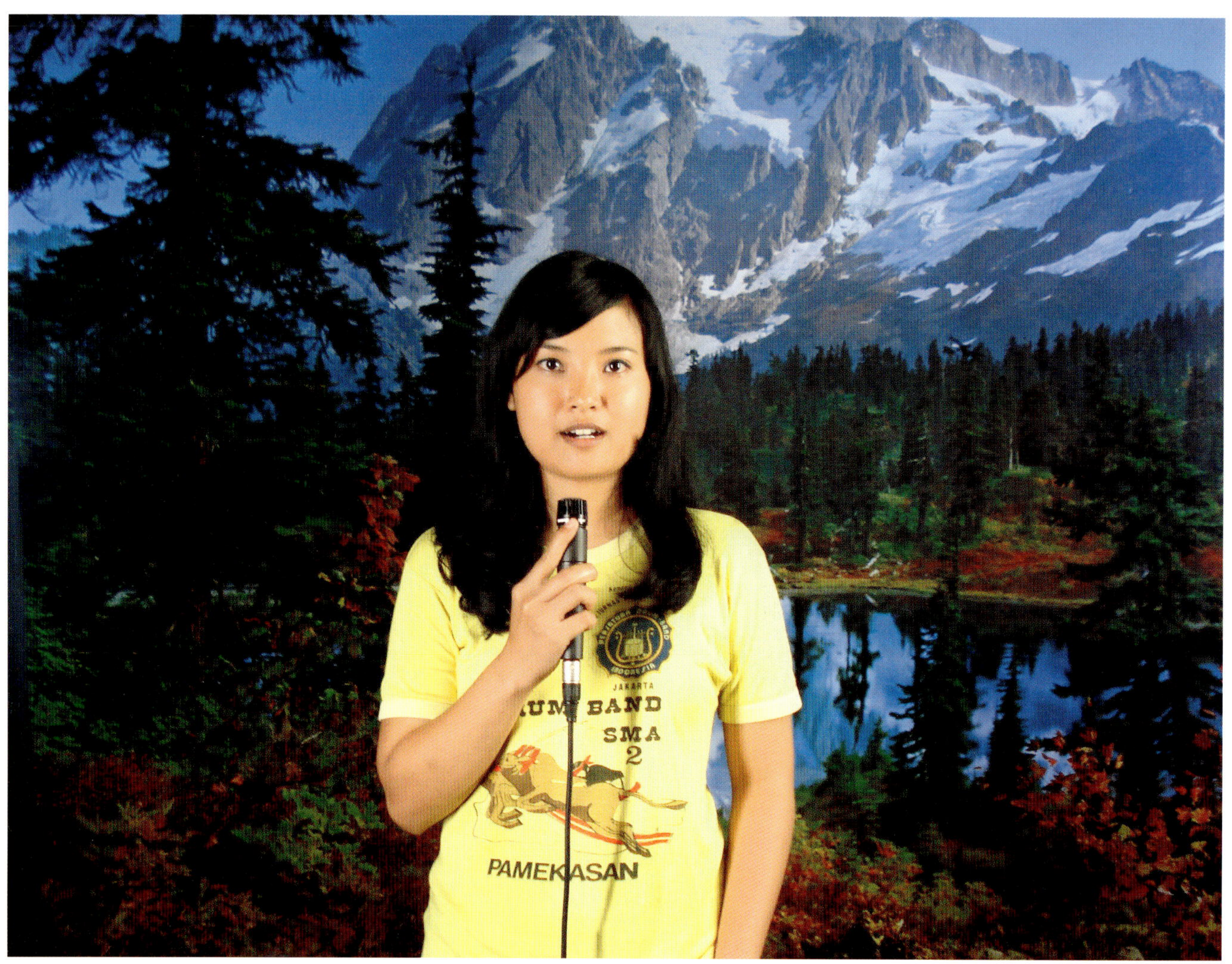
UM BAND
SMA
2
PAMEKASAN

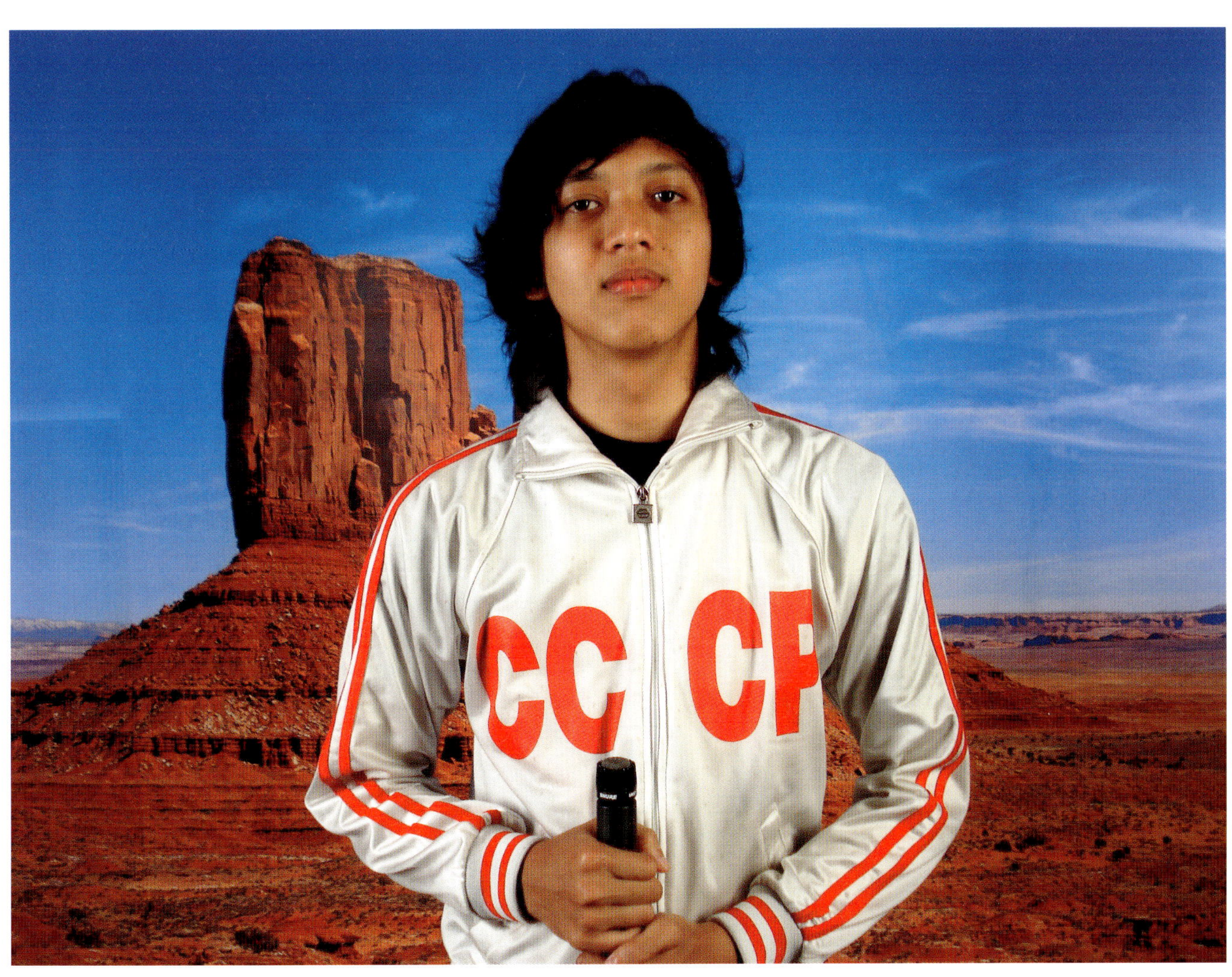

dunia tak akan mendengar

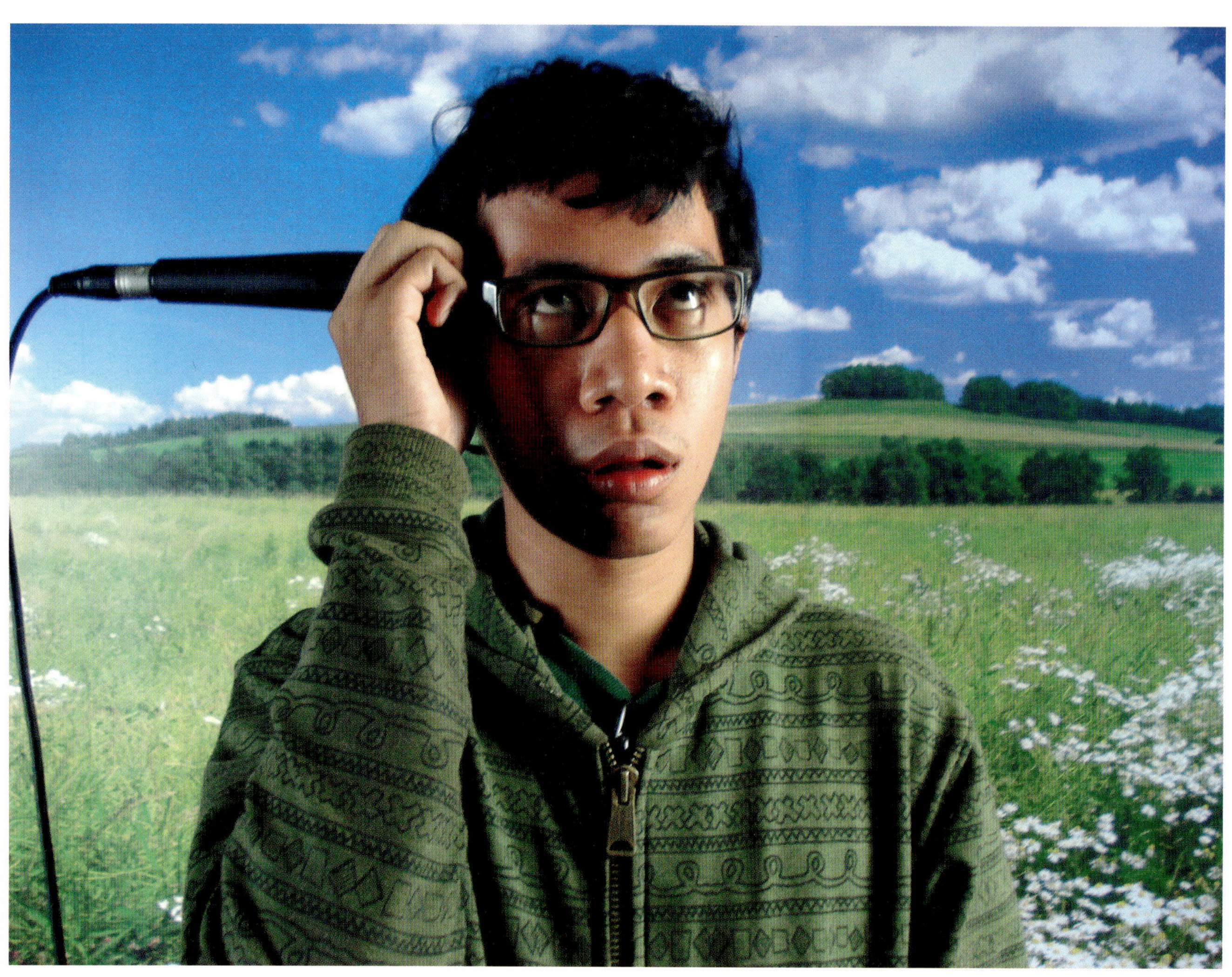

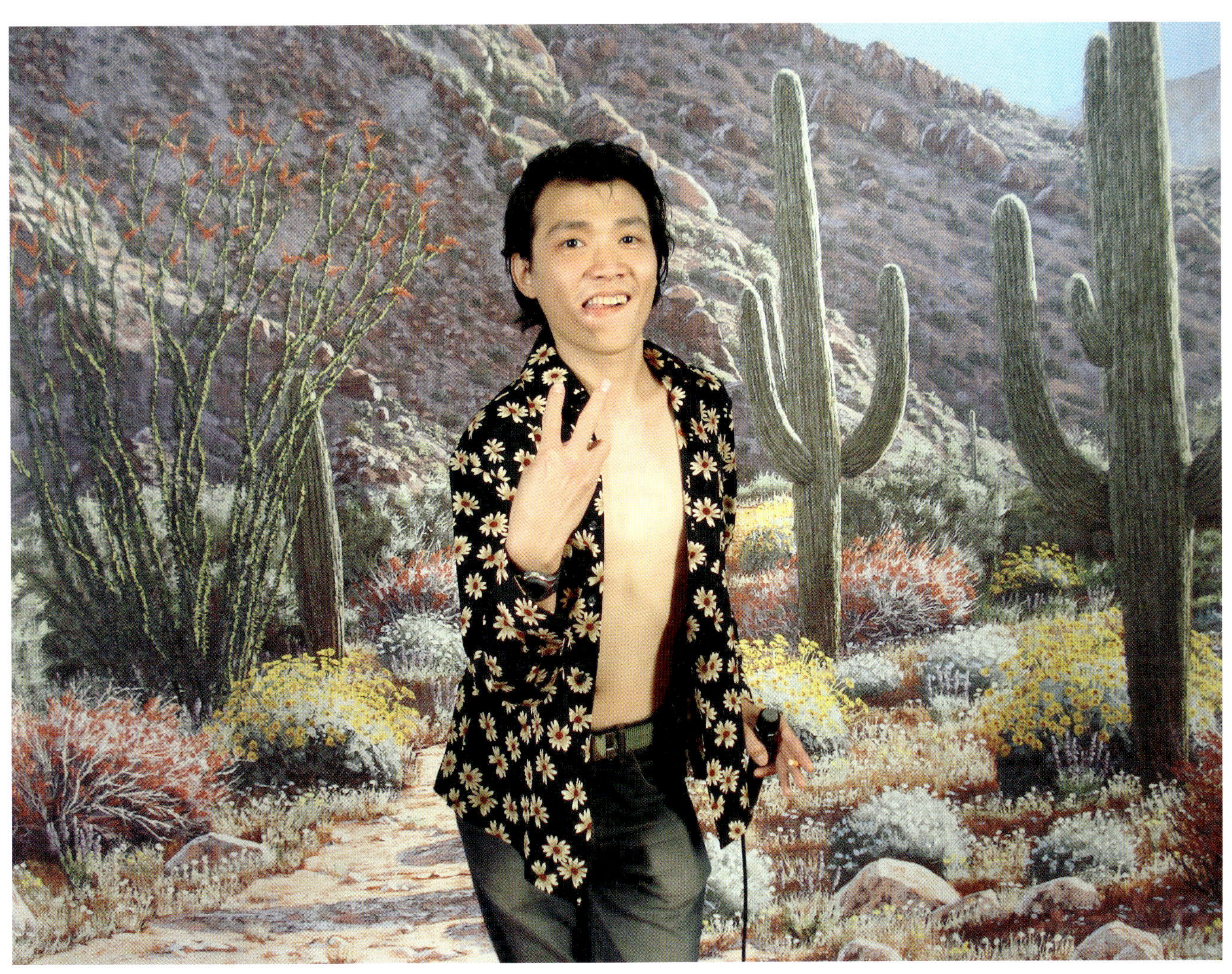

dunia tak akan mendengar

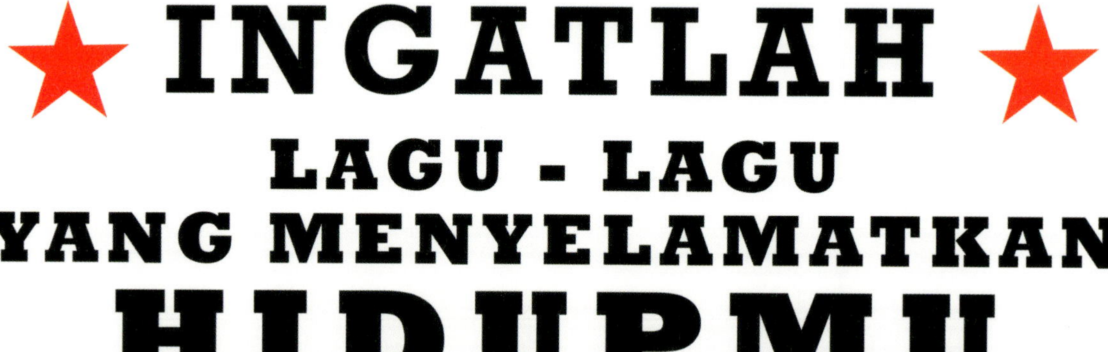

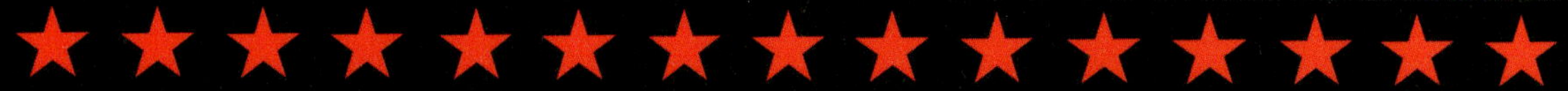

the smiths

KARAOKE

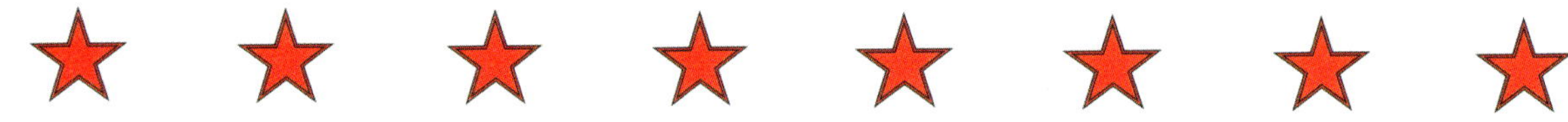

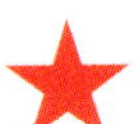

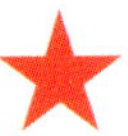

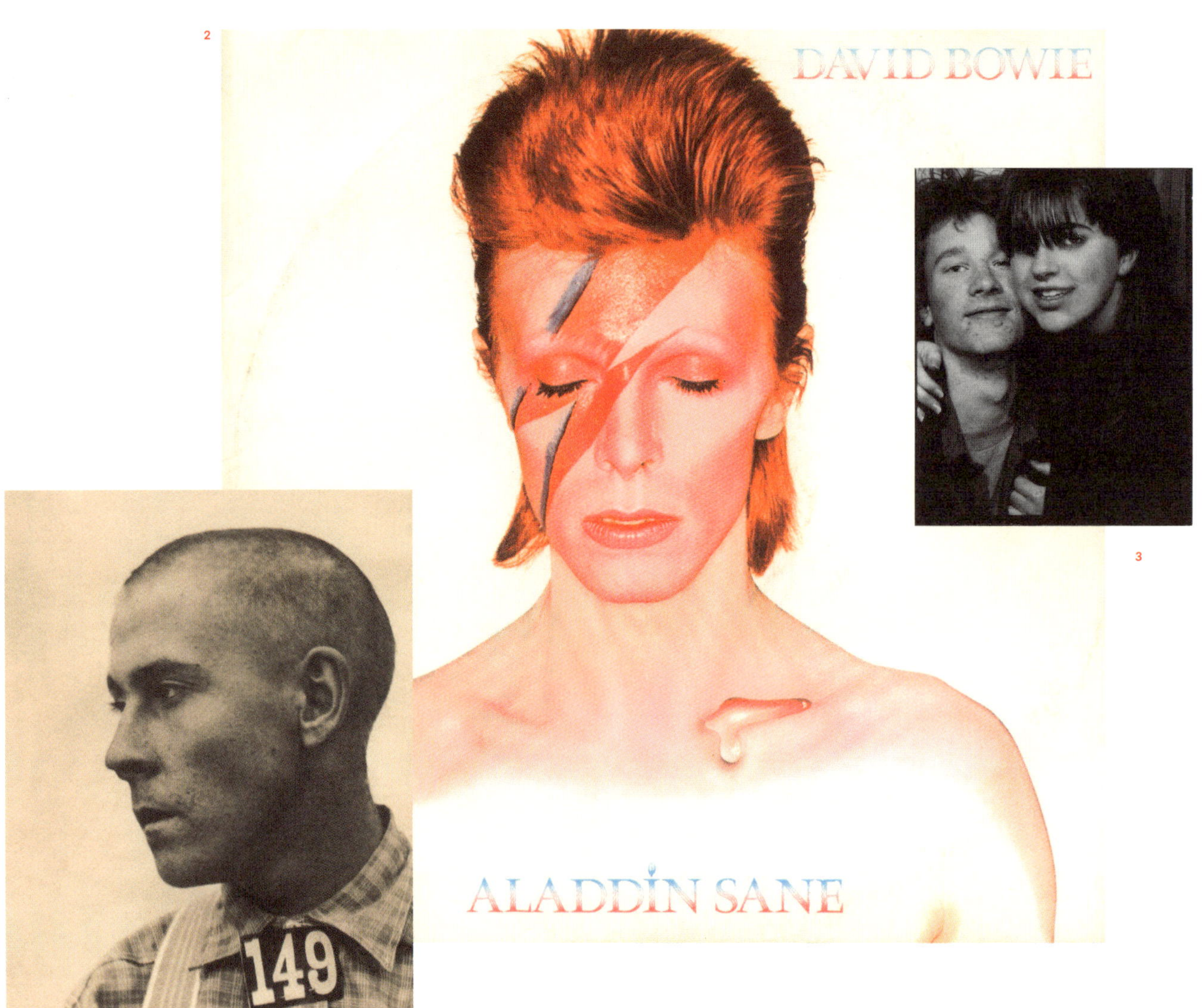
DAVID BOWIE
149
ALADDIN SANE

*Edited excerpts from a series of taped conversations between Phil Collins and Suzanne Weaver,
Scotland, May 7 – 10, 2007*

SW

Once the recording is on and the tape is rolling, I become so self-conscious. Why is that?
Do you feel self-conscious?

PC

Yeah, completely — so stop making me feel extra self-conscious, Suzanne! I was bad
enough before. No, honestly, I think at heart a lot of my work is built precisely around
that. When you start recording, what is it that you immediately lose? How does it feel
to clam up? Maybe it's because the minute a camera comes out, or a taperecorder appears,
I start acting woefully out of character, as if I'm in a court of law about to be sent down
for fifteen years for bad behavior.

SW

Can anyone act natural?

PC

Well, some people can do a better job than others, I have to say. Some people seem to
eke out a lifelong career out of the appearance of self-confidence. I only hope that inside
they're a horrible mess of nerves and doubt.

One thing about recording devices though is that while they inhibit some kinds
of activities, they definitely provoke others. This tape recorder, for example, may possibly
encourage us to solemnly meditate upon the more profound sides of life because we
hope to —

SW

Immortalize our brilliance?

PC

Mmm, yes, precisely. Please.

SW

You were talking about your work being what happens in front of a recording device,
a camera —

PC

Yes, it is. I mean, I've always been fascinated how in photography, since its earliest days,
there seems to exist an acute concern with the relationship between portraiture and
authority. Among the Victorians, there is a an overwhelming interest in specifically
marginalized characters — criminals, hysterics, homosexuals — and how the photographic
portrait might yield up otherwise invisible asocial traits. These photographs have always
had a devastating effect and been an enormous influence on me.

85

Equally with film. I've always seen the person behind camera as a central element of the equation. Would you take your clothes off if there wasn't a camera present and me behind it? Would you sing a karaoke song if we weren't recording? The witness to these very fragile and beautiful moments, the person who sits and takes the picture, is very much implicated — the one who directly influences the activity.

SW

I would like to discuss influences that have motivated your choices in content and form.
How has music influenced you?

PC

Pop music for me, as for you, is something that has profoundly affected me from an early age. As a child I used to sing myself to sleep. And sometimes wake myself up singing. From about 1978 onward, I began tape-recording the charts and filling ring-bound notebooks with the careers of forgettable pop stars. My fingers were forever on record-play-pause. (In fact, my little fingers are still damaged by the stretch!) I also amassed huge scrapbooks on Bowie, Siouxsie and the Banshees, Yazoo, Soft Cell. Even now I can recall my horror when David Bowie reincarnated himself as Margaret Thatcher in 1983. From that day on, I was definitely on the lookout for something new.

SW

What touched you about Bowie?

PC

I think that initially it was the fundamental sexual terror that Bowie inspired in me. I remember distinctly fingering the cover of my older cousin's copy of *Aladdin Sane*, praying that no one would come into the room as I traced my fingers over the record sleeve, unable to tear myself away. I knew it would be hideously embarrassing to be found staring so intently at this alien, whose implicit promise seemed that he could somehow liberate you from the everyday.

SW

When did you discover The Smiths?

PC

I was thirteen when The Smiths were first on *Top of the Pops*. It was their second single, "This Charming Man," which went to about number twenty-five. When The Smiths arrived, you have to remember what an appalling wasteland the charts were, and how little they reflected the desolation of Britain, especially the North, at that time. You had mass unemployment and inner-city riots all over the country, and at the same time "Club Tropicana" or "Ay Ay Ay Moosey" on every station. Doddery old has-beens rolling up their shoulder-padded jackets and squirting in their Sun-In. The air was horribly stale with the crass but discernible waft of cashing in and cover versions — pop being hung out to dry. If you look at the charts of 1982 or 1983, they are still quite physically and psychologically disturbing.

And then The Smiths arrived like avenging angels, assailing the Thacherite confection of pop with a sharpened scythe, and I was literally swept away. They unquestionably governed my formative years.

I stole "What Difference Does It Make?" from the local mobile disco and from then on I was hooked. I loved the whole package: the cover stars, the Pat Phoenix interview, the *Smash Hits* cover with Pete Burns, the appearance on *Pop Quiz*. Merciless taste on a grand scale. I got "Hatful Of Hollow" and "Meat Is Murder," and became a vegetarian at the tender age of thirteen, living on this horrifying gruel they called Beanfeast. No, really! Bean feast!

SW

Your obsession or addiction has been a constant throughout your life?

PC

Yes, it has been probably the only current in my life for the past twenty-four years. I've played their records every single day, and in that sense I've always approached The Smiths karaoke as much as a fan, on a pretty equal level as the singers, as I have as an artist. I really do understand what it is to live with this thing.

SW

And then there are the clubs . . . when did you start going to clubs?

PC

I started going to clubs when I was about fourteen, when I would trundle into Manchester or Liverpool on the train and head down to the Number One Club, Berlin Bar, the Lisbon, or Planet X, and later to the Hacienda. I worked in the cloakroom, and later the bar, of the Hacienda for four years, whilst I was a student, when it was like the Wild West in there. Of course, it was a dreadful mistake working in the cloakroom when at four a.m. you're suddenly faced with thousands of people completely off their tits, unsure where they'd put their ticket, what their coat looked like, or even what their name was. It didn't help either that I felt exactly the same way.

SW

Let's focus on your three-part video project, *the world won't listen*. Why did you travel to Bogotá in 2004, the year you began the first part?

PC

Cocaine, paramilitaries, and great salsa music — Suzanne, who could resist? *the world won't listen* began in a bar in Bogotá. I went there briefly in early 2004, to give a couple of lectures at the university and art school, and had been going out in the evening, as you do. Bogotá is a city of around ten million, and in the bars around Séptima, one of its main run-down thoroughfares, you can drink *aguadiente*, the local firewater, and stumble around inelegantly to the best salsa you'll hear in the world.

It was when I visited La Rebeca, an artist-run space in the city where I met Michèle Faguet, who would be instrumental in the realization of the project, that the idea started to germinate. I knew I wanted to go back to Colombia, so I did, and I spent a couple of months there in the autumn of 2004.

Bogotá is a city where paranoia is firmly cemented into basic social relations. Armed guards at Starbucks. The taxi driver gives you a code when he picks you up, and then hilariously (or sensibly, you be the judge) you give him the last four digits of your phone number, so he knows you're not going to kidnap him. And away you go, into this seemingly endless, chaotic metropolis. Istanbul and Jakarta have the similar sense of scale and unknowability, and it was probably some of those things that, at least partly, motivated me to work there.

SW

Why did you select The Smiths's 1987 album *The World Won't Listen*?

PC

It could well have been the title, although whatever I picked would have surely provoked a bun fight among the rarely satisfied, pernickety Smiths fans.

SW

What was your production process? For example, how was the music created for the karaoke machine? How did you solicit Smiths' fans?

PC

The re-creation of the album in its entirety was like climbing a mountain. Michèle introduced me to Alejandro Gomezcaceres Bertel, the guitarist from Los Aterciopelados, Colombia's biggest rock group, who had, I found out by chance, busked "Bigmouth Strikes Again" ten years earlier on the streets of London. What serendipity! Alejo also had squirreled away a dusty copy of *Guitar Player* magazine with an interview with Johnny Marr about his notoriously complicated tunings — which was lucky for us as we hadn't got any sheet music. So we relied on Alejo's magnificent ear and patience to rerecord, quite precisely, each and every guitar line for the entire album, note for note. I don't know if you can imagine what an endeavor it was. (But believe me — it was!)

The album was mixed at Voces e Imagen studio in Bogotá. Drummer, bassist, backing singers — everybody, unbelievably — learned each line by ear and proceeded to lay them down with effortless grace and real dedication. During this period I worked with a couple of video editors to make the visuals. The lyrics would appear at exactly the right moment, line by line. This is a karaoke machine for initiates and devotees, but more importantly, it's a karaoke machine that works like any other, like one you may find down at the local.

Parallel to all this frantic activity, we set out on a publicity offensive. I lectured in any college that would have us — some of that was very memorable for me — and ran

a citywide poster campaign with beautiful block-print posters that look somewhere
between an ad for a boxing match and one for a political rally. We flyered incessantly
at every bar in town until we bored everyone stupid, went on the radio in the evenings
and TV in the mornings. I wanted to have the widest possible draw for the project,
and to try at least to offer it to people from all over the city, every age, every background.
In the end, we had one participant who flew in from Medellín. And they say the drugs
don't work!

SW

What is fascinating is that the performers sang line by line in English, which is not
their language.

PC

Yes, and in all of the locations, some people had a very rudimentary grasp of English.
But they knew the songs so devastatingly well through repetition, every breath and every
ad lib, which, considering the importance of lyrics in the songs, their arch and archaic
constructions, as well as the prelinguistic wail at the heart of them, is pretty amazing.
In Colombia people often did simultaneous or prepared translations into Spanish. Which,
you might say, is going a bit far and showing off, but, well, I am very easily impressed.

SW

There must be a relationship between MTV, *American Idol*, and karaoke machines and
the contestants on these shows being so slick. It is just a feeling I have because so many
of the singers seem to be trying to be the next Mariah Carey, who I think is terribly
uninteresting.

PC

With *American Idol*, there is no real reason for it to be so sickeningly conservative. Why
can't we have someone on *American Idol* singing the Cocteau Twins or Tiny Tim? It should
be a program that is wide open, but every single season it is about complete conformity
around the idea of the songbook. Karaoke, of course, is egalitarian by design. If you have
had enough to drink and you fancy it, anybody can do it. Except that there is nothing
anyone in their right mind would want to sing.

Other people sometimes find karaoke embarrassing, or laughable, or delusional —
the idea that someone gets up and thinks they can sing. But I find it moving and incredibly
courageous. As a format, karaoke offers a promise of completion — this act will somehow
make me whole — but at the same time it's predicated on the idea of vulnerability and
failure, with its countless false starts, its blind terror. The way the pub falls away, and you
can clearly see the spot where someone stands. The way they find themselves lost in the
middle of a song, but unable to escape until it finishes. It's like a mild form of heroism.

SW

What is the relationship between the karaoke machine and the singer? Is the person who
is singing with the karaoke machine wanting to be the performer whose lyrics are being
shown on the screen? Or is it something else?

COL MI MORBID COL MI PEIL
CALL ME MORBID, CALL ME PALE

I'VE SPENT SIX YEARS ON YOUR TRAIL
AI ESPENT SIXIARS ON YUR TREIL
SIX LONG YEARS ON YOUR TRAIL
SIX LONG YIARS ON YUR TREIL
CALL ME MORBID, CALL ME PALE
COL MI MORBID, COL MI PEIL
I'VE SPENT SIX YEARS ON YOUR TRAIL
AI ESPENT SIXIARS ON YUR TREIL
SIX FULL YEARS OF MY LIFE ON YOUR TRAIL
SIX FUL YIARS OF MAI LAIF ON YUR TRAIL

AND IF YOU HAVE FIVE SECONDS TO SPARE
AND IF YU HAV FAIV SECONDS TU ESPER
THEN I'LL TELL YOU THE STORY OF MY LIFE:
DEN AIL TEL YU DE STORY OF MAI LAIF
SIXTEEN, CLUMSY AND SHY
SIXTIN CLOMSI AND CHAI
I WENT TO LONDON AND DIE
AI VVENT TU LONDON AND DAI
I BOOKED MYSELF IN AT THE Y....W.C.A
AI BUKED MAISELF IN AT THE UAI DOBL YU, CI, EI.
I SAID: "I LIKE IT HERE - CAN I STAY ?..........I LIKE IT HERE - CAN I STAY ?
AI SEID AI LAIKIT HIR CAN AI ESTEI ...
AND , DO YOU HAVE A VANCANCY FOR A BACK-SCRUBBER ?"
AND DO YU HAV E VACANCI FOR E BAC-SCROBER ?
SHE WAS LEFT BEHIND, AND SOUR
CHI WAS LEFT BIJAIND, AND SAUER
AND SHE WROTE TO ME ON THE HOUR
AND CHI WROUT TU MI ON DI OUER
SHE SAID: "IN THE DAYS WHEN YOU WERE HOPELESSLY POOR
CHI SED IN DE DEIS WEN YU WER HOPESLY PUR
I JUST LIKED YOU MORE.."
AI JUST LAIK YU MOR
SO IF YOU FIVE SECONDS TO SPARE

AND IF YOU HAVE FIVE SECONDS TO SPARE

THEN I'LL TELL YOU THE STORY OF MY LIFE:

SIXTEEN, CLUMSY AND SHY

I WENT TO LONDON AND DIE

I BOOKED MYSELF IN AT THE Y....W.C.A

I SAID: "I LIKE IT HERE - CAN I STAY ?   I LIKE IT HERE - CAN I STAY ?

AND , DO YOU HAVE A VANCANCY FOR A BACK-SCRUBBER ?"

CALL ME MORBID, CALL ME PALE

I'VE SPENT TOO LONG ON YOUR TRAIL
AIV ESPENT TU LONG ON YUR TREIL
FAR TOO LONG CHASING YOUR TRAIL   OH OH OH
FAR TU LONG CHEISING YUR TREIL
AND IF YOU HAVE FIVE SECONDS TO SPARE

THEN I'LL TELL YOU THE STORY OF MY LIFE: SIXTEEN, CLUMSY AND SHY, THAT'S THE STORY OF MY

LIFE.......
I THAT'S THE STORY
THE ST
THAT'S THE
THAT'S THE   THAT'THE / THE / THAT

PC

Karaoke is a form of joyful treason in which you quite materially supplant your idol. So it's different from singing into the hairbrush in your bedroom. And the beauty of this kind of treachery is that for the first time you are not singing along, you are in fact *the* singer, suddenly thrown into the spotlight without a guiding voice, which makes for all kinds of uncertainties and mistakes. In that very simple sense, it's what makes it so compelling for me. Karaoke also raises all the issues of the "original" and the "copy," but who is to say which is the most valid? Is a South American performance of a desperate northern English love song any less, or more, valid than a northern English performance? If The Smiths symbolize a sense of prototypical Englishness, then this Englishness is in no way in and of itself stable. The Smiths themselves were, of course, all from Irish families.

The first time I ever did karaoke was in Dickens in Manchester, a gay club above a chip shop that felt like it had never made it past the fifties. It had a stinky chicken-in-a-basket café in the middle and lots of wig-on-wonky, hard-as-nails trannies at the bar. No matter how many times you went, a small shutter opened at the front door and, before they let you in, someone asked if you'd been before, and then, to prove it, where the toilets were. People were always saying Julie Goodyear was a regular, but I don't know. I never saw her, or she was very well camouflaged. So, Dickens was my first time. I sang "If I Fell" by The Beatles, and, luckily for me, everyone joined in.

SW

During the filming, it must have been intense with you and these other fans working together.

PC

Singing is such an intimate act, and almost entirely transformative, so it's doubly intense when it becomes shared in a public situation. It can quite literally take you out of yourself, which has very little to do with whether you can carry a tune. Like Bob Dylan or Lou Reed, Morrissey was always a singer who encouraged passion rather than perfection. In "Sing Your Life," off *Kill Uncle*, his 1991 solo album, he sings:

> *and make no mistake, my friend*
> *your pointless life will end*
> *but before you go*
> *can you look at the truth?*
> *You have a lovely singing voice*
> *a lovely singing voice*
> *and all of those*
> *who sing on key*
> *they stole the notion*
> *from you and me*

A validation of the amateur. And who ever wanted pop music to be sung by someone who can necessarily hold a tune anyway?

You're right when you say the production set of *the world won't listen* was intense. Maybe it's because the music itself and the vocals are so unremittingly passionate that the fans are very serious about the event. Jakarta and Bandung were actually the best examples of how prepared they were. Very few British bands played concerts in Indonesia (or, for that matter, Colombia or Turkey) so there was an overdetermined response to the arrival of our very modest karaoke machine, which, because it was not a joke in itself, and because it treated the idea of interaction in an impeccably serious manner, was able to meet this intensity head on. When people heard the backing tracks and realized that they were not cobbled together in an afternoon on a Casio synthesizer in a bathroom, but were made by a full band playing a full album, they could see this was an act of realization, of becoming, in some way, which is, quite naturally, a very intense enterprise.

SW

In each city, how did you create the best possible situation for filming in nightclubs and other places?

PC

Well, that changed as we went along according to the budget, or what we had been able to negotiate that afternoon. But generally it's always been important to find somewhere very central, where people can drink, where we can play our music very loud, at all times of day or night, but where the space would also be very focused and concentrated. In Jakarta I recorded for four days in Déjà Vu (I know!), a nightclub that had somewhat

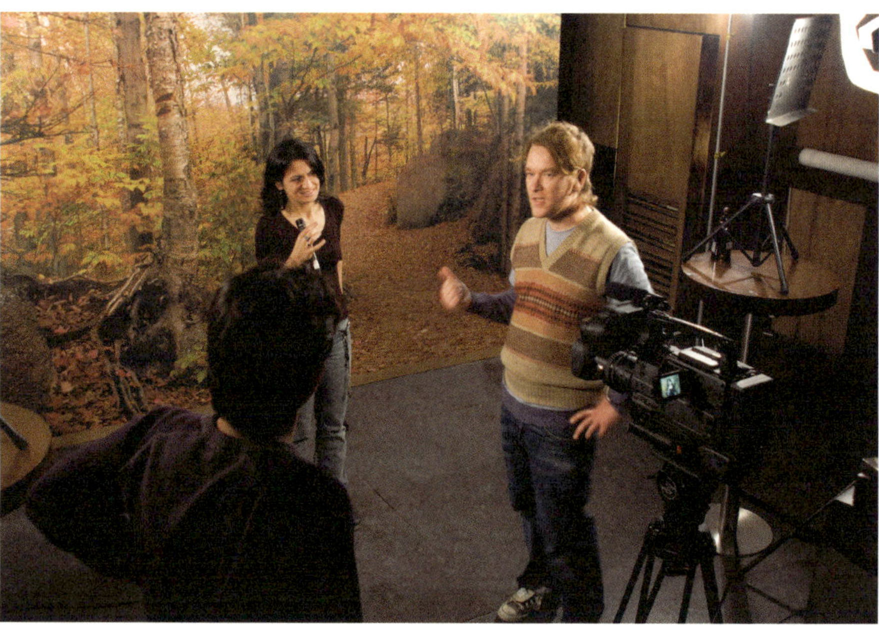

Balans Music Hall, Istanbul, 2005

lost its way and was now empty except for the barmaid singing . . . yes, karaoke.
To herself. But in Bandung we were able to secure Gedung Merdeka, the Asia-Afrika
Conference Center, a building of enormous importance for the history of the Non-
Aligned Movement that Indonesia co-founded. And in Istanbul, I had a nightclub,
Balans Music Hall, for four days and four long nights on the promise we'd throw
a party there at the end. How was I to know that twelve hundred people would turn
up on the night, when the karaoke version of *The World Won't Listen* was recreated live,
which at times descended into complete chaos, most memorably when everybody
stormed the stage for "Oscillate Wildly."

SW

What kind of cameras did you use?

PC

Whatever I can afford, really. There's this idea in art that things simply appear,
just like that, out of thin air, but what with money not growing on trees it can take me
a year or more to save up to go and make a work. The Colombian and the Indonesian
chapters weren't made within any institutional frame, or for any other reason than I
wanted to make them. Bogotá is the most anti-glam — it's a Canon XL1 left on autofocus
— so there's this constant tension between things being clear and then quite badly
blurred. And then in Istanbul, and later in Indonesia, we started renting modest
studio cameras.

SW

When did you decide to do the second part? Was it when you were invited to be in the
Ninth Istanbul Biennial?

PC

I'd wanted to make a trilogy right from the beginning but at first the idea was to record
all three in South America. Brazil, Chile, Argentina . . . hell — maybe even Uruguay!
But in Istanbul I was put in touch with a fantastic visual arts producer Derya Demir,
who led me by the hand to all the dank, claustrophobic basement bars of the city where
I was instantly convinced that we might be able to run the project successfully. So in
the process, it became obvious that we could tour the machine to different continents.
Besides, it was always important for me that the production should stay outside first-world
circuits of pop and cultural industries, and in places where it might appear as much an
imposition as a gift.

SW

When you went to Indonesia, there must have been new challenges. You arrived at the
time Jakarta was experiencing the worst flood in centuries, thousands of people, I think
around three hundred thousand, were displaced and fifty died.

PC

Yes, it was bad timing in lots of ways. I went over Christmas to do a recce, so I spent a very memorable Christmas Day alone in a red-light bar being served cake by a sympathetic madame. I hadn't noticed it was that kind of establishment, until it dawned on me that every light in the place was actually red. Oh, dear! It was quite lonely floating around the streets of Bandung, even though on every street corner there was someone serenading the traffic. Honestly — every street was full of singers singing to car windows! When I saw this and started following bands like The Brandals and Goodnight Electric around, and then when I heard it was the fourth most populous country in the world but that the last international artist to sing there had been Phil Collins ten years ago, I knew I had to go back. Jakarta also has a strong mod and skin scene — Lambrettas and Harringtons and oxblood Doc Martens. And in Malaysia I unaccountably ended up at a skinhead party where the mood got wilder the more bottles got smashed. I'd never seen anything like it. Well not in Kuala Lumpur, obviously. I booked my return ticket almost on the spot.

When I went back in January, Jakarta was completely flooded. There were outbreaks of dengue fever, and around 70 percent of the city was affected by the flood waters. So there I was, with my rucksack and my packs of duty-free cigarettes, in a godforsaken Internet café, trying to organize a Smiths karaoke in the middle of a major disaster. In a funny way, it fitted the mood quite well.

SW

How many fans came and how much time was each allotted?

PC

Indonesia was the only country where I filmed in two different cities. Apart from Jakarta, Clarissa Adinegoro, my brilliant co-producer, and I felt that Bandung, as the spiritual home of indie music in Java, couldn't be ignored. In Jakarta and Bandung we had a really big turnout, the biggest by far — about 132 appointments, and many of those are, of course, groups of people. So we must have done something right. Most people get about twenty to thirty minutes where they basically call the shots. There's this very charged atmosphere on the set, with people meeting, having a bevvie, smoking, and chatting before they're called up. And most people sing in a way well beyond the frame, the songs becoming very explicitly and self-consciously a love letter to elsewhere.

SW

What is the process of editing? It is must be a tedious and lengthy task. How do you choose who stays in and who gets cut?

PC

It's torturous because you're so attached to everyone, and you're looking at them not in an objective way, but like a lover. I'm often completely paralyzed by choice because, well there's just so much. I have reams of tapes of unused takes of "There Is A Light That Never Goes Out," and "Ask," and "Bigmouth Strikes Again." In Turkey "Half A Person" was enormously popular, while in Indonesia the favorite by far was "Asleep."

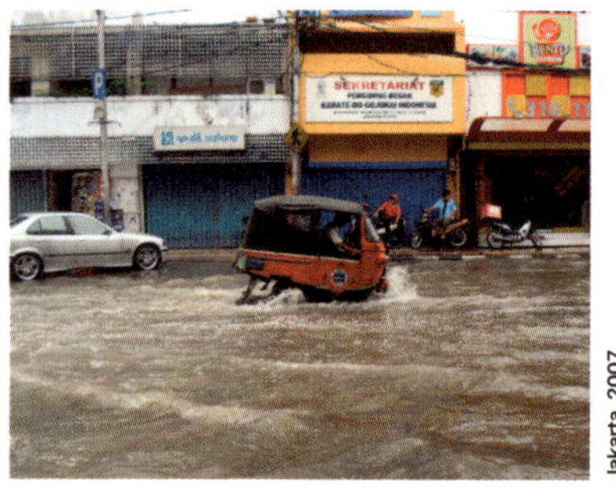

Mailbag

Rock is dead— killed by musicians

"ROCK IS DEAD." Originally it was meant to be primitive. A lot of critics, musicians and fans have voiced the opinion that rock has become a new form of musical expression by virtue of its musical simplicity.

If this is true, then I would say that rock music has in fact killed itself, because when rock musicians try to do something new they are beginning to complicate the music and therefore making it contrary to the simplicity which is supposed to be inherent.

So it would appear that if rock music is to survive it must do so by its own momentum — and I'd say that it cannot do this.

I feel that rock has come as far as it can come. Groups like the Who, Deep Purple, the Stones are the last remaining rock groups.

Bands like Yes, Genesis, and King Crimson are hybrids who rake in jazz, classical and rock to express themselves. But they are not rock in the true sense of the word.

Rock is dying as I see it. And it's not due to rising costs or taxes and expenses. It is due to the boundaries rock has set itself. — RONAN GUILFOYLE, Crosthwaite, Park West, Dun Laoghaire, Co Dublin, Ireland.
■ LP WINNER.

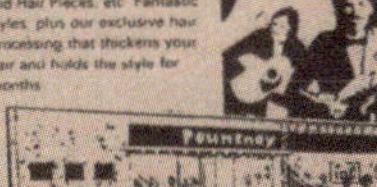

THE WHO's ROGER DALTREY: last rocker?

Diamond girl

WELL said, Brian Murphy (Mailbag 16.8.75)! The music press and general public seem all too often to overlook the excellent work of Joan Baez. These days, the release of a Baez album is a far rarer event than the release of a Dylan one.

Yet it is never front-page news. "Diamonds And Rust" got a small column several weeks after its release in this country — no track by track analysis, just a rather superficial review.

And yet Joan Baez is equally as important an artist as Bob Dylan — perhaps more so. It should not be forgotten that it was Baez who did much to promote Dylan in 1963/64 by bringing him on as a guest at her concerts, thus providing him with a ready-made audience.

It was Baez who was really the leader of the traditional folk-revival of the Sixties, and there can be very few female folk-type singers who can honestly claim not to have been influenced by her.

Throughout, she has remained true to her beliefs and acted on her conscience, although it has made her unpopular in many quarters and has brought her two terms of imprisonment. Dylan, on the other hand, has deviated from the views and ideas expressed in his early songs, claiming that he wrote them only to gain recognition and success. Thus, we have cause to doubt his sincerity.

Now financial trouble, caused by too many benefit concerts and donating record royalties to charity, has forced her to make what she calls "a commercial album." True, "Diamonds And Rust" is non-political — her first for many years — but it is full of damn good music.

Surely the pictures presented are of the Baez-Dylan relationship of 1963-65 and not, as Karl Dallas suggested, of her and David Harris?

Joan Baez is one of the truly great musicians of our time. Whatever the press does or does not say, she will have a large and very devoted following. If you admire Dylan you cannot ignore the lady who was instrumental in gaining him world-wide recognition. — ELIZABETH M. THOMSON, Heddon Road, Cookfosters, Herts.

Remember Al

SEPTEMBER 3 was the fifth anniversary of Alan "Blind Owl" Wilson's death. Wilson was a highly-talented musician whose loss has never yet been successfully chronicled.

The Canned Heat albums up to "Hooker And Heat" all bore the Wilson trademarks: the soaring, explosive harmonica; the dynamic and highly-original guitar work; the high-piercing vocal lines; the dramatic intensity of his songs.

He wrote of love, society, conservation and paranoia with a chilling realism. Other people have been glorified for lesser works — Wilson still remains in the shade.

The later Canned Heat albums only show the sterility of the band without Wilson's driving force, and although Canned Heat were more than a one-man-band, Wilson was so inimitable and irreplaceable, that I, for one, am surprised the band didn't change their name. Without him they certainly could no longer live up to the "electric white country blues" tag (their last albums have seen them ensconced within a rather dated rock field).

So on this sad date, I urge anyone who believes that music is based on emotion — and not commerce — to wade through the plastic twelve bars of today's rock, to shun the neon stars of technoflash and discover the music of Alan Wilson. It contained so much skill, personal truth and beauty that it remain timeless and is just as rewarding and enjoyable today as originally (not a common factor in music) — JOHN HARRIS, Beech Street, Preston.

Genesis: this is the end, beautiful friend

AS A long-time Genesis fan, I thank Chris Welch for his MM tribute on the passing of a great British band. In the past, I've not always agreed with Welch's comments on Genesis' career; his initial review of "The Lamb" I found particularly irritating.

But here he has written a very fair obituary on the death of Britain's best and most creative rock band. And it is the end, make no mistake.

Phil Collins' promise to "carry on as if nothing had happened" shows commendable optimism, but a distinct lack of realism.

While admitting Gabriel contributed no more and no less to the band's musical skill than the others, it must be said that he personified the very essence of Genesis.

The sinister, yet endearing, shy yet charismatic, young public school Englishman became the visual embodiment of what Genesis were all about, with or without bizarre costumes.

In losing him Genesis have lost their focal point. The core has been cut out of the apple, and it cannot survive without it.

No new singer brought in to replace him can ever do that. And no new singer will be accepted by the fans.

The damage has been done — already people accept Genesis will never be the same, nor as good. — IAN KNIGHT, Windlesham Road, Shoreham by Sea, Sussex.
■ LP WINNER.

■ Congratulations to Derek Jewell on his Jethro Tull Sounds Interesting. Who would have thought the Beeb could air such a great programme? Ironic, though, it's on BBC 3. Maybe some of those BBC 1/2 DJ's could get on the right track and please cut the crap? — JEFF WILSON, Normans Place, Altrincham, Cheshire.

Aero-vision

AEROSMITH are one of those American dance-a-rama scenic bands with enough punch to see the Stones on pensions and enough make-up to last them through the winter. Their music is that of confused struggle, with vocalist Steven Tyler sounding as though he is using the microphone to brush his teeth.

They are as original as a bar of soap and have as much to offer Seventies rock as Ena Sharples.

Aerosmith are just another street-corner rock 'n' roll band, using notorious Zeppelin riffs in an effort to steal our love and devotion.

But when one ruminates over the fact that "Toys In The Attic" is the band's THIRD album!

Thanks, but no thanks. Aerosmith, I'll stick with the New York Dolls for my rock 'n' thrills. — STEVE MORRISSEY, Kings Road, Stretford, Manchester.

Disgusted . . .

■ I AM disgusted with Peter Gabriel's split with Genesis. Genesis are (were) in my opinion one of the few rock bands with a distinctive character. The theatrical genius and distinctive value of Gabriel merged extremely well into the superb musicianship of Banks, Hackett, Collins, and Rutherford.

Followers of Genesis will be very lucky indeed to pick out the sound of a flute in future Genesis recordings. I can't imagine what Genesis concerts will be like in the future without the boundless stage presence of Gabriel.

I hope I'm proved wrong, because life without Genesis would be very dull. — ROB STATEN, Foxcroft, Flitwick, Bedfordshire.
■ LP WINNER.

Marley : just a composer. . .

I WHOLEHEARTEDLY agree with Bret Ewins (MM August 16) concerning Bob Marley. I just fail to see why everybody makes such a big fuss out of the bloke. I mean he composes some great songs and stuff but that's about all.

Personally, I dig other established JA artists singing his songs. Why, recently the Maroons had a smash hit with "Falling Star" and Johnny Clarke has his new record, a version of "No Woman No Cry" — which is in my opinion far heavier and rootsy than Marley's soulful version.

Why is it that the naive think Marley is the king of reggae at the moment? Perhaps because all the musical papers blow him up as some kind of God?

He isn't. And it would seem that Bob Marley is the only reggae artist in existence, because the names of real reggae stars never appear.

Their singles never get reviewed, (Bob Marley's did through) and neither do their albums. I mean, how about educating the people who don't know about the reggae music of today?

Reggae to the majority is Johnny Nash! Susan Cadogan/Typically Tropical vibes and they don't realise how heavy and involved the whole thing is.

There are some great records out at the moment by fantastic artists, such as Honey Boy, Big Youth, Prince Jazzbo and Jah favourite I, Roy; and of course reggae music has its "Dark Side Of The Moon"/"Sgt. Pepper" album — King Tubby Meets The Upsetter At The Grass Roots Of Dub" by Jah Natty Locks. — PAUL NAGLE, Dover Court, Southgate Road, London.
■ LP WINNER.

What's happening at Pountney's Hounslow Hair Salon ?

Pountney's has been famous with Melody Maker readers for many years. It is always been ahead on modern hair-styling with both sexes. Probably London's most up-to-date salon and certainly the largest ground floor hair establishment, with specialist departments.

Hair loss clinic. Men's toupees and Hair Pieces etc. Fantastic styles, plus our exclusive hair processing that thickens your hair and holds the style for months.

Pountney

THAT'S WHAT'S HAPPENING AT POUNTNEY'S HAIR FASHIONS — 20-24 STAINES ROAD, HOUNSLOW, MIDDX. TELEPHONE: 01-570 9656/7/8

This is also Britain's most modern Transplant Clinic, using the most advanced techniques under medical supervision.

INSTAMATIC POP

THE PHOTOS/MARK ANDREWS & THE GENTS
Manchester Polytechnic

WENDY WU might easily be clutching a well-worn copy of 'Plastic Letters' as she skips playfully up to the microphone to pose the ultimate question: Do YOU have fun with YOUR friends?

The photos are a "fun band", but smooth with it. In fact, The Photos are so smooth that they almost slip off the stage.

'Do You Wanna Dance?' sings well-flavoured Wendy, but really, you have no choice. The Photos took Manchester by the throat and wouldn't let go until everyone had danced themselves six inches into the ground.

They even have a heartrending ballad about an old haunt of their's, 'Barbarellas' ("Why did they have to close it down?"). Thrillsville 1980. And Wendy Wu, garishly wrapped in a pair of discarded curtains, NEVER bothers with people she hates, and tells you so in 'The Lady Is A Tramp' (so outrageous!). But isn't all this hub-hub a mite primitive? Of course it is. The Photos take extravagant strides backwards as they suicidally cling to a sixties danceband" format which has already dug its own grave. Possibly their only saving grace is their drummer Ollie whose playing is excellent. Will anything happen?

Less loved support group Mark Andrews & The Gents defy analysis. Looking as if they ought to be playing 'Moonriver' in any Butlins resort, there's a nervous twang with a Blackpool pier organ piping away. When you realise just how serious they are, you know it's worth swallowing. Mark Andrews & The Gents are musically and vocally faultless, and will be tap dancing on The Photos' heads before they know it. They excel on 'I Want It All On A Plate' and 'You're Talking With Your Body'.

But no songs are suicide. I miss the old days.

STEVEN MORRISSEY

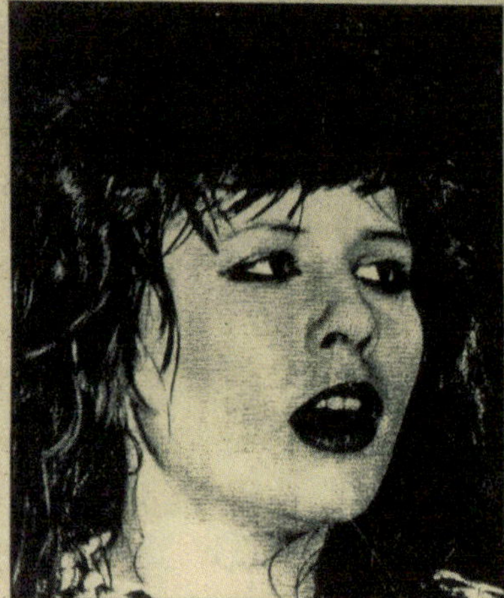

WENDY WU takes you by the throat.

DEXY'S MIDNIGHT RUNNERS
Newcastle Polytechnic

WHEN CONTINUALLY being force-fed a diet of squalid, ska-infested music (via the Beat, Madness, Selecter etc). for the past few months the last thing you need is to have it from yet another band.

Having been surpassed (in commercial terms) by the aforementioned names, it's hard not to conclude that Dexy's Midnight Runners have just missed the train for the gold pot and been left standing. Mind you, it's hardly surprising when listening to a set that consisted of a dozen ultra-shapeless songs; the only redeeming factor being the set length — one hour, including encores (a midnight rip-off?).

To be able to run on the spot for an hour is the prime qualification you need to join the clan of any reggae / ska band, and most of the eight Dexy's are sure enough qualified. But hey, what about the music? Well, it was pretty desperate for most of the time. Strictly speaking, DMR are a mixture of everything, soul, rock, reggae, you name it. Not unexpectedly they sounded a mess. Two renditions of 'Geno' weren't needed to convince anyone to steer 'clear of the new single. 'Respect' was never like this and absolutely pulverised while an umpteenth cover of 'Breaking Down The Walls Of Heartache' didn't inspire a single tap of the foot.

Their own songs cried out for mass injections of inspiration as they crawled around the hall, passed through one ear, out another before flopping to a close. At one point, vocalist Kevin Rowland gave us all a larf and a half by playing a guitar that ended up stringless, but that didn't seem to matter too much as he wasn't plugged in anywhere. Next . . .

AIDAN CANT

SQUEEZE / WRECKLESS ERIC
Brighton Top Rank

TWO BANDS who don't leave themselves open to classification. After a smash-hit with 'Cool For Cats', Squeeze have been spending their time seemingly trying to carve a sucure niche in the (over?) populous of disco chartmakers.

No trend-setters, here, even Wreckless Eric's punk label was not enough to pull the wool over the eyes of an enthusiastic audience. He takes the stage after the others have assembled, bounding to the mike, grasping it with both hands and spits out every word of their first number with venomous energy.

The most enigmatic aspect that the set reveals is of the front-man image, so inappropriate for a band who knit themselves together with such harmonious solidarity; Eric himself repeatedly overshadowed by the qualities of talent around him. While the jaunty, catchy rhythms of 'Pop Song' assert themselves as a hallmark, some excellent Chuck Berry-like guitar riffs remind me that this is no dance band alone. In fact Eric seems to have hedged his bets pretty well, applying himself to a broad spectrum of rock 'n' roll, while with the slower numbers like 'It'll soon be the weekend', there's enough pop-potential for him to rival any Two-Tone dance band.

This is where their paths most evidently cross with Squeeze, and which makes the pairing of them less curious than I first supposed. Squeeze belatedly come on stage after a rapturous Eric encore. Straight into 'Slap And Tickle' — with an eight-piece drum set, elaborate keyboard desks and a visual decor of colourful precision, the stamp of class gives an immediate contrast to Eric's rough-and-ready demeanour. The sound, though, is more obscurely differential. While Tilbrook's vocals seem to carry the slower moods particularly aptly in 'Another Nail In My Heart', they always sound more comfortable with the pace that proved such a winner for 'Cool For Cats'.

Perhaps, though, what separates and distinguishes their style most from Wreckless-like contemporaries like in keyboardist Holland's vital contribution to the finished sound. DAVE JORDAN

THE PSYCHADELIC FURS/A CERTAIN RATIO/ECHO & THE BUNNYMEN/TEARDROP EXPLODES/MANICURED NOISE
The Lyceum, London

MANICURED NOISE, first on in Curd's Sunday night package, are a four-piece band which use a sax as a full-time instrument. With clear vocals, they have a full, balanced, almost jazz-based sound — not tomorrow's latest thing, but certainly competent. Favourites were 'Dreams Money Can Buy' and 'Survival Time'.

Stars of the evening were Teardrop Explodes, whose melodies and personalities stood out against the posing to follow. Simple keyboards punctuate their sad love stories and northern anecdotes. Most songs discuss some hitherto undiscovered theme. 'Poppies In The Field' has a galloping rhythm — The Lone Ranger almost rides in and tramples down Julian Cope's poppies. 'Treason', the new single, drives home the point, it's just a story, with mesmerizing effect.

Cope's voice sounds a little like Sting's — but then it always did, I don't think the Teardrops are jumping on the policewagon. They encored with their fearless version of Aretha Franklin's 'Save Me'.

Next on were Teardrop's friends and rivals, Echo & The Bunnymen. Too much reverb spoilt Ian Maculloch's vocals, turning his shaky, quavery intensities into something of a mush.

Towards the end of the set, they picked up speed, and began to sound more coherent. If they'd only cared a little more earlier on, the whole set could have been a success, and not just the finish.

This brings us to A Certain Ratio (I'd rather it didn't) — with their Devo orientated, head-banging noises, desperately trying to attain status as being weird. They stand, backs to audience, wearing uniforms of shirts and baggy shorts. Instead of the desired shock effect this was obviously meant to have, they just looked like a bunch of dumb mounties who'd lost their horses, and undoubtedly lost their way.

Last on, They Psychadelic Furs, opened with 'India', and went on to plug the rest of the tracks from their new album.

A few tracks into the set, and I was just beginning to vaguely like the Furs brand of Bowie beat, when singer, Butler Rep, informed the audience, "Some girls just like to get ——, and some like to get married". What a remarkable understanding and experience of women this guy has.

Despite their naivety, the Furs can produce a few good, brainwashing tunes. 'Sister Europe' is one of these.

Getting to like the Furs, is like getting to notice how few good new bands there are around today — clutching at covers of what used to be good, and still remains so.

The Furs' adolescent ideology of what a good band is all about, has worked to a certain effect — it just forgets to innovate. GILL PRINGLE

PRAYING MANTIS / WHITE SPIRIT
Music Machine, London

CONNOISSEUR'S rock that everybody could get into. Don't believe me? You should have seen Praying Mantis and White Spirit proving that a mixture of high-quality craftmanship and sharp slices of bad boy boogie can be a potent recipe for a good time.

White Spirit are among the hottest keyboard combos I've seen in ages. This was their second Music Machine date, and as on the previous occasion, they took the place by storm. Graeme Crallen (drums) and Phil Brady (bass) provided a constant co-ordinated backdrop over which Mal Pearson wove atmospheric keyboard patterns. Guitarist Janick Gers drove his instrument through the inner sanctums of Santana, Blackmore and Beck. However, the band's most devastating asset was definitely diminutive vocalist Bruce Walker, who reminded me in terms of both his phrasing and range of a younger Ronnie Dio.

Highlights of their 45 minute set were a trio of originals in 'Back To The Grind' (a version of which is due out as their first Neat Records single), mystic heart-searcher 'A Fool For The Gods' and the sci-fi swagger of 'Red Skies', plus a scintillating cover of Judas Priest's 'The Ripper'.

In the past, the only complaint I've had against Praying Mantis has been that occasionally their excellent battery of street-hard rockers have sounded a little muted. On this night, that problem just never arose. Numbers such as 'Johnny Cool', 'Rock 'n' Roll Fever' and newie 'High Roller' were given a lick of arrogance and a dash of dirt that transformed them into scorching, customised earthshakers. Mantis's more expansive tones, for instance 'Lovers To The Grave' (an anthem for the undead) and their most recent composition 'Means Of Ebony', still carried the band's hallmark of richly resonant three-part harmonies. MALCOLM DOME

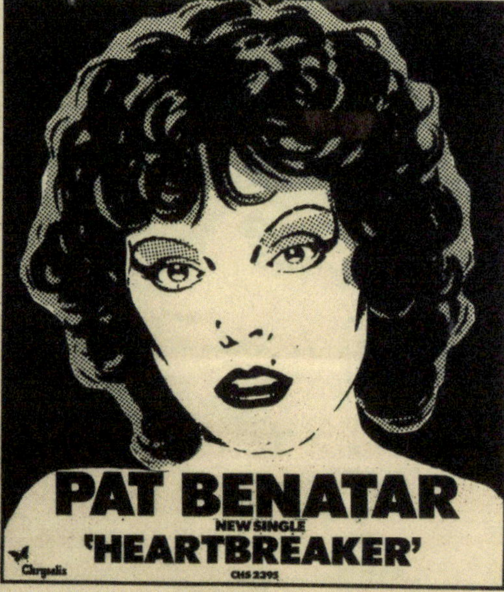

SW

Let's talk about your exhibition at the Dallas Museum of Art, where all three videos
will be shown together. Besides my winning personality and persistence, what interested
you about presenting this project in Dallas?

PC

The last few minutes of *Live in Dallas*, at the Starplex Amphitheater in 1991, have seared
themselves into my memory for all time. There's a massive stage invasion at the end
of the gig, during "Everyday Is Like Sunday," where the audience literally takes over
the stage as our hero beats a hasty retreat, abandoning the band to finish the song.
Well, so would anyone . . . have you seen those orange cotton shorts and the mullets?
The final moments of the front row weeping to an enormous backdrop of Edith Sitwell
as Shirley Bassey's "Ave Maria" booms through the sound system — Suzanne, there was
no way we couldn't do it in Dallas.

SW

Why is the work envisaged as three parts now become one complete piece?

PC

It's so exciting to imagine all the pieces of the jigsaw finally coming together, like
a chorus, or a fight. I'd wanted something bigger than you could possibly encounter in
a single glance, something that would open up in room after room, delivering the same
content, again and again, till you would like nothing more than to crawl out on your
hands and knees and go and smoke yourself senseless in a corner of a bar somewhere.
That is, unless there's a smoking ban where you are.

SW

Not surprising, Dallas has a liberal non-smoking law as well as a liberal gun-toting law.
So, if you have a permit, you can take your concealed weapon into a bar (if it does not
open up to a restaurant) and smoke yourself, as you say, senseless. I have one more question
about your Dallas exhibition. What are the screenprints that have been added?

PC

These are all blowups of the pages from British rock weeklies, to which an adolescent
Morrissey had obsessively written in the seventies. Magazines like *Sounds*, the *New
Musical Express*, *Melody Maker*, and *Record Mirror*, whose letter pages were an extremely
funny battleground between fans, at such an important time in music history, between,
let's say, prog rock and punk. Morrissey's letters are interesting in that they don't
deviate in any way from anything we know of him. It almost seems as if his tastes haven't
particularly changed and were either fully formed, or arrested, at the age of fourteen
or fifteen. He is mainly writing asking for more coverage of the New York Dolls and
Jobriath, which, thirty years later, he's still doing. But as social documents, the pages

themselves speak of this slightly more amateurish and desperate world of pen pals, and fan clubs, and yes, hair salons in Hounslow. I mean, it sounds exactly like the world of The Smiths.

SW

Looking back, how has this four-year, three-part video project changed your work? Has it changed you?

PC

Well, I guess you could say that it has changed my life. I've been working on it for four years now, so it's played a really central part of my life during that time. And through it, I've had the good fortune to meet hundreds of people who have touched me in ways I'd never have expected. How will someone give of themselves in such a situation? And how carefully must we, who are entrusted with this tenderness, handle it?

I think *the world won't listen* marked a shift in my practice as well in that it provoked a move for the work away from the symbolic terrain of representation and toward its literally becoming the thing itself, a modest but real insertion into the social fabric. So, it's not a representation of a karaoke machine, it *is* a karaoke machine; it's not a representation of the press conference, it *is* a press conference. And, if nothing had been recorded, well, really, the work would still exist.

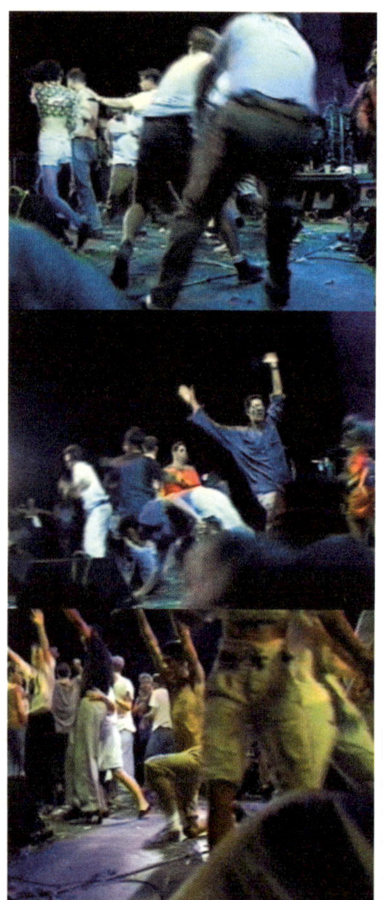

Morrissey, *Live in Dallas*, 1991

Phil Collins

1970	Born in Runcorn, England
1990–94	University of Manchester
1998–2000	University of Ulster, Belfast
	Currently based in Glasgow, Scotland

Selected Solo Exhibitions

2007 *the world won't listen*, Dallas Museum of Art, Dallas, Texas
Victoria Miro Gallery, London
Ausstellungshalle zeitgenössische Kunst, Münster, Germany
Forum 59: Phil Collins, Carnegie Museum of Art, Pittsburgh, Pennsylvania

2006 *New Work: Phil Collins*, San Francisco Museum of Modern Art, San Francisco, California
erreala denaren itzulera / el retorno de lo real, sala rekalde, Bilbao, Spain
they shoot horses, Tate Britain, London
Tanya Bonakdar Gallery, New York
Stedelijk Museum voor Actuele Kunst, Ghent, Belgium

2005 *yeah . . . . . you, baby you*, Milton Keynes Gallery, Milton Keynes, England
phil collins: they shoot horses, Wexner Center for the Arts, Columbus, Ohio

2004 *el mundo no escuchará*, Espacio La Rebeca, Bogotá, Colombia

2003 *real society*, Ormeau Baths Gallery, Belfast, Northern Ireland

2002 *siniša and sanja*, The Wrong Gallery, New York
bad infinity, Kerlin Gallery, Dublin, Ireland
becoming more like us, Temple Bar Gallery and Studios, Dublin, Ireland

2001 *face value*, Context Gallery, Derry, Northern Ireland

Selected Group Exhibitions

2007 *Time Present Time Past*, Istanbul Museum of Modern Art, Istanbul, Turkey
You Have Not Been Honest, British Council Touring Exhibition
Breaking Step: Displacement, Compassion and Humour in Recent Art from Britain,
Museum of Contemporary Art, Belgrade, Serbia
War and Discontent, Museum of Fine Arts, Boston, Massachusetts
Turbulence, Third Auckland Triennial, Auckland Art Gallery, Auckland, New Zealand
Raised by Wolves, Art Gallery of Western Australia, Perth, Australia

2006 *Hearth: Concepts of Home*, Irish Museum of Modern Art, Dublin, Ireland
Turner Prize 2006, Tate Britain, London
Deutsche Börse Photography Prize 2006, The Photographers' Gallery, London

2005 *British Art Show 6*, National Touring Exhibition
Istanbul, Ninth International Istanbul Biennial, Deniz Palas Apartments,
Istanbul, Turkey

Populism, Stedelijk Museum, Amsterdam, Netherlands; Frankfurter Kunstverein, Frankfurt, Germany; and Contemporary Art Centre, Vilnius, Lithuania

Belonging, Seventh Sharjah International Art Biennial, Sharjah Art Museum and Expo Centre, Sharjah, United Arab Emirates

Universal Experience: Art, Life, and the Tourist's Eye, Museum of Contemporary Art, Chicago, Illinois; and Hayward Gallery, London

2003 *Now: Images of Present Time*, Le Mois de la Photo, L'Espace Vox, Montreal, Canada

Art Now: Lightbox 01, Tate Britain, London

Undesire, apexart, New York

Witness: Contemporary Artists Document Our Time, Barbican Centre, London

2002 *Onufri*, National Gallery of Arts, Tirana, Albania

Reality Check: Recent Developments in British Photography & Video, British Council Touring Exhibition

Frontline Compilation, Donostiako Arte Ekinbideak, San Sebastián, Spain

2001 *Intentional Communities*, Rooseum, Malmö, Sweden

Uniform: Order and Disorder, P.S.1 Contemporary Art Center, New York

2000 *Borderline Syndrome*, Manifesta 3, Moderna galerija, Ljubljana, Slovenia

Selected Bibliography

Bishop, Claire. "The Social Turn: Collaboration and Its Discontents." *Artforum* 44, no. 6 (February 2006): 178–83.

Bishop, Claire, Francesco Manacorda, Kate Bush, Todd Haynes, and Bill Horrigan. *yeah . . . . you, baby you*, edited by Siniša Mitrović. Milton Keynes and Hove, England: Milton Keynes Gallery and Shady Lane Publications, 2005.

Dawsey, Jill. *New Work: Phil Collins*. San Francisco: San Francisco Museum of Modern Art, 2006.

Edelsztein, Sergio. "Phil Collins." In Sergio Edelsztein et al., *Ice Cream: Contemporary Art in Culture*, 88–91. London: Phaidon Press, 2007.

Farquharson, Alex. "Minority Report." *frieze* (London), no. 94 (October 2005): 196–201.

Lazzarato, Maurizio, Edgar Schmitz, and Leire Vergara. *the return of the real*, edited by Leire Vergara and Siniša Mitrović. Bilbao, Spain: sala rekalde, 2007.

Mac Giolla Léith, Caoimhin, Siniša Mitrović, and Andrew Renton. *i only want you to love me*, edited by Siniša Mitrović. Brighton, England: Brighton Photo Biennial and Photoworks, 2003.

Sholis, Brian. "Phil Collins." In Rodrigo Alonso et al., *Vitamin Ph: New Perspectives in Photography*, 58–61. London: Phaidon Press, 2006.

1. *the world won't listen*, 2004–07
Synchronized three-channel color video
projection with sound, approx. 60 min.
Poster installation, dimensions variable
Courtesy of the artist
and Tanya Bonakdar Gallery, New York

Original recording: The Smiths
The World Won't Listen © 1986 Warner
Music UK Ltd. Lyrics by Morrissey;
music by Marr, except "Golden Lights"
by Twinkle. Adapted by Alejandro
Gomezcaceres; guitars, keyboards,
synthesizers, and programming:
Alejandro Gomezcaceres; bass guitar:
Alfonso Robledo; drums and
tambourines: Mauricio Montenegro;
backing vocals: Andrea Piñeros
and Ana Maria Gonzales

Guitars, bass guitar, keyboards,
synthesizers, and programming
recorded and engineered by Alejandro
Gomezcaceres at Casa en el Aire,
Bogotá; drums, tambourines, and
backing vocals recorded and engineered
by Toño Castillo at Voces e Imagen,
Bogotá; mixing and mastering:
Toño Castillo at Voces e Imagen,
Bogotá; Logic and Pro Tools assistance:
Andrés Otoya; produced by Alejandro
Gomezcaceres

Karaoke machine graphics: María
Margarita Jiménez, Roberto Herrera,
and Felipe Soler

Post production: Creativemedia AV
Audiovisual installation:
Sue MacDiarmid

Part one
el mundo no escuchará, 2004
Produced by Phil Collins and
Michèle Faguet; camera: Phil Collins;
sound: Carlos "Champi" Bonavides;
filmed at Espacio la Rebeca, Bogotá,
November 2004

Part two
dünya dinlemiyor, 2005
Produced by Phil Collins and
Derya Demir; camera: Metin Çavus;
sound: Metin Bozkurt; filmed
at Balans Music Hall, Istanbul,
August 2005

Part three
dunia tak akan mendengar, 2007
Produced by Phil Collins and
Clarissa Adinegoro; production
co-ordinators: Indra Ameng,
Detty Wulandari; camera:
Anggun Priambodo; camera assistants:
Carita Chandra, Angela A. Rikarastu
Rainy; sound: Adam Joshwara;
set: Iis Rajab (Jakarta), Team Sound
(Bandung); lights: Ary Sendy; filmed
at Déjà Vu (Jakarta), Gedung Merdeka
(Bandung), March 2007

2. *MELODY MAKER*,
September 6, 1975, 2006
Silkscreen print on paper, framed
49 ¼ × 37 in. (125 x 94 cm) unframed
Courtesy of the artist,
Victoria Miro Gallery, London
and Kerlin Gallery, Dublin

3. *SOUNDS, December 27, 1975*, 2006
Silkscreen print on paper, framed
49 ¼ × 37 in. (125 x 94 cm) unframed
Courtesy of the artist,
Victoria Miro Gallery, London
and Kerlin Gallery, Dublin

4. *SOUNDS, December 11, 1976*, 2006
Silkscreen print on paper, framed
49 ¼ × 37 in. (125 x 94 cm) unframed
Courtesy of the artist,
Victoria Miro Gallery, London
and Kerlin Gallery, Dublin

5. *MELODY MAKER*,
February 27, 1977, 2006
Silkscreen print on paper, framed
49 ¼ × 37 in. (125 x 94 cm) unframed
Courtesy of the artist,
Victoria Miro Gallery, London
and Kerlin Gallery, Dublin

6. *SOUNDS, August 12, 1978*, 2006
Silkscreen print on paper, framed
49 ¼ × 37 in. (125 x 94 cm) unframed
Courtesy of the artist,
Victoria Miro Gallery, London
and Kerlin Gallery, Dublin

7. *SOUNDS, October 27, 1979*, 2006
Silkscreen print on paper, framed
49 ¼ × 37 in. (125 x 94 cm) unframed
Courtesy of the artist,
Victoria Miro Gallery, London
and Kerlin Gallery, Dublin

8. *Record Mirror, March 29, 1980*, 2006
Silkscreen print on paper, framed
49 ¼ × 37 in. (125 x 94 cm) unframed
Courtesy of the artist,
Victoria Miro Gallery, London
and Kerlin Gallery, Dublin

Bruce Hainley is a writer who lives in Los Angeles. He is a contributing editor of *Artforum* and is the author of *Foul Mouth* (Los Angeles: 2nd Cannons, 2006) and, with John Waters, *Art—A Sex Book* (London: Thames and Hudson, 2003). His work has appeared in *Bidoun*, *Parkett*, *frieze*, and the *New York Times*.

Liz Kotz writes on postwar and contemporary art. She teaches in the Department of Art History at the University of California, Riverside, and is the author of *Words to Be Looked At: Language in 1960s Art* (Boston: MIT Press, 2007).

Simon Reynolds is the author of *Bring the Noise: 20 Years of Writing about Hip Rock and Hip Hop* (London: Faber and Faber, 2007), *Rip It Up and Start Again: Postpunk 1978-84* (London: Faber and Faber, 2005), and *Energy Flash: A Journey through Rave Music and Dance Culture* (1988; expanded and updated London: Picador, 2008). A freelance contributor to the *New York Times*, the *Guardian*, and *Salon*, he also maintains the weblog Blissblog at http://blissout.blogspot.com/.

Suzanne Weaver, the Nancy and Tim Hanley Associate Curator of Contemporary Art, has been at the Dallas Museum of Art for ten years. During that time, she has curated over twenty *Concentrations*, a series of project-based exhibitions featuring the work of leading younger international and American artists such as Doug Aitken, the collaborative team of Jennifer Allora and Guillermo Calzadilla, Matthew Buckingham, Anne Chu, Maureen Gallace, Jim Lambie, Anri Sala, and Charline von Heyl.

Pages 39, 54
dünya dinlemiyor, 2005.
Posters, offset print on paper,
27 ½ × 19 ¾ in. (70 × 50 cm).

Page 56
₁ Yvonne Rainer, *The Mind Is A Muscle*,
Judson Memorial Church, N.Y.C.,
May 24, 1966. Photo: Peter Moore.
© Estate of Peter Moore/VAGA, NYC.
₂ *they shoot horses*, 2004. Video still.
₃ Max Factory, *who we were and why
didn't we get what we wanted*, 1996.
© Max Factory.

Page 58
how to make a refugee, 1999. Video still.

Page 59
baghdad screentests, 2002. Video stills.

Page 60
Courtesy of the artist and Neue
Kunsthalle St. Gallen, Switzerland.

Page 61
Yvonne Rainer of the Judson Dance
Theater; dance with facial expressions,
1965. © Hulton-Deutsch Collection/
Corbis.

Pages 62–63
Bruce Nauman, *Walking in an Exaggerated
Manner around the Perimeter of a Square*,
1967-68. © 2007 Bruce Nauman/
Artists Rights Society (ARS), New York;
image courtesy of EAI.

Page 66
eight hours is not a day #2, 1998.
Lambda print, framed;
39 ⅜ × 27 ⅝ in. (100 × 70 cm)
unframed.

Pages 67, 82
dunia tak akan mendengar, 2007.
Posters, digital print on paper,
27 ½ × 19 ¾ in. (70 × 50 cm).

Pages 68–81
dunia tak akan mendengar, 2007.
Production stills.

Page 84
₁ George Marsh, age 19, 1909.
Chelan County, Wash.; grand larceny,
escaped. *Least Wanted: A Century
of American Mugshots*. © 2006 Steidl
Publishers, Göttingen, and
Steven Kasher Gallery, New York.
₂ David Bowie, *Aladdin Sane* (London:
Virgin, 1973); record cover. © Virgin.
₃ Photograph from personal archive,
c. 1983.

Page 90
el mundo no escuchará, 2004.
Lyric sheet, Bogotá, November 2004.

Page 92
dünya dinlemiyor, 2005. Production set,
Balans Music Hall, Istanbul.
Photo: Metin Çavus.

Page 94
Jakarta, February 2007.

Page 95
MELODY MAKER, September 6, 1975,
2006. Silkscreen print on paper, framed;
49 ¼ × 37 in. (125 × 94 cm) unframed.

Page 96
Record Mirror, March 29, 1980, 2006.
Silkscreen print on paper, framed;
49 ¼ × 37 in. (125 × 94 cm) unframed.

Page 98
Video stills. © 2000 EMI Records Ltd.

Page 107
dunia tak akan mendengar, 2007.
Production set, Gedung Merdeka,
Bandung, March 2007.

Pages 108–09
the world won't listen, 2004-07.
Production and video stills,
installation view. Photos: Phil Collins,
Michèle Faguet, Istanbul Foundation
for Culture and Arts (IKSV), and
Tanya Bonakdar Gallery, New York.

Pages 110–11
Bandung, March 2007.

Pages 112–13
West Pacific, Jakarta, March 2007.

Page 114
dunia tak akan mendengar, 2007.
Production still.
Facing: Letter (unauthenticated).
"Morrissey Misses Chelsea, Kinda
Sorta." Living with Legends:
HotelChelsea Blog. http://legends
.typepad.com/living_with_legends_the_
h/2007/01/morrissey_misse.html.

Dallas Museum of Art
John R. Lane, The Eugene McDermott Director
Suzanne Weaver, The Nancy and Tim Hanley
        Associate Curator of Contemporary Art
Tamara Wootton-Bonner, Director of Exhibitions
        and Publications
Eric Zeidler, Publications Coordinator
Jeff Zilm, Rights and Reproductions Coordinator

Siniša Mitrović, Associate Editor

Copyedited by Frances Bowles
Designed by Scott Williams and Henrik Kubel of A2/SW/HK
Typeface design by A2/SW/HK
Printed and bound in Belgium by Die Keure

Cover: Phil Collins, *the world won't listen*, 2004–07

Distributed for the Dallas Museum of Art by
Yale University Press, New Haven and London
www.yalebooks.com

Library of Congress Cataloging-in-Publication Data
Weaver, Suzanne, 1951–
Phil Collins : the world won't listen / Suzanne Weaver;
with contributions by Bruce Hainley, Liz Kotz, Simon Reynolds.
        p. cm.
"This catalogue has been published in conjunction with the
exhibition *Phil Collins: the world won't listen*, no. 52 in the series
Concentrations, organized by the Dallas Museum of Art,
November 9, 2007–March 23, 2008."—T.p. verso.
Includes bibliographical references (p.   ).
ISBN 978-0-300-13292-2
1. Collins, Phil, 1970– —Exhibitions. 2. Karaoke—Exhibitions.
3. Smiths (Musical Group)—Exhibitions. I. Hainley, Bruce.
II. Kotz, Liz. III. Reynolds, Simon, 1963– IV. Dallas Museum
of Art. V. Title.
ML141.D25C65 2008
709.2—dc22

                        2007029860

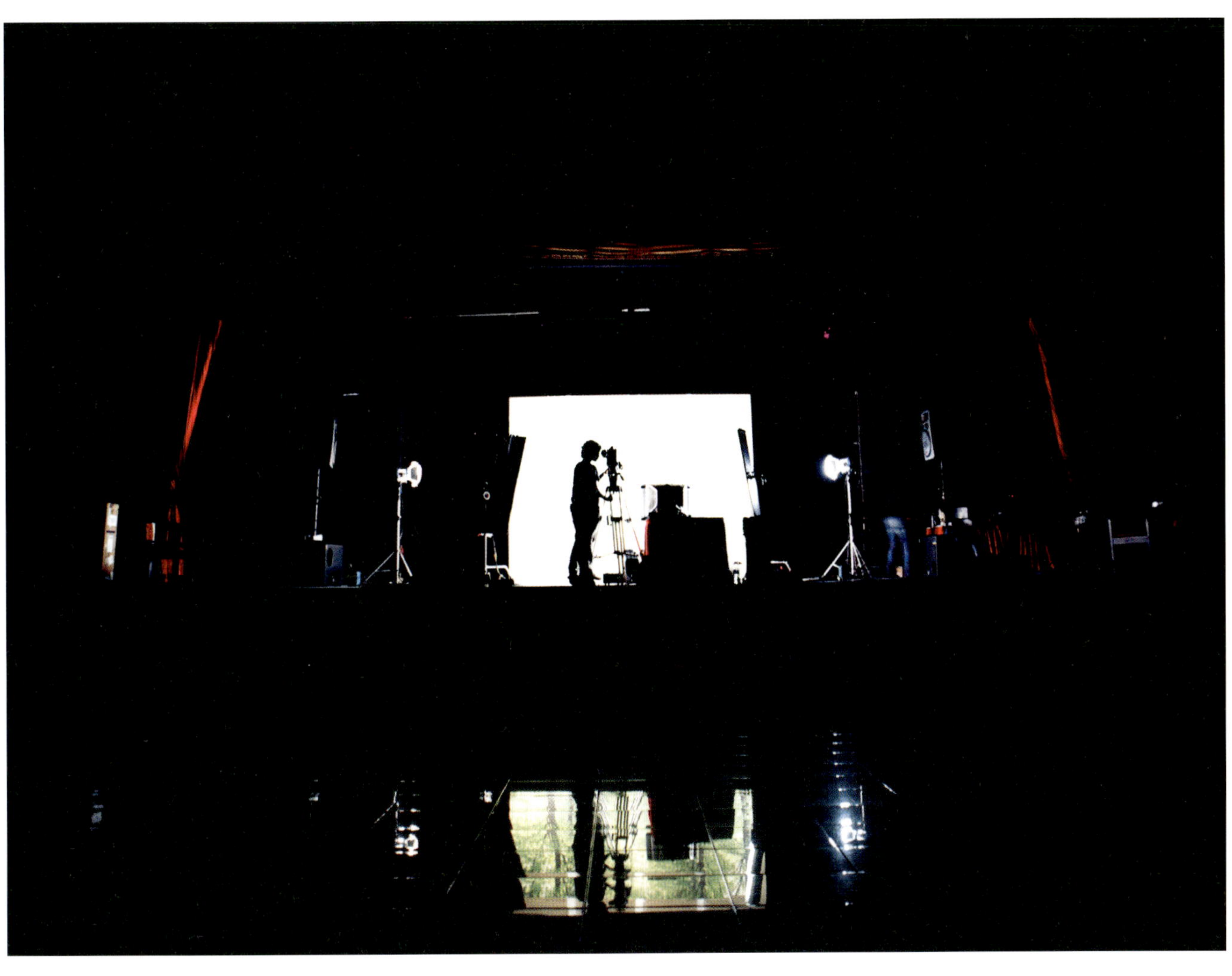

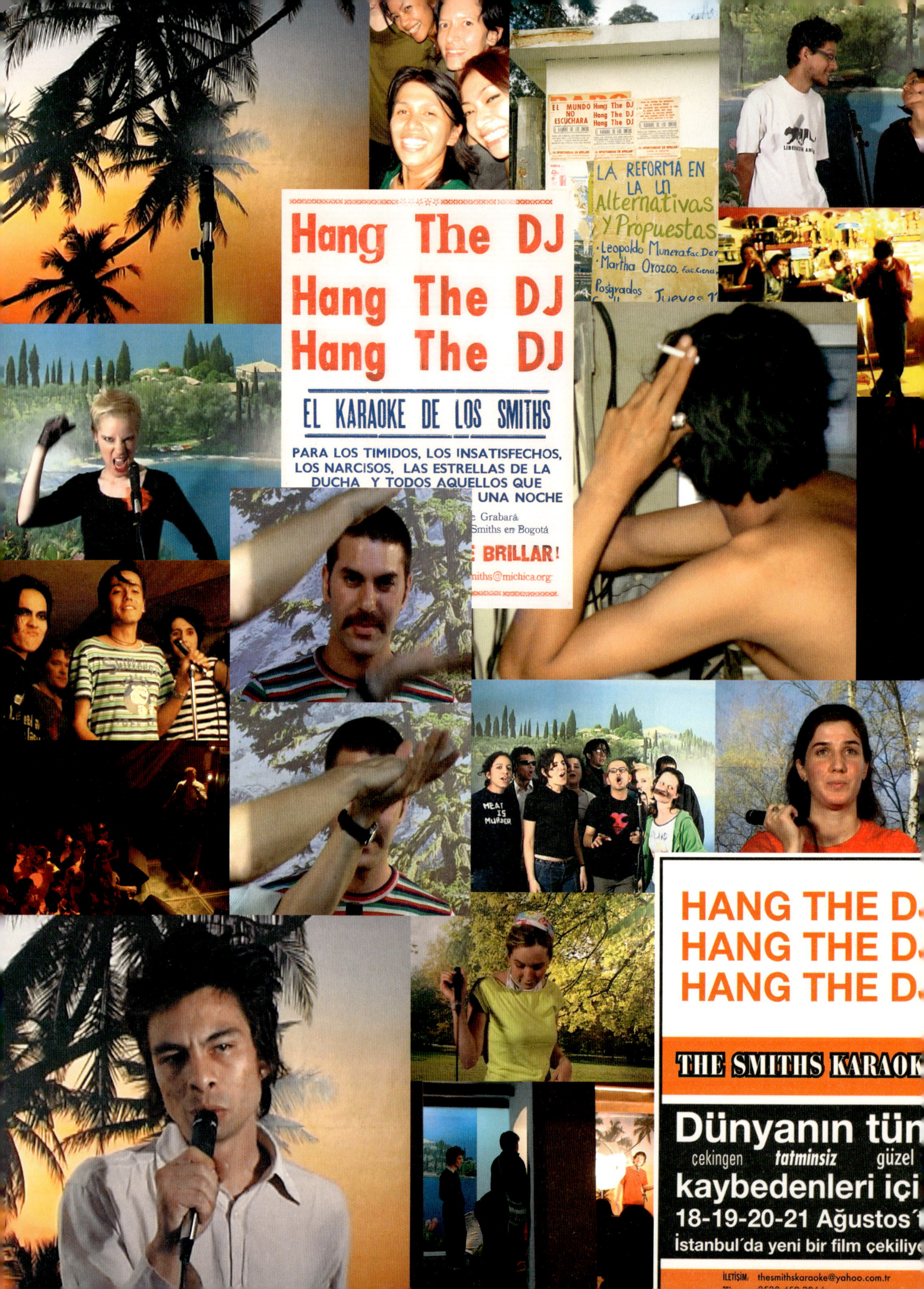
Hang The DJ
Hang The DJ
Hang The DJ
EL KARAOKE DE LOS SMITHS
PARA LOS TIMIDOS, LOS INSATISFECHOS,
LOS NARCISOS, LAS ESTRELLAS DE LA
DUCHA Y TODOS AQUELLOS QUE
UNA NOCHE
Grabará
Smiths en Bogotá
BRILLAR!
miths@michica.org
LA REFORMA EN
LA UN
Alternativas
Y Propuestas
· Leopoldo Munera.fac.Der
· Martha Orozco. fac.Cien.
Posgrados
Jueves
EL MUNDO   Hang The DJ
NO   Hang The DJ
ESCUCHARA   Hang The DJ
MEAT
IS
MURDER
HANG THE D
HANG THE D
HANG THE D
THE SMITHS KARAOK
Dünyanın tün
çekingen   tatminsiz   güzel
kaybedenleri içi
18-19-20-21 Ağustos
İstanbul'da yeni bir film çekiliy
İLETİŞİM: thesmithskaraoke@yahoo.com.tr

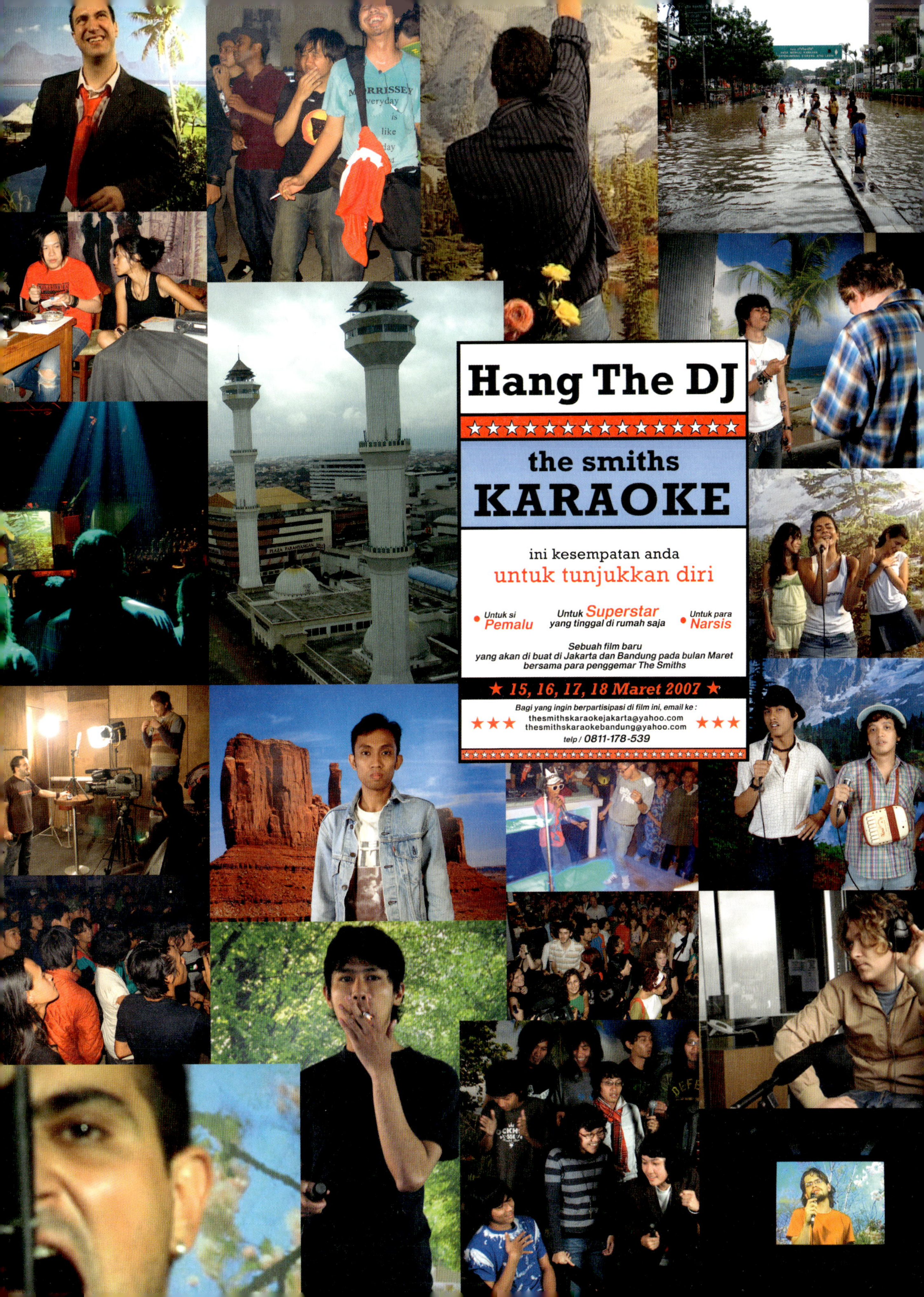

Hang The DJ
the smiths
KARAOKE
ini kesempatan anda
untuk tunjukkan diri
Untuk si Pemalu
Untuk Superstar yang tinggal di rumah saja
Untuk para Narsis
Sebuah film baru
yang akan di buat di Jakarta dan Bandung pada bulan Maret
bersama para penggemar The Smiths
15, 16, 17, 18 Maret 2007
Bagi yang ingin berpartisipasi di film ini, email ke :
thesmithskaraokejakarta@yahoo.com
thesmithskaraokebandung@yahoo.com
telp / 0811-178-539

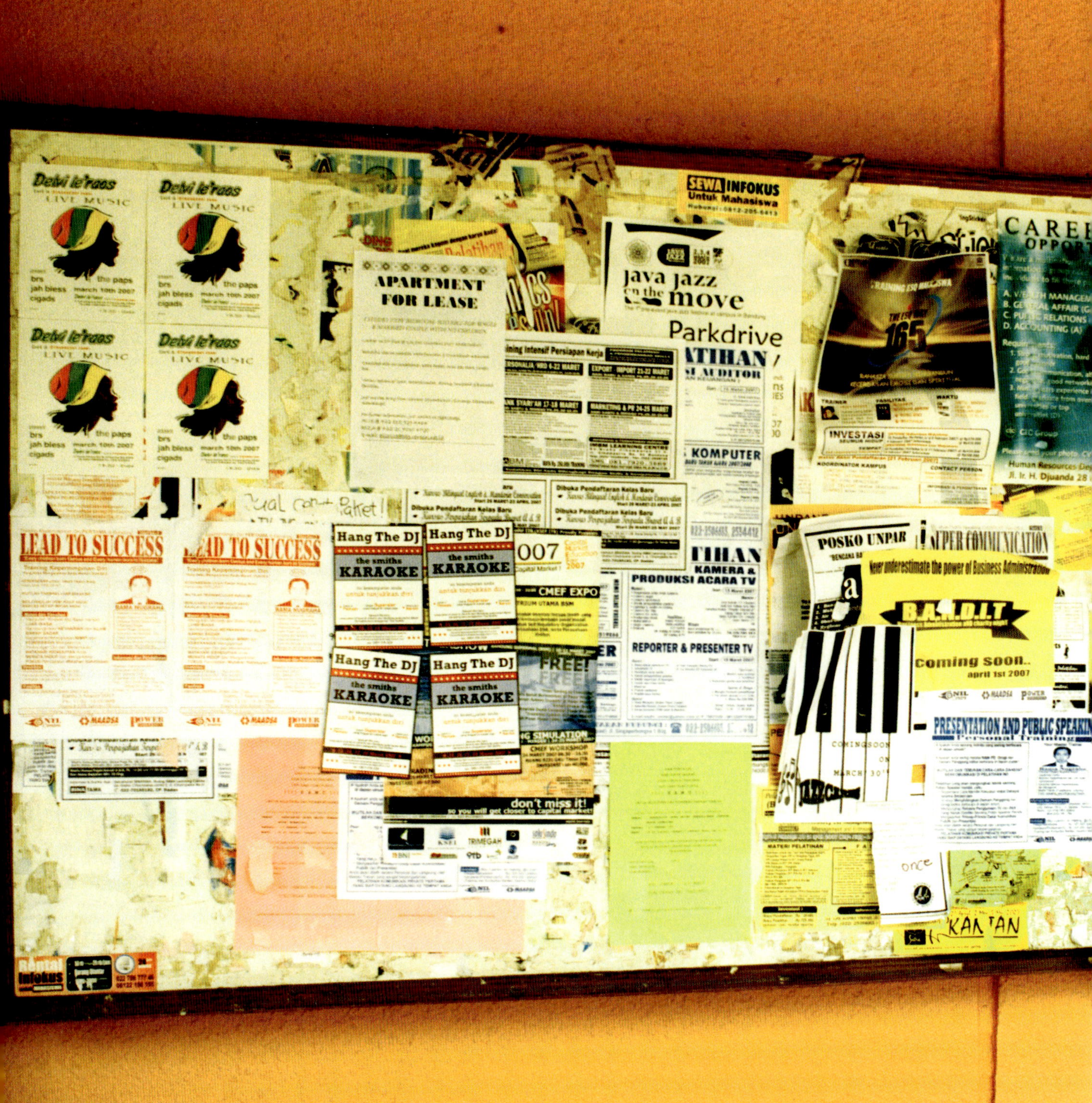

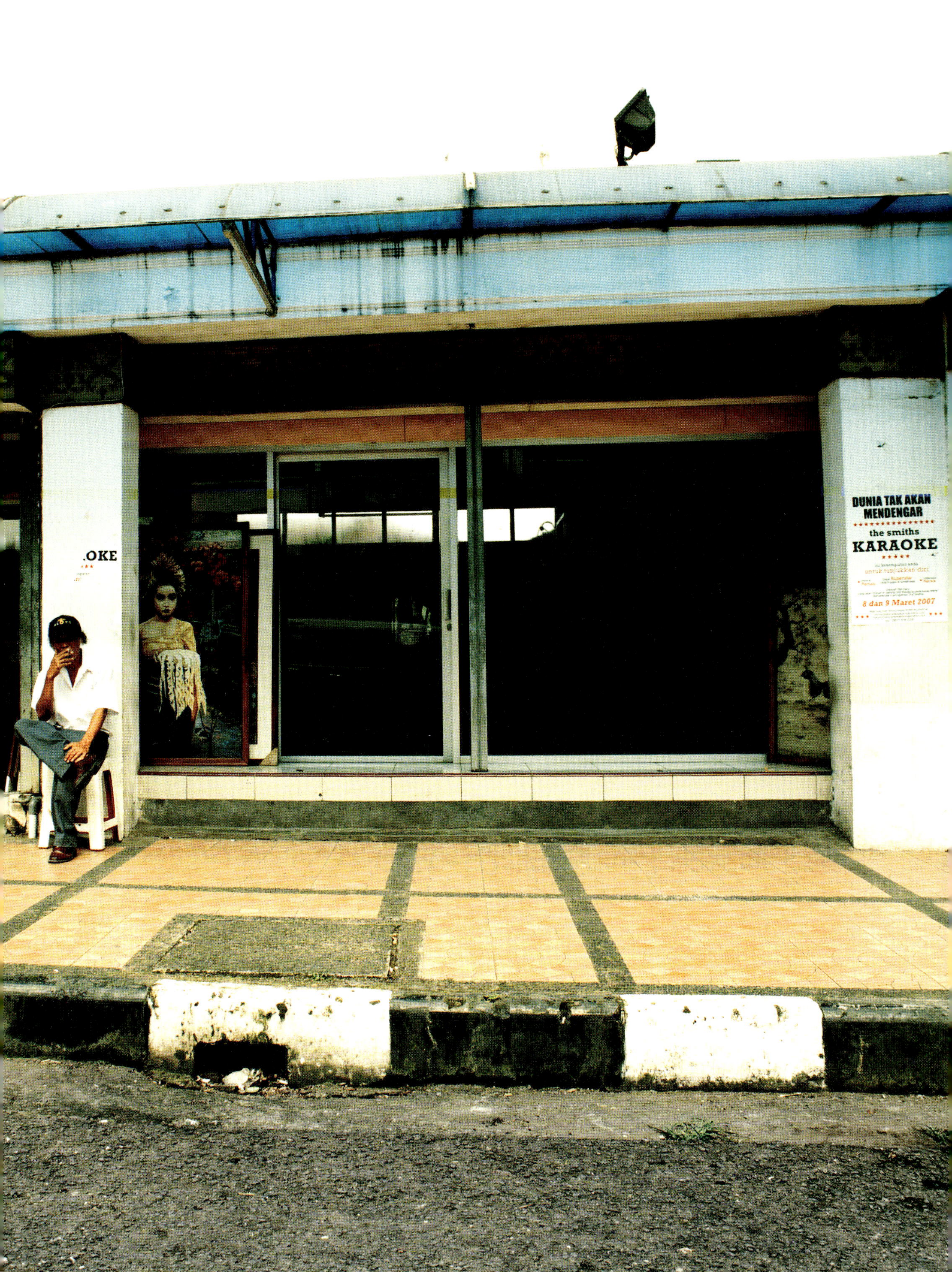
.OKE
DUNIA TAK AKAN
MENDENGAR
the smiths
KARAOKE
untuk tunjukkan diri
8 dan 9 Maret 2007

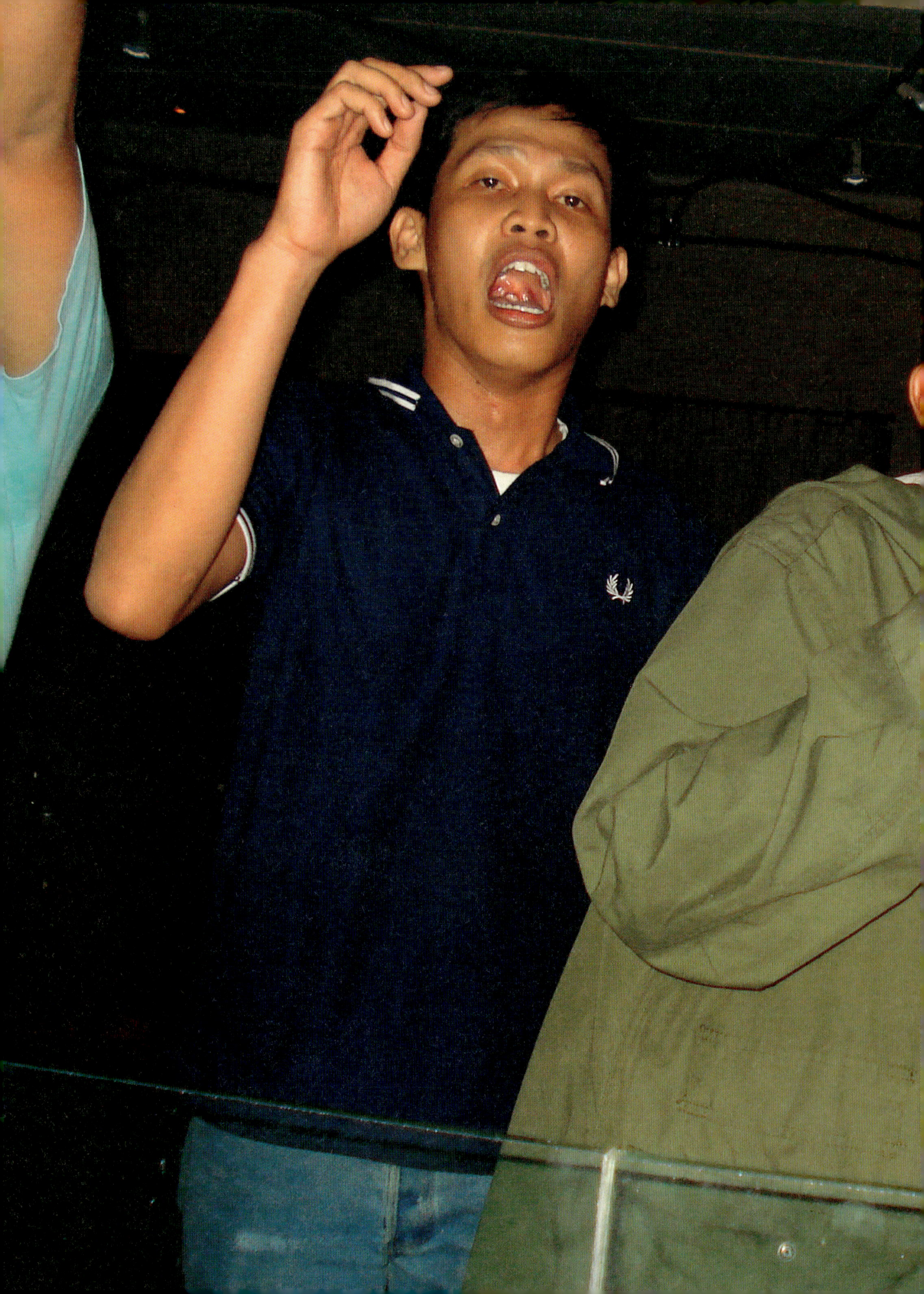

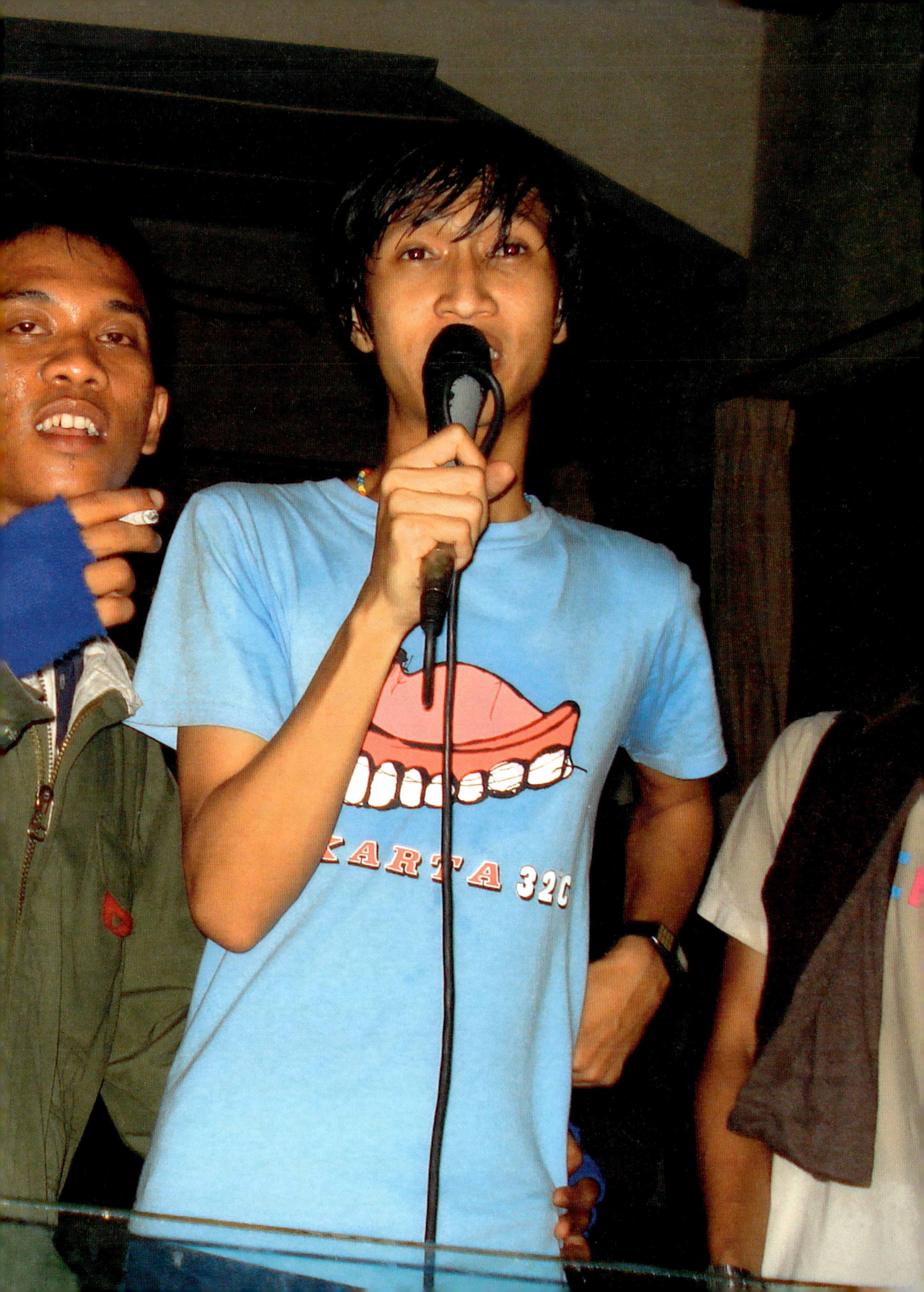

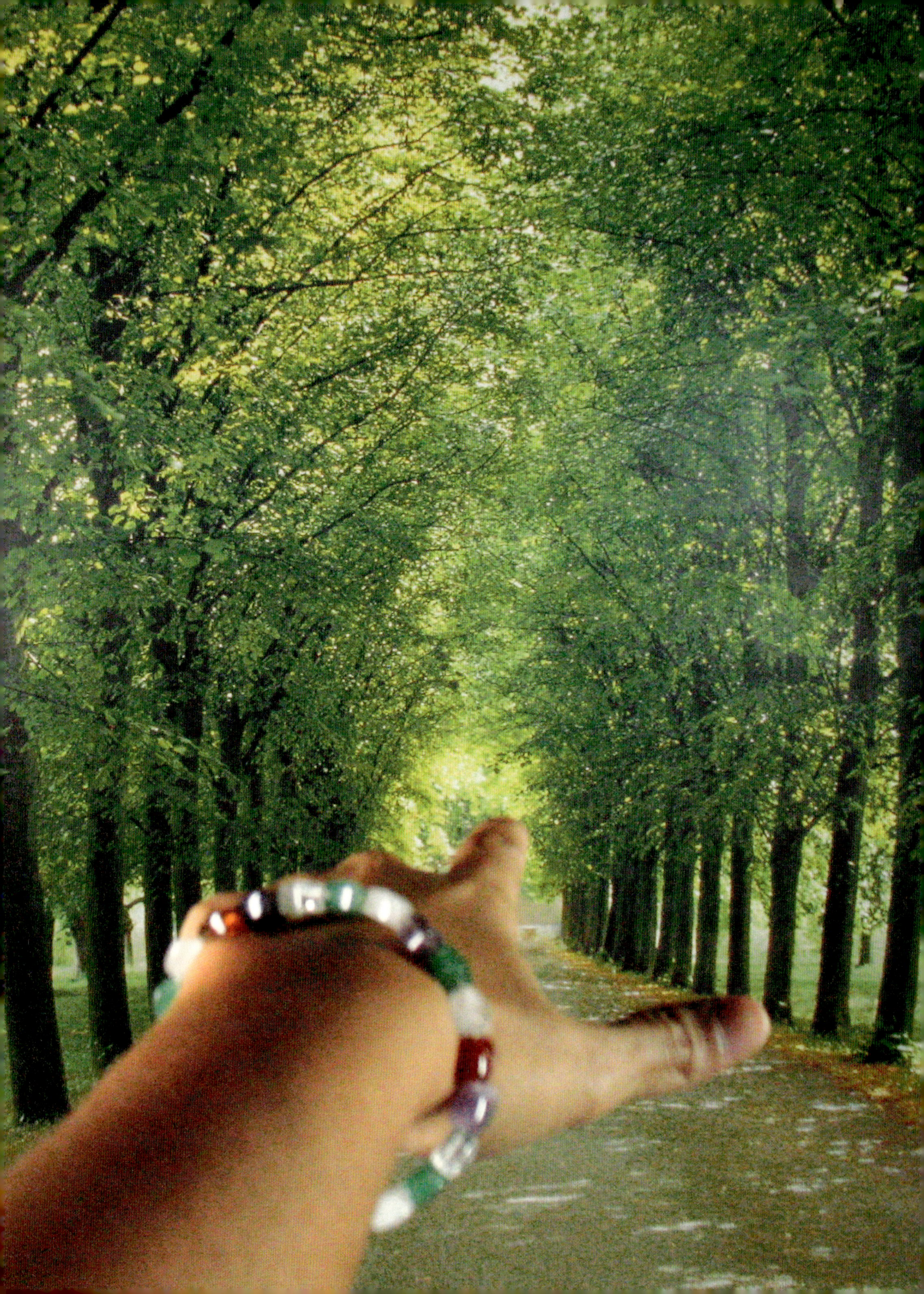

Jan 16, 1981

Dear Jon,
    Yes, I told you I'd cultivate
Texas! Those dear cowboys! So
Sweet! So dull... and really, the
English and Americans have so much
in common — except, of course, language.
But there is no Art here, and I
am consequently mis-placed. I will
go to New York and have my
photograph taken with the dear old
Chelsea serving as an insignificant background.
I hope you got your rided. At the
moment I have Eve Arden in " So This
Is Brooklyn"?
            Love & trash,
            Steven Morrissey

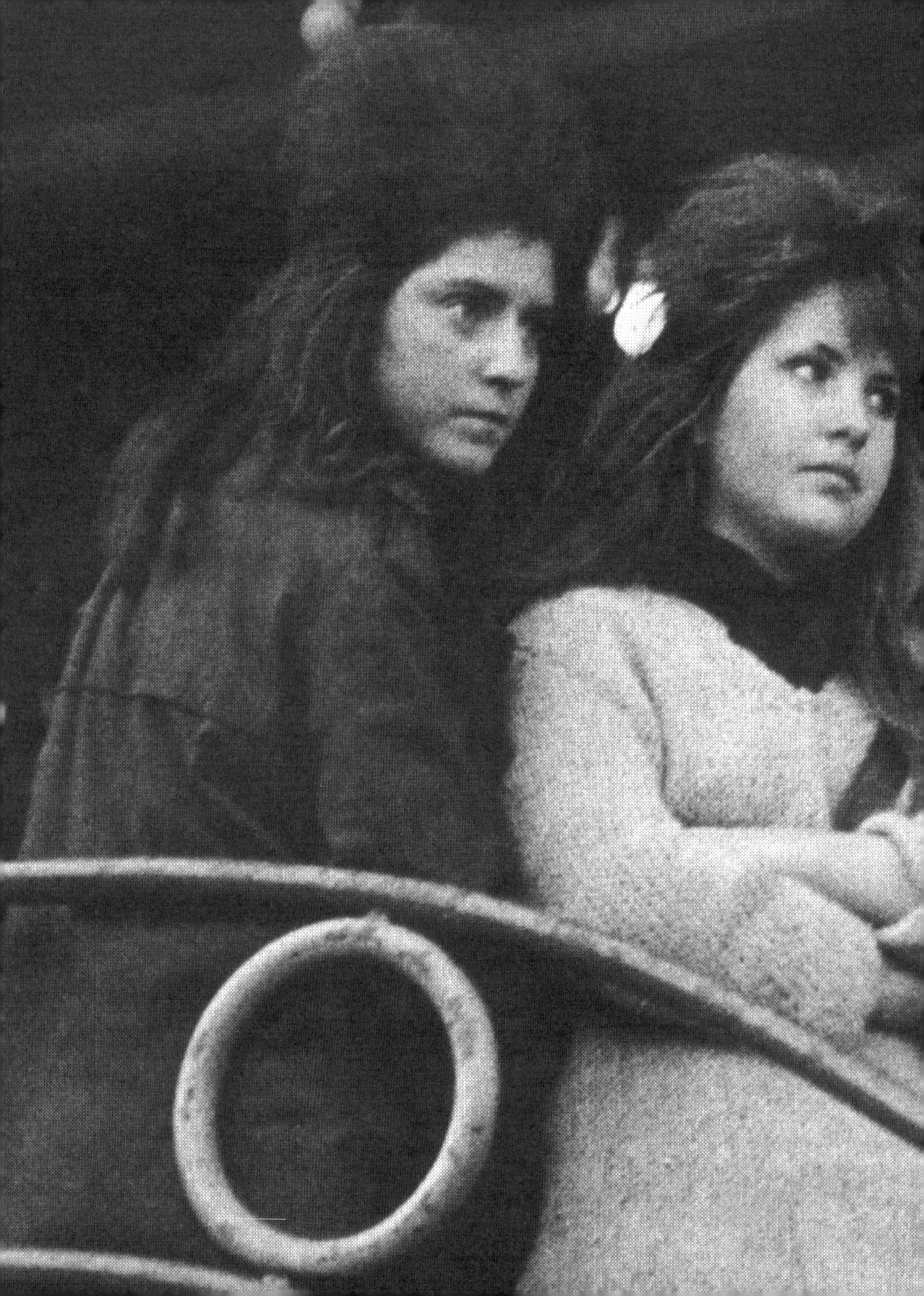